A Brief Excursion into Human Cognition

Hans Kankam

A Brief Excursion into Human Cognition

The Evolving Influence of Social Media & Artificial Intelligence

palgrave
macmillan

Hans Kankam
General Internal Medicine, Psychotherapy
ExoVital Institute for Psychological-Medicine
Zug, Switzerland

ISBN 978-3-031-89751-1 ISBN 978-3-031-89752-8 (eBook)
https://doi.org/10.1007/978-3-031-89752-8

This Palgrave Macmillan imprint is published by the registered company Springer Nature Switzerland AG.
The registered company address is: Gewerbestrasse 11, 6330 Cham, Switzerland

To Daniel, Damian, and Alvar.

Preface

At first glance, human cognition, behavior, and emotion may seem easy to grasp, as we assume they guide us through our environment and enable social interactions. However, this perception does not capture the full complexity of what occurs behind scenes. As we begin to understand the limitations of our perceptions and the filters that influence our decision-making processes, we become aware that our assumptions do not always match reality. Every one of our decisions, whether they relate to government/politics, economics, education, or any other aspect of human life, is subject to the biases and limitations of human cognition.

An awareness of these limitations and complexities and our tendencies to reconcile them to create coherent understanding significantly influenced my decision to write this book. As a physician and cognitive behavioral psychotherapist (CBT), I value the substantial contributions from my colleagues in fields such as biology, psychology, psychiatry, philosophy, linguistics, neuroscience, and social science. This list extends to include political science, culture, education, and physiology, among others. Occupying a central position in bridging theory and practice, a clinician utilizes insights from various disciplines to shape therapeutic interventions, gaining profound insights into the intricacies of human behavior.

The American academic, neuroscientist, and primatologist Robert Sapolsky in his book Behave (Sapolsky, 2017) describes the complexity of human cognition, shaped by physiology, sensory cues, prenatal environment, and ecological pressures. This complexity makes the field incredibly fascinating, as it pertains to us—our daily interactions with our environment, our decision-making processes, our establishment of alliances, and our propensity to foster animosities, among many other aspects of human experience.

Social media and gaming platforms exploit cognitive aspects to secure their online dominance, leading to a high prevalence of addiction among their users (Jitoku et al., 2024). Evidence from a variety of cross-sectional, longitudinal, and empirical studies implicate smartphone and social media use in the increase in mental health disorders, self-injurious behavior, and suicidality among youth (Abi-Jaoude et al., 2020). This growing concern is echoed globally, as more individuals are reported with mental health issues due to excessive engagement with these platforms.

The field of artificial intelligence (AI) prompts critical questions about how our cognitive limitations may influence the technologies we create (Mbalaka, 2023). There is a concern that our misperceptions and biases could be embedded in AI systems, potentially leading to widespread unintended consequences or even catastrophic outcomes (Vakali and Tantalaki, 2024). Given historical trends, it seems likely that our imperfections will indeed be reflected in these advanced systems. As we continue to develop increasingly sophisticated AI technologies, which are intrinsically tied to our human cognition, it becomes paramount that we proactively identify and mitigate our inherent biases and limitations. It is crucial to ensure that these technologies contribute positively to society and do not exacerbate our existing shortcomings and failures. However, the task of navigating this complex landscape is daunting, particularly when considering the current geopolitical tensions, prevalent dysfunctional leadership, and the integration of AI in warfare systems, to mention just a few challenges. These factors collectively cast a shadow of pessimism on the prospects of achieving the responsible and ethical integration of AI into our society.

This book aims to serve as a helpful resource designed to support both students and professionals who are eager to deepen their understanding of the vast and intriguing field of human cognition. Whether you are refreshing existing knowledge or delving into this subject for the first time, the insights explored here aim to inspire and inform your journey through the complexities of cognitive processes.

Furthermore, it is relevant to add that this book has its limitations in trying to cover this vast, interesting, and intricate topic; thus, it is but a brief excursion into human cognition.

There are many people and fortunate moments over the years that have made this book possible. First, I want to thank my team in California, USA—Pattie Rhoades, Vanessa Gilmore, Amanda Berumen, and Erika

Ramirez—for giving me the most valuable resource: time. Without you, this book would not have been possible. I also want to thank my ever-diligent editor, Catherine McNamara, who has offered invaluable input and advice. Finally, my thanks go to Daniel T. Kankam-Rusch for spending countless hours vetting research documents and rechecking data.

Zug, Switzerland Hans Kankam

References

Abi-Jaoude, E., Naylor, K. T., & Pignatiello, A. (2020). Smartphones, social media use and youth mental health. CMAJ: Canadian Medical Association journal = journal de l'Association medicale canadienne, 192(6), E136–E141. https://doi.org/10.1503/cmaj.190434

Jitoku, T., Tanaka, S., & Yamamoto, H. (2024). Explicit and implicit effects of gaming content on social media on the behavior of young adults. Journal of Media Psychology, 45(2), 123–137. https://doi.org/10.3389/fpsyg.2024.1332462

Mbalaka, B. (2023). Epistemically violent biases in artificial intelligence design: The case of DALLE-E 2 and Starry AI. Digital Transformation and Society. https://doi.org/10.1108/DTS-01-2023-0003

Sapolsky, R. M. (2017). Behave: The biology of humans at our best and worst. Penguin Press.

Vakali, A., & Tantalaki, N. (2024). Rolling in the deep of cognitive and AI biases. arXiv. https://arxiv.org/abs/2407.21202

Competing Interests

The author has no competing interests to declare that are relevant to the content of this manuscript.

Contents

About the Author

Hans Kankam the author, is a practicing clinician in Switzerland and Germany, specializing in General Internal Medicine, Psychotherapy (CBT), Addiction and Palliative Medicine. He obtained his Medical Degree and completed his dissertation at Philipps University in Marburg an der Lahn and obtained an MBA from the Paul Merage School of Business at the University of California, Irvine.

CHAPTER 1

Introduction to Human Cognition

Overview of Human Cognition

The Oxford English Dictionary (OED) notes that cognition traces its roots to the Latin cognit ("a getting to know, acquaintance, notion, knowledge, etc.") (Oxford English Dictionary, n.d.). *Eric Partridge's Origins: A short etymological dictionary of Modern English notes that cognition originates from the Latin cognōscere ("to know, to learn about")* (Partridge, 2008).

Human cognition is a mental architecture that enables individuals to comprehend their environments, learn from experiences, communicate through language, and navigate complex social and physical worlds (Eysenck & Keane, 2020). It is at the heart of what allows humans to reason, innovate, adapt, and meaningfully engage with the challenges and opportunities they encounter (Gazzaniga et al., 2019).

In other words, *human cognition* has developed through our evolutionary history as a means to navigate the complexities of our environment (Diamond, 1997). In the past, this environment was largely defined by nature, and our cognitive abilities evolved to help us survive in the conditions that our ancestors faced thousands of years ago in savannah grasslands (Diamond, 1991). Although our world has undergone rapid changes—within a relatively brief time span marked by technological, social, and environmental transformations—these developments stand in sharp contrast to the much longer timescales typically required for

H. Kankam, *A Brief Excursion into Human Cognition*,
https://doi.org/10.1007/978-3-031-89752-8_1

evolutionary changes in cognitive processes. Basic cognitive traits can evolve within a few hundred to a few thousand generations, whereas complex cognitive abilities may require millions of years to emerge. Even so, these evolutionary processes define how we perceive and interact with the world around us (Henrich, 2016). However, this creates a dilemma, as some of these processes are out of sync with the demands and challenges of modern society in this urban world of our creation. In the era of our forebears, human decisions had minimal influence on the environment and society at large. Small tribal communities operated within a narrow scope and had a limited impact on other nearby groups (Trigger, 2003). Communication was confined primarily to the immediate circle, and any negative consequences arising from the actions of these individuals were inconsequential to other groups or the environment in general. In today's technologically advanced world, with tightly interwoven societies, powerful weapons of mass destruction, and vast industrial complexes that significantly impact our planet's environment, human decisions, per proxy, can carry considerable weight (Brynjolfsson & McAfee, 2014).

The transition from hunter-gatherer societies to the modern industrial age is a complex process that spans tens of thousands of years (Diamond, 1997). Approximately 12,000–10,000 years ago, the Agricultural Revolution took place in various parts of the world.

During this time, humans transitioned from hunter-gatherer lifestyles to settled farming communities. The domestication of plants and animals has allowed for more stable food sources and led to population growth and the development of complex societies (Trigger, 2003). The first cities and states emerged approximately 5000–4000 years ago in Mesopotamia, Egypt, India, and China. The rise of urban centers and the development of writing, law, and administration were significant advancements in human society. The Scientific Revolution, which took place between the sixteenth and eighteenth centuries, laid the foundation for the modern understanding of the natural world. This period saw significant developments in mathematics, physics, astronomy, biology, and chemistry (Shapin, 1996). The Industrial Revolution began in the mid-eighteenth century, initially in Britain, and later spread to other parts of the world. This period marked the shift from agrarian economies to industrial economies, with mechanized production, steam power, and factories playing crucial roles. The Industrial Revolution brought about significant social, economic, and technological changes that continue to shape the modern world.

In roughly 12,000 years, *Homo sapiens* evolved from a hunter-gatherer lifestyle to the Industrial Age, with the onset of the Agricultural Revolution marking the initial substantial stride toward contemporary society. This period is relatively brief when viewed in the context of evolutionary history (Diamond, 1997). In addition, the digital revolution, fueled by globalization, just began approximately 25 years ago. Compared with the time scale of a species' evolutionary adaptation processes, this is indeed a remarkably short period. One could infer that this underlines the challenges our species face in utilizing the tools that we created without falling prey to them. This brings up concerns on several levels: cognitive overload due to the constant stream of information and stimuli that can overwhelm our human brain, dependence on technology that reduces our skills in areas that are dominated by machines, job displacement and economic inequality through AI and automation transforming the labor market, as some segments of society may benefit disproportionately from these technological changes and others may not. Existential risks are posed by increasingly powerful AI systems with misaligned objectives, potentially causing unintended consequences with catastrophic outcomes. Social fragmentation and polarization, exacerbated particularly by social media, create echo chambers and spread misinformation. Ethical and moral challenges occur as AI systems become more capable, as they increasingly make decisions previously made by humans. Privacy and surveillance issues emerge due to advancements in AI and data analytics that allow for unprecedented levels of surveillance and data collection in the process outpacing legal and ethical frameworks designed to protect individual rights (Brynjolfsson & McAfee, 2014).

To understand more about the process of cognition, it is essential to understand what this encompasses. *Human cognition* refers to the mental processes by which we acquire, process, store, and use information to interact with our environment (Eysenck & Keane, 2020). Cognition encompasses a wide range of processes, including perception, attention, memory, language, reasoning, problem-solving, decision-making, learning, and emotion (Gazzaniga et al., 2019). These processes enable us to recognize and interpret sensory input, form and retrieve memories, communicate with others, solve complex problems, and make informed decisions on the basis of available information. It involves an intricate interplay between our sensory organs, which have evolved to gather vital information, enabling us to thrive in our environment. Essential sensory input refers to the information or data that are received by our sensory organs—our eyes, ears, nose, tongue, and skin. These organs detect various stimuli in the environment, such as light, sound, odor, taste, and touch, and convert them into electrical signals that are then transmitted to the brain for processing (Goldstein, 2010). Sensory inputs are essential for our perception and understanding of the world around us and play a crucial role in our ability to interact with and respond to our environment.

Importance of Studying Cognition

Studying cognition is central to understanding the inner workings of the human mind—how we perceive, think, learn, remember, solve problems, and make decisions (Eysenck & Keane, 2020). Its relevance extends far beyond academic inquiry, influencing practical applications across numerous fields. The study of cognition was initially the key field of research in psychology and neuroscience, as it provides insights into how humans process, store and utilize information. Consequently, this has had a significant effect on various other fields, including education, mental health, technology, politics, and marketing (Fiske & Taylor, 2013). In education, understanding how students learn and retain information can improve teaching practices and curriculum design (Mayer, 2011). The study of the cognitive aspects of mental health disorders can lead to better diagnoses, treatments, and interventions (Fernández et al., 2013), which is particularly useful in the context of aging and cognitive decline. Insights into human cognition aid the development of technologies such as artificial intelligence (AI) and human–computer interaction (HCI) (Brynjolfsson & McAfee, 2014). In politics, cognition research helps inform policymakers about cognitive biases and heuristics, aiding them in decision-making and the crafting of policies. Similarly, in marketing and advertising, the knowledge of cognitive processes is used to design more effective campaigns.

The increase in social media platforms and their online dominance has increased the relevance and importance of research into human cognition, particularly for the corporations that own and operate these platforms. Social media platforms utilize cognition in several ways, both in terms of the design of their platforms and the manner in which they engage users.

Social media platforms are designed to capture and hold users' attention, using visually appealing interfaces, notifications, and personalized content feeds to encourage frequent and prolonged engagement (Shanmugasundaram & Tamilarasu, 2023). The advantage of using users' cognitive biases to make social platforms more engaging is that they utilize confirmation bias through showing users' content that aligns with their existing beliefs and interests, which helps to keep users on the platform longer (Kahneman, 2011). Complex algorithms that are able to analyze users' behaviors, preferences, and social connections are used to curate personalized content feeds. This tailored content maintains users' interest and engagement by presenting them with information that irresistibly appeals to their interests in life. Social platforms leverage users' natural tendencies, and these tendencies become hooks that begin to condition opinions and behavior. Features such as likes, shares, and comments can create a sense of social validation or pressure, which encourages users to engage with content or adopt certain viewpoints. All successful social media platforms are designed to elicit strong emotional responses from users. Content that evokes emotions such as happiness, anger, or fear is more likely to be shared, commented on, or liked; therefore, platforms prioritize this type of content in users' feeds (Shanmugasundaram & Tamilarasu, 2023). Habit formation through features such as notifications, infinite scrolling, and easy access to new content is encouraged to increase the likelihood that users will check the platform regularly and spend more time on it. Easy access to information is facilitated, which can affect users' memory and retrieval processes. Users tend to be more likely to rely on a platform for information rather than to recall it themselves, as the platform can provide instant answers and store content for later retrieval. Social media platforms are engineered to elicit immediate reactions from users, tapping into our fast and automatic cognitive processes, a concept well articulated by Daniel Kahneman in his dual-process theory of thinking (Kahneman, 2011).

This often leads to responses that are impulsive and less considered, lacking the balance and refinement that might come from engaging our slower, more deliberate cognitive processes. Such hastily made comments can result in social backlash or exclusion, as the online community reacts, potentially leading to significant negative consequences for the user.

By understanding and leveraging cognitive aspects, social media platforms craft engaging and immersive experiences that capture users' attention, foster psychological dependence, and, in many cases, influence cognitive perceptions (Fiske & Taylor, 2013).

Historical Perspectives on Cognitive Science

Cognitive science is an interdisciplinary field that emerged in the mid-twentieth century, drawing on insights from psychology, linguistics, philosophy, anthropology, neuroscience, and computer science (Thagard, 2005). However, the groundwork for future cognitive research started much earlier, with intuitive inquiries from philosophers such as Descartes, Locke, and Hume, who explored questions related to the nature of the mind, perception, and knowledge (Hatfield, 2002).

In the early twentieth century, behaviorism dominated psychology, with a focus on the study of observable behaviors and the role of reinforcement in shaping behavior (Skinner, 1953).

However, behaviorism's limited focus on observable behaviors has left many questions about the internal processes of the mind unanswered.

In the mid-twentieth century, the cognitive revolution emerged as a response to the limitations of behaviorism. Researchers had begun to shift their focus toward the internal processes of the mind, spurred by developments in computer science, information theory, and the advent of new experimental techniques (Miller, 2003; Neisser, 1967). William Dember was the first to use the terminology "the cognitive revolution" (Dember, 1974). In his article, Dember discussed the shift in psychology from behaviorism to cognitive psychology. He argued that the cognitive revolution was characterized by a focus on mental processes, such as perception, memory, and problem-solving, rather than exclusively observable behavior.

The establishment of cognitive science as an interdisciplinary field in the 1970s and 1980s brought together researchers from various disciplines, such as psychology, linguistics, and artificial intelligence, to study the human mind from multiple perspectives (Gardner, 1985).

Notably, cognitive research has been shaped by several key figures who have made significant contributions to the field. Some of the most notable individuals include Ulric Neisser, often referred to as the "father of cognitive psychology." Neisser's research and theories laid the groundwork for the field as we know it today. His seminal book, *Cognitive Psychology* (Neisser, 1967), helped define the discipline. Jean Piaget, a renowned Swiss psychologist, is widely recognized for his significant contributions to developmental psychology, specifically his influential theory of children's cognitive development (Piaget, 1952). His research and ideas have greatly influenced educational practices and our understanding of cognitive growth. The linguist and philosopher Noam Chomsky revolutionized the study of language and cognition. His theories on generative grammar and the innate language ability of humans have had a profound impact on cognitive science and psychology (Chomsky, 1965). George A. Miller's work on short-term memory and cognitive processing helped establish the field of cognitive psychology. His groundbreaking paper, "The Magical Number Seven, Plus or Minus Two," remains influential in understanding human information processing (Miller, 1956). Elizabeth Loftus, a prominent figure in memory research, is best known for her work on false memories and the malleability of human memory. Her research has had important implications for the legal system and eyewitness testimony (Loftus, 1979).

Daniel Kahneman, a Nobel Prize-winning psychologist, is known for his work on decision-making and judgment. His research, in collaboration with Amos Tversky, led to the development of prospect theory and has been influential in understanding cognitive biases and heuristics (Kahneman, 2011). Turing was primarily known as a mathematician and computer scientist, yet his work on artificial intelligence and the "Turing Test" (the Turing Test is a measure of a machine's ability to exhibit intelligent behavior equivalent to, or indistinguishable from, that of a human) has had a lasting impact on cognitive science and the study of human cognition (Turing, 1950). These key figures, along with many others (Warren McCulloch, Walter Pitts, Allen Newell, Marvin Minsky), have played crucial roles in shaping cognitive research and broadening our understanding of the human mind.

Over the past few decades, cognitive science has continued to evolve, incorporating new methodologies, such as neuroimaging techniques and computational modeling, and exploring the intersections between cognition and other fields, such as *social cognition*, *affective neuroscience* (Damasio, 1994),[1] and *embodied cognition* (Lakoff & Johnson, 1980).[2]

Notes

1. Affective neuroscience is a multidisciplinary field investigating how the brain generates and regulates emotions, moods, and other affective states. Researchers use neuroimaging (fMRI), EEG, and animal studies to map neural circuits, brain regions, and neurotransmitter systems linked to both basic (e.g., happiness, fear) and complex emotions, as well as social and cognitive–emotional interactions. These insights illuminate how emotions influence behavior, decision-making, and well-being and guide interventions

for psychiatric and neurological conditions such as mood and anxiety disorders, addiction, and autism.

2. Embodied cognition highlights how bodily experiences and interactions with the environment shape our thinking.

   This theory argues that cognition is not just brain-based but also influenced by physical movements, sensory–motor skills, and mental simulations of actions. This approach has transformed research in multiple fields, from psychology and neuroscience to AI and robotics, offering new ways to study and treat cognitive processes and disorders.

References

Brynjolfsson, E., & McAfee, A. (2014). *The second machine age: Work, progress, and prosperity in a time of brilliant technologies*. W. W. Norton & Company.

Chomsky, N. (1965). *Aspects of the theory of syntax*. MIT Press.

Damasio, A. (1994). *Descartes' error: Emotion, reason, and the human brain*. Putnam.

Dember, W. N. (1974). Motivation and the cognitive revolution. *American Psychologist, 29*(2), 161–168. https://doi.org/10.1037/h0035907

Diamond, J. (1991). *The rise and fall of the third chimpanzee*. Radius.

Diamond, J. (1997). *Guns, germs, and steel: The fates of human societies*. W. W. Norton & Company.

Eysenck, M. W., & Keane, M. T. (2020). *Cognitive psychology: A student's handbook* (8th ed.). Taylor & Francis.

Fernández, A., Goldberg, E., & Michelon, P. (2013). *The sharp brains guide to brain fitness: How to optimize brain health and performance at any age* (2nd ed.). SharpBrains, Inc.

Fiske, S. T., & Taylor, S. E. (2013). *Social cognition: From brains to culture* (2nd ed.). Sage.

Gardner, H. (1985). *The mind's new science: A history of the cognitive revolution*. Basic Books.

Gazzaniga, M. S., Ivry, R. B., & Mangun, G. R. (2019). *Cognitive neuroscience: The biology of the mind* (5th ed.). W. W. Norton & Company.

Goldstein, E. B. (2010). *Sensation and perception* (8th ed.). Wadsworth.

Hatfield, G. (2002). *Psychology, philosophy, and cognitive science: Reflections on the history and philosophy of experimental psychology*. Clarendon Press.

Henrich, J. (2016). *The secret of our success: How culture is driving human evolution, domesticating our species, and making us smarter*. Princeton University Press. https://doi.org/10.2307/j.ctvc77f0d

Kahneman, D. (2011). *Thinking, fast and slow*. Farrar, Straus and Giroux.

Lakoff, G., & Johnson, M. (1980). *Metaphors we live by*. University of Chicago Press.

Loftus, E. F. (1979). *Eyewitness testimony*. Harvard University Press.

Mayer, R. E. (2011). *Applying the science of learning*. Pearson.
Miller, G. A. (1956). The magical number seven, plus or minus two: Some limits on our capacity for processing information. *Psychological Review, 63*(2), 81–97.
Miller, G. A. (2003). The cognitive revolution: A historical perspective. *Trends in Cognitive Sciences, 7*(3), 141–144. https://doi.org/10.1016/S1364-6613(03)00029-9
Neisser, U. (1967). *Cognitive psychology*. Appleton-Century-Crofts.
Oxford English Dictionary. (n.d.). *Cognition*. Retrieved July 5, 2022.
Partridge, E. (2008). *Origins: A short etymological dictionary of modern English* (6th ed.). Routledge. Retrieved July 5, 2022.
Piaget, J. (1952). *The origins of intelligence in children*. International Universities Press.
Shanmugasundaram, M., & Tamilarasu, A. (2023). The impact of digital technology, social media, and artificial intelligence on cognitive functions: A review. *Frontiers in Cognition, 2*, 1203077. https://doi.org/10.3389/fcogn.2023.1203077
Shapin, S. (1996). *The scientific revolution*. University of Chicago Press.
Skinner, B. F. (1953). *Science and human behavior*. Macmillan.
Thagard, P. (2005). *Mind: Introduction to cognitive science* (2nd ed.). MIT Press.
Trigger, B. G. (2003). *Understanding early civilizations: A comparative study*. Cambridge University Press.
Turing, A. M. (1950). Computing machinery and intelligence. *Mind, 59*(236), 433–460.

CHAPTER 2

Foundations of Cognitive Psychology

Early Theories and Models of Cognition

During the formative years of cognitive psychology, various theories and models emerged to elucidate the manner in which the human brain processes information, leading to the development of several important early concepts.

The *theory of structuralism* was introduced by Wilhelm Wundt and Edward Titchener, who concentrated on deconstructing mental processes into their fundamental components, or "structures" (Titchener, 1910; Wundt, 1880/1897). They primarily utilized introspection as a means to examine the composition of conscious experiences.

Conversely, William James, James Angell, and John Dewey highlighted the adaptive aspects of mental processes and introduced the term *Functionalism.* Functionalist thinkers seek to comprehend the objectives of mental activities such as thinking, feeling, and perceiving, as well as their role in facilitating an organism's survival and adaptation to its environment (Angell, 1907; Dewey, 1896; James, 1890).

Drawing inspiration from philosophers such as Aristotle, David Hume, and John Locke, *Associationism* proposed that intricate mental processes could be comprehended as amalgamations of basic ideas or sensations linked through association principles such as contiguity, similarity, and contrast (Hume, 1748/2007; Locke, 1690/1980).

H. Kankam, *A Brief Excursion into Human Cognition*,
https://doi.org/10.1007/978-3-031-89752-8_2

Gestalt Psychology

Emerging in the early twentieth century, *Gestalt psychology* is an intellectual perspective that underscores the comprehensive nature of human cognition and perception. Notably, Gestalt psychologists such as Max Wertheimer, Wolfgang Köhler, and Kurt Koffka posited that the mind interprets and processes data as complete configurations or "Gestalten" (originating from German), as opposed to isolated components (Koffka, 1935; Köhler, 1947; Wertheimer, 1923/1938). Various core principles of Gestalt psychology are noteworthy, as they fundamentally influence how humans perceive and decipher diverse environments and stimuli, and these principles are extensively applied in digital contexts such as social media.

Figure-ground: the mind arranges sensory input into discrete figures (objects) that are prominent against a backdrop;

Proximity, similarity, and continuity: the mind tends to group elements that are in close proximity, exhibit similar appearances, or possess continuous forms;

Closure: the mind attempts to complete ambiguous or unfinished figures by supplying missing information on the basis of previous experiences and anticipations.

Gestalt psychology has substantially impacted cognitive psychology, particularly in the realms of perception, problem-solving, and learning.

Information Processing Approach

The *information processing approach*, which gained prominence in the 1950s and 1960s, views the human mind as a system that processes information, much like a computer (Miller, 1956). This approach focuses on understanding the steps and stages involved in various cognitive tasks, such as perception, memory, and decision-making (Atkinson & Shiffrin, 1968). The information processing approach is a framework used in cognitive psychology that considers mental processes similar to the workings of a computer in terms of input, processing, storage, and output.

The key pioneers of this approach include George Miller, who is known for his work in cognitive psychology. He is especially famous for his paper, "The Magical Number Seven, Plus or Minus Two: Some Limits on Our Capacity for Processing Information" (Miller, 1956), where he suggested that the number of objects an average human can hold in working memory is about seven.

Donald Broadbent developed the *Filter Model of Attention*, which describes how we selectively attend to the most important information (Broadbent, 1982). Imagine you are at a busy train station, trying to listen to an announcement about your train departure over the loudspeaker. There are several sources of sensory information:

1. The loudspeaker announcing train times
2. The chatter of people around you
3. The sounds of trains arriving and departing

According to Broadbent's model, each of these sensory inputs initially enters a sensory buffer. However, as you are unable to address these stimuli at once, your attention acts as a filter. In this way, you would "set" your filter to focus on the sound of the loudspeaker. This allows important information (the train times) to pass through the filter and be processed by your conscious mind. Moreover, the other sensory information (people talking, trains, etc.) is not attended to and therefore does not pass through the filter to be processed for meaning.

Baddeley is known for his work on working memory, especially his model of working memory, which includes the *central executive* (responsible for coordinating and integrating information); the *phonological loop* (a component of working memory that is responsible for the temporary storage and manipulation of auditory or verbal information); the *visuospatial sketchpad* (responsible for the temporary storage and manipulation of visual and spatial information); and the *episodic buffer* (Baddeley, 2000) (a temporary storage system that integrates information from the phonological loop, the visuospatial sketchpad, and long-term memory to create and maintain a unified representation of ongoing events or experiences). It also plays a critical role in the integration of information across time, allowing individuals to maintain a sense of continuity and coherence in their experiences.

Atkinson and Shiffrin developed the *multi store model* of memory, which includes a *sensory register* (the first stage of memory processing, in which incoming sensory information is briefly stored in its original form before being transferred to working memory, which holds information only for a fraction of a second), *short-term memory,* and *long-term memory* (Atkinson & Shiffrin, 1968)

Herbert Simon, John Clifford Shaw, and Allen Newell (the Newell-Shaw-Simon consortium) are known for their early work in artificial intelligence (Newell et al., 1958); they developed the concept of a *logic theorist* and were among the first to view the brain as an information processing system. *The logic theorist* is one of the earliest computer programs developed for artificial intelligence and automated reasoning in 1955 at the RAND Corporation.

Marvin Minsky, a cofounder of the Massachusetts Institute of Technology's AI laboratory, has made many contributions to the fields of artificial intelligence, cognitive psychology, mathematics, computational linguistics, robotics, and optics (Minsky, 1967). With John McCarthy, Nathaniel Rochester, and Claude Shannon, Minsky coined the term *artificial intelligence* (AI) in 1956 at the Dartmouth Conference. These are just a few of the many scientists who have contributed to the development of the *information processing approach* over the years. The key components of this process, which has played a significant role in shaping models and theories related to cognitive processes, include the following:

Serial processing: the mind processes information in a linear, step-by-step manner, with one stage completed before the next begins;

Stages and components: Cognitive tasks can be broken down into distinct stages or components, such as encoding, storage, and retrieval in memory;

Capacity limitations: the mind's processing resources are limited, constraining the amount of information that can be processed simultaneously or stored in memory.

Connectionism and Neural Networks

Another key concept is *connectionism and neural networks. Connectionism*, also known as *parallel distributed processing* (PDP), is an approach to cognitive modeling that emerged in the 1980s. Connectionist models are based on artificial neural networks, which are simplified simulations of biological neural networks in the brain (McClelland et al., 1986; Rumelhart et al., 1986). Warren McCulloch and Walter Pitts introduced the concept of artificial neurons and the first simple neural network model in their 1943 paper, "A Logical Calculus of the Ideas Immanent in Nervous Activity" (McCulloch & Pitts, 1943).

The key features of connectionist models and neural networks include the following:

Nodes and connections: connectionist models consist of interconnected nodes or units, analogous to neurons, which transmit and process information through weighted connections, similar to synaptic connections in the brain;

Parallel processing: unlike the serial processing approach, connectionist models process information simultaneously across multiple nodes and connections;

Learning and adaptation: Connectionist models can learn and adapt through adjusting the weights of connections on the basis of experience and feedback, a process known as learning algorithms, e.g., backpropagation: the backpropagation algorithm works by first propagating the input forward through the network to produce an output. Then, the error between the predicted output and the actual output is calculated, and this error is propagated backward through the network to adjust the weights and biases of the neurons in the network (Rumelhart et al., 1986; McClelland et al., 1986; Hinton et al., 2006).

References

Angell, J. R. (1907). The province of functional psychology. *Psychological Review, 14*(2), 61–91. https://doi.org/10.1037/h0071667

Atkinson, R. C., & Shiffrin, R. M. (1968). Human memory: A proposed system and its control processes. In K. W. Spence & J. T. Spence (Eds.), *The psychology of learning and motivation* (Vol. 2, pp. 89–195). Academic Press. https://doi.org/10.1016/S0079-7421(08)60422-3

Baddeley, A. D. (2000). The episodic buffer: A new component of working memory? *Trends in Cognitive Sciences, 4*(11), 417–423. https://doi.org/10.1016/S1364-6613(00)01538-2

Broadbent, D. E. (1982). Task combination and selective intake of information. *Acta Psychologica, 50*(3), 253–290. https://doi.org/10.1016/0001-6918(82)90043-9

Dewey, J. (1896). The reflex arc concept in psychology. *Psychological Review, 3*(4), 357–370. https://doi.org/10.1037/h0070405

Hinton, G. E., Osindero, S., & Teh, Y. W. (2006). A fast learning algorithm for deep belief nets. *Neural Computation, 18*(7), 1527–1554. https://doi.org/10.1162/neco.2006.18.7.1527

Hume, D. (2007). *An enquiry concerning human understanding*. Oxford University Press. (Original work published 1748).

James, W. (1890). *The principles of psychology* (Vol. 1–2). Henry Holt.

Koffka, K. (1935). *Principles of Gestalt psychology*. Harcourt Brace.

Köhler, W. (1947). *Gestalt psychology: An introduction to new concepts in modern psychology*. Liveright.

Locke, J. (1980). In P. H. Nidditch (Ed.), *An essay concerning human understanding*. Clarendon Press. (Original work published 1690).

McClelland, J. L., Rumelhart, D. E., & The PDP Research Group. (1986). *Parallel distributed processing: Explorations in the microstructure of cognition. Vol. 2: Psychological and biological models*. MIT Press.

McCulloch, W. S., & Pitts, W. (1943). A logical calculus of the ideas immanent in nervous activity. *The Bulletin of Mathematical Biophysics, 5*, 115–133. https://doi.org/10.1007/BF02478259

Miller, G. A. (1956). The magical number seven, plus or minus two: Some limits on our capacity for processing information. *Psychological Review, 63*(2), 81–97. https://doi.org/10.1037/h0043158

Minsky, M. (1967). *Computation: Finite and infinite machines*. Prentice-Hall.

Newell, A., Shaw, J. C., & Simon, H. A. (1958). Elements of a theory of human problem solving. *Psychological Review, 65*(3), 151–166. https://doi.org/10.1037/h0048495

Rumelhart, D. E., Hinton, G. E., & Williams, R. J. (1986). Learning internal representations by error propagation. In D. E. Rumelhart, J. L. McClelland, & The PDP Research Group (Eds.), *Parallel distributed processing: Explorations in the microstructure of cognition. Vol. 1: Foundations* (pp. 318–362). MIT Press.

Titchener, E. B. (1910). *A text-book of psychology*. Macmillan.

Wertheimer, M. (1923/1938). Laws of organization in perceptual forms. In W. D. Ellis (Ed.), *A source book of Gestalt psychology* (pp. 71–88). Routledge & Kegan Paul. (Original work published 1923).

Wundt, W. (1880/1897). *Outlines of psychology* (C. H. Judd, Trans.). Wilhelm Engelmann. (Original work published 1880).

CHAPTER 3

Perception and Attention

Perception and attention are fundamental cognitive processes that allow humans and other animals to interpret and interact with the environment (Freeman & Ambady, 2011).

Perception refers to the process through which living beings interpret and derive meaning from sensory information obtained from their surroundings; it involves multiple organs and neurotransmitters in the processing of information about their surrounding environment. Information is gathered through sensory organs (such as the eyes, ears, and skin) and processed by the brain (especially within the thalamus, the primary sensory cortex, and the association cortex) to create an internal representation or mental model of the surroundings. In essence, *perception* is crucial for organisms to navigate the world, recognize objects and people, and respond to changes in the environment. There are various types of *perception*, including visual, auditory, tactile, olfactory (smell), and gustatory (taste) perception.

The cognitive process of attention allows us to selectively focus on specific aspects of the environment or information while ignoring others. This allows us and other organisms to prioritize and allocate mental resources to the most relevant or salient stimuli, which is critical for decision-making and goal-directed behavior (Posner & Petersen, 1990; Eysenck & Keane, 2020). Attention can be influenced by both bottom-up (stimulus-driven) and top-down (goal-directed) factors.

H. Kankam, *A Brief Excursion into Human Cognition*,
https://doi.org/10.1007/978-3-031-89752-8_3

A bottom-up stimulus refers to a situation where attention is captured by external sensory stimuli that are salient or unexpected.

Here is an example: imagine you are walking down a busy street, engrossed in your own thoughts. Suddenly, you hear a loud crash followed by the sound of breaking glass. Your attention is immediately drawn to the source of the sound. In this scenario, sudden and unexpected noise acts as a bottom-up stimulus that captures one's attention involuntarily. Your attention is shifted toward the sound because it stands out from the background noise and grabs your attention automatically, without any conscious effort on your part.

Top-down *attention* is the cognitive process that allows us to voluntarily focus our attention on specific aspects of our environment according to our goals or interests instead of simply responding to stimuli that are the most salient or noticeable. This is controlled by the individual and can be guided by factors such as previous knowledge, expectations, or specific goals.

Let us consider a real-life scenario to illustrate this: imagine you are at a crowded party with music playing, people talking, glasses clinking, and all sorts of smells from different types of food. Amidst all of this sensory input, someone tells you that your favorite celebrity is also at the party. Suddenly, your attention becomes oriented toward finding this celebrity. You might start scanning faces, listening for their voice among the chatter, or looking for other indications of their presence. This stimulus—the information that your favorite celebrity is at the party—is a top-down attention stimulus. It is directing your attention in a particular way on the basis of your existing knowledge and interests rather than the most salient or noticeable features of your environment.

Another example we could consider would be studying for an exam. If you are reading a textbook and actively looking for information that you know will be on the test, that is top-down attention. The stimulus here is your knowledge of which particular topics will be on the exam, and this will therefore guide your attention as you study.

Examples of *attention* include *selective attention* (focusing on one thing while ignoring others), *sustained attention* (maintaining focus over an extended period), and *divided attention* (attending multiple things at once), which is related to multitasking. Importantly, the human brain is not necessarily well suited for multitasking, particularly in regard to tasks that require significant cognitive resources or focus. While we can divide our attention, doing so often results in decreased performance or accuracy with respect to the tasks at hand.

Both *perception* and *attention* work together to ensure that organisms can efficiently process and respond to the vast amount of sensory information they encounter. While *perception* provides an internal representation of the environment, *attention* filters and prioritizes this information on the basis of relevance, goals, or other factors, helping organisms make informed decisions and carry out goal-directed behaviors.

Visual and Auditory Perception

Let us explore how our sensory organs function. *Visual* and *auditory perceptions* are the cognitive processes that allow us to interpret and make sense of the information received through our eyes and ears, respectively (McGurk & MacDonald, 1976).

Visual perception involves the processing of light information to recognize objects, colors, textures, and motion. The key stages of visual perception include the following:

Early visual processing: Retinal cells convert light into neural signals, which are processed by the primary visual cortex;

Feature detection: specialized cells in the visual cortex detect specific features, such as edges, lines, and colors;

Object recognition: higher-level visual areas integrate these features to recognize objects and scenes.

Auditory perception involves the processing of sound waves to recognize and locate sounds. The key stages of *auditory perception* include the following:

Early auditory processing: hair cells in the cochlea convert sound vibrations into neural signals, which are transmitted to the primary auditory cortex;

Feature detection: specialized cells in the auditory cortex detect specific features, such as pitch, loudness, and timbre;

Sound recognition and localization: Higher-level auditory areas integrate these features to recognize sounds and determine their sources.

Although *auditory processing* is an essential part of human perception and communication, humans are considered to be more visually focused, with the visual system playing a dominant role in many aspects of perception and cognition. The visual system provides a rich source of information about the environment, allowing for efficient navigation, object recognition, and interaction.

Nick Chater is a behavioral and cognitive scientist known for his work on various aspects of human cognition, including *visual perception*, and he is the author of the exceptional book "*The Mind Is Flat*" (Chater, 2018). One of his key ideas is that our minds do not have a rich, detailed model of the world, as we might intuitively think. Instead, our brains construct a "grand illusion" on the basis of very minimal data. The theory posits that our perception of a rich and detailed world is largely an illusion created by our brain.

According to this perspective, our brains do not fully perceive or process all the information from our surroundings. Instead, the brain creates a convincing illusion of a detailed world from the relatively sparse sensory data it receives.

For example, in *visual perception*, the detail and color that we perceive are only present in the very center of our vision (the foveal view). Our peripheral vision is far less detailed, yet we perceive a uniformly detailed world around us because our brain fills in the gaps on the basis of what it expects to see, on the basis of past experiences and learned information.

This theory challenges the intuitive idea that human perception works like a camera, recording a fully detailed picture of our surroundings. Instead, it posits that our brains are actively constructing our perceptual experiences in a much more efficient, albeit less accurate, manner.

This concept has broad implications for understanding human cognition, artificial intelligence, and fields such as virtual reality, where creating the illusion of a fully detailed world can be done without needing to render every detail of the scene.

However, it is important to note that this is a theory and, like all scientific theories, is subject to further debate and empirical testing.

In the context of *visual perception*, this translates to the idea that we only perceive a small fraction of our surroundings at any given moment. We construct a coherent mental picture of our environment by "filling in the gaps" using expectations on the basis of past experiences. This "grand illusion" theory suggests that our brains are efficient processors of information, focusing on the most crucial details and using past data to fill in the rest.

Notably, while this perception process may have deficits with respect to its failure to be completely accurate or adequately detailed, processing the vast amount of visual information we encounter every waking moment of each day remains highly efficient.

Object Recognition and Face Processing

Object recognition and *face processing* are two related but distinct processes within the realm of *visual perception*. While both involve the identification and interpretation of visual stimuli, they have evolved for specific and diverse purposes.

Object recognition is the ability to identify and categorize objects within the visual environment. It involves the processing of various features, such as shape, color, and texture, to distinguish objects from their surroundings and recognize them as distinct entities. *Object recognition* relies on the hierarchical processing of visual information, with lower levels detecting basic features and higher levels integrating these features to form a coherent representation of the object. *Object recognition* is a cognitive process that enables us to identify and categorize objects on the basis of their features and our prior knowledge. Two influential theories of *object recognition* are as follows:

Template-matching theory: This theory proposes that the visual system matches the sensory input with stored templates or prototypes to recognize objects (Fischler & Elschlager, 1973);

Feature-based theory: This theory suggests that the visual system extracts key features from the sensory input and uses them to recognize objects by comparing them to stored representations (Treisman & Gelade, 1980; Biederman, 1987; Marr, 1982);

Face processing, on the other hand, is a specialized aspect of *visual perception* that involves the recognition and interpretation of faces. The human brain has evolved to be highly sensitive to facial features, as they convey important social and emotional information. As a result, face processing involves a more refined and specialized neural system than general object recognition does. The *fusiform face area* (FFA), a region in the inferior temporal cortex, is known to be specifically involved in face perception. We see, however, in work carried out by Isabel Gauthier on FFA, that this is much more complicated.Isabel Gauthier is a cognitive psychologist at Vanderbilt University, best known for her work on the *Fusiform Face Area* (FFA). As mentioned, the FFA located in the fusiform gyrus on the ventral surface of the brain has been identified in neuroimaging studies as being particularly active when people are looking at faces, as opposed to other types of objects. In contrast, Gauthier and her colleagues proposed an alternative view known as the "expertise hypothesis." This finding suggests that the role of the FFA is not exclusive to face perception; rather, it becomes active when individuals recognize any type of object with which they are familiar. To support this hypothesis, Gauthier conducted experiments with "Greebles," a specific object that people were trained to recognize ("Greebles" are a type of novel, computer-generated stimulus that resembles three-dimensional, abstract objects; they are designed to be similar in complexity to faces, with several parts that can vary in shape, size, and configuration). Gauthier reported that after extensive training, the FFA in these individuals also responded to Greebles in addition to faces. This finding indicated that the FFA could be involved more broadly in the recognition of highly familiar or expertly known objects, not just faces (Gauthier & Tarr, 1997).

While *object recognition* and *face processing* share some common underlying mechanisms, such as the hierarchical processing of visual information, they also exhibit unique properties due to their distinct functions. Faces, for example, are processed more holistically, meaning that the brain perceives the face as a whole rather than as a collection of individual features. This is known as the *configural* or *holistic* processing of faces, which is different from the *feature-based processing* often used for *object recognition.*

A classic demonstration of the importance of *configural processing* in face recognition is the "Thatcher Effect." If we take a photograph of a face and rotate it upside-down after inverting the eyes and mouth, it looks fairly normal. However, if we flip it right-side-up, it becomes clear that the mouth and eyes are also upside-down (a manipulation that is hard to detect when the whole face is upside-down). This illusion shows that disrupting the usual *configuration* of facial features significantly impacts our ability to recognize faces, indicating the importance of *configural processing* in this task (Thompson, 1980).

In contrast to *configural* or *holistic* processing, *feature-based processing* (used for object recognition) involves perceiving and recognizing individual components or features of an object rather than perceiving the object as a whole. This contrasts with the *holistic* or *configural processing* typically used for facial recognition. Let us take the example of recognizing a car. When we observe a car, we do not necessarily see it as a single, unified whole. Instead, we likely recognize it on the basis of its individual features, for example, its shape; the presence of wheels, windows, headlights, doors; and the distinctive logo or emblem of the manufacturer. Each of these features contributes to our perception and recognition of the object as a car.

Another example could be the recognition of a letter of the alphabet, such as "A." We identify the letter "A" on the basis of a combination of individual lines and angles—a horizontal line ("-") sandwiched between two diagonal lines ("/") in a specific configuration.

In each of these cases, we focus on the individual components or features of an object rather than perceiving the object in a holistic manner. The brain pieces together these features to recognize the object. This type of processing is typically employed for recognizing objects for which we have not developed specific expertise or for objects that lack a standard configuration, as we experience with faces (Treisman & Gelade, 1980; Biederman, 1987; Marr, 1982).

Attentional Processes and Selective Attention

Attention is a cognitive process that allows us to selectively focus upon specific aspects of our environment while filtering out irrelevant information. There are key attentional processes that are relevant:

Selective attention enables us to focus on specific sensory inputs, thoughts, or actions while ignoring others. Models of selective attention include Broadbent's *filter model* (Broadbent, 1958), Treisman's *attenuation model* (Treisman, 1964),[1] and Deutsch and Deutsch's *late selection model* (Deutsch & Deutsch, 1963).[2]

Selective attention allows one to filter out irrelevant or less important information and concentrate on the information that is most important for the task at hand. It is a critical capability for functioning in a world full of constant sensory inputs. A few examples: suppose you are studying in a bustling coffee shop. You hear the sound of the espresso machine, the chatter of other customers, the music playing over the speakers, you smell the aroma of coffee, etc. Despite these various distractions, you manage to focus your attention on the material you are studying. Similarly, when driving, especially in heavy traffic, there are numerous elements vying for your attention: traffic lights, road signs, pedestrians, other vehicles, your car's speedometer, maybe even a conversation with a passenger. However, you are able to selectively attend to the most essential elements to keep yourself and others safe.

Divided attention involves allocating attentional resources to multiple tasks or stimuli simultaneously. However, our capacity for divided attention is limited, and performance often suffers when tasks compete for the same attentional resources.

Let us consider an example: you are cooking dinner while also keeping an eye on a football match on the TV and listening to your child tell you about their day at school. In this case, you are dividing your attention between cooking, watching the game, and listening to your child. A regular domestic challenge!

Research has shown that trying to perform multiple tasks at once can result in more mistakes or can lead to tasks taking longer to complete than if they were done sequentially. This is because switching back and forth between tasks can cause *cognitive interference*, essentially creating a bottleneck in our information processing.

With practice, some tasks can become automated or require less cognitive effort, making it easier to perform them alongside other tasks. For example, an experienced driver might be able to navigate familiar roads while also carrying out a conversation with a passenger. However, if a task requires focused attention or is new or complex, it is usually better to address this with undivided attention.

Sustained attention refers to maintaining focus on a task or stimulus over an extended period, also known as "vigilance." Examples include meditation, which involves focusing one's attention on a particular object, thought, or activity for lengthy stretches of time.

Similarly, when preparing for an exam, the student needs to maintain a focus on his or her study materials for extended periods. Whether one is reading, writing notes, or practicing mathematics problems, these activities require *sustained attention*.

Spatial attention involves directing attention to specific locations in space, which can be guided by both bottom-up (stimulus-driven) and top-down (goal-driven) factors (Posner, 1980). In other words, it refers to the ability to focus on a particular location or area within our visual field while ignoring other areas. It is a form of selective attention but is specific to the spatial layout of the scene or environment we find before us.

Here is an example: imagine you are at a tennis match, seated in the stands. The players are small from your perspective, and there is a lot going on around you—other spectators chatting, vendors selling snacks, people moving around. Despite these distractions, you manage to focus your attention on the specific part of the court where the game is taking place. You keep track of the small, fast-moving ball, the positions of the players, and you anticipate where the ball will go next. This is all possible owing to your ability to direct your spatial attention to the game while ignoring irrelevant stimuli in other locations. In fact, your focus on the game is so intense that when someone suddenly waves to you from the other end of the stands, you might not even notice them—that is because your spatial attention is directed elsewhere. The famous "invisible gorilla" experiment, officially called the "*selective attention test*," is a powerful demonstration of both *spatial attention* and a related concept called *inattentional blindness* (Simons & Chabris, 1999).

In this experiment, participants are asked to watch a video of people passing a basketball to each other and to count the number of passes made by the team wearing white.

During the video, a person in a gorilla suit walks through the scene, beating their chest. Amazingly, roughly half of the participants do not notice the gorilla at all, despite it being plainly visible. This demonstrates that our attentional resources are limited: when we are focusing on one task (in this case, counting the number of passes), we can become blind to other, unexpected stimuli in our visual field, even those that are quite salient and would be easy to notice if we were not preoccupied with another task.

While the gorilla experiment is often discussed in terms of *inattentional blindness*, it certainly also involves *spatial attention*. The participants are directing their *spatial attention* to the players passing the ball and, as a result, fail to notice the unexpected stimulus (the gorilla) that appears in a different location.

This experiment clearly reveals how our cognitive and perceptual systems work, showing that we often see what we expect to see or what we are focusing on and can miss a great deal of information that is right in front of our eyes.

Digital Media and Attention Deficits

Research on *digital media* and *attention deficits* has gained considerable attention in the past few decades (no pun intended), particularly with the rise of smartphones, social media, and other forms of screen-based entertainment and communication. Some studies have reported a correlation between the amount of time spent on screens (especially engaging in rapid-task switching, such as checking *social media*, then reading an article, then watching a video) and difficulties in *sustained attention*; in this case, heavy media multitaskers have been found to be more susceptible to distractions (Rosen et al., 2011; Cain et al., 2016). Many digital platforms, especially social media apps, are designed to capture and maintain users' attention.

Features such as notifications, “likes,” and endlessly scrolling feeds can promote “neurological fast food,” rewarding the brain’s desire for novelty but potentially undermining sustained and focused attention. Heavy digital media usage can lead to symptoms commonly associated with “Attention Deficit Hyperactivity Disorder” (ADHD), such as impulsivity and difficulty focusing. While it is not clear whether digital media use can cause ADHD, there is evidence that those with ADHD might be more drawn to digital media and that excessive use might exacerbate attentional challenges. Inherently, there is particular concern regarding children and adolescents, whose brains are still developing. Excessive screen time during these formative years might influence the development of attentional capacity (Swing et al., 2010; Marciano et al., 2022). The American Academy of Pediatrics recommends limited screen time for children, emphasizing the importance of quality over quantity. The COVID-19 pandemic greatly increased the reliance on digital media for both work and leisure, leading to an increase in research on the effects of this sudden shift. Some findings have suggested that prolonged screen time and online activities could worsen attention difficulties.

Alternately, studies have shown that digital media, when used properly, could assist those with attention deficit disorders. For example, certain educational apps and software could help individuals with ADHD manage their symptoms and improve their focus (Powell et al., 2018). Other digital tools and platforms can be used to train attention and mindfulness. For example, digital meditation apps such as *Headspace* or *Calm* have been shown to promote mindfulness and could counteract some of the attention-scattering effects of other forms of digital media. The concept of “digital minimalism,” popularized by computer science Professor Cal Newport (Newport, 2019), advocates for a more intentional and limited use of digital tools to prevent their potential negative impacts on attention and well-being.

While these trends provide some insight, research in this area is ongoing and complex, with many factors at play.

Multisensory Integration

Multisensory integration is the process by which information from different sensory modalities, such as vision, audition, and touch, is combined to form a coherent perception of the environment. This integration can enhance perception, improve accuracy, and result in faster processing of sensory information.

The key principles of *multisensory integration* include the following:

Temporal and Spatial Congruence: Multisensory integration is more likely to occur when sensory inputs are temporally and spatially aligned or close in time and space (Stein & Meredith, 1993; Spence & Driver, 2004; Vatakis & Spence, 2007; Wallace & Stevenson, 2014). This is a complex concept, as spatial congruence can be interpreted in several ways.

Temporal congruence refers to two or more events occurring at the same time or in synchronization with each other. The events are congruent in terms of time, meaning that they align or coincide. Let us consider the simple case of listening to music. The different elements of a song (consider the beat of the drum, the melody of the guitar, the vocals, etc.) must all occur in *temporal congruence* with each other for the song to sound harmonious. If one element is out of sync, the music sounds off. In another example, when you watch a movie, you expect the audio and visual components to be in sync. If they are not (for example, if the sound of a character speaking does not match up with the movement of their lips), it can jar and disrupt the viewing experience. This is because the brain expects *temporal congruence* between audio and visual stimuli.

Spatial congruence in this context refers to when sensory stimuli from different modalities occur in the same spatial location, which can make this integration process more efficient or effective (Stein & Meredith, 1993; Spence & Driver, 2004). At a live concert, you can see the band playing their instruments (visual) and hear the music they are producing (auditory) from the same location. The *spatial congruence* of these sensory experiences helps the brain integrate them into a single perceptual event (Vatakis & Spence, 2007; Wallace & Stevenson, 2014).

Inherently, both *spatial* and *temporal congruence* are relevant in any form of communication. The *congruence* between what we say (verbal communication) and how we say it (nonverbal communication, for example, body language) influences how our message is perceived. A message is likely to be received more positively if the verbal and nonverbal messages are congruent both in time (*temporal congruence*) and in their content (which we can think of as a type of *spatial congruence*). Conversely, if they are incongruent, it can lead to confusion or miscommunication (Posner, 1980; Alais & Burr, 2004).

The principle of *inverse effectiveness* in multisensory integration is based on the idea that the more ambiguous or weak a stimulus is in one sense, the more it can benefit from the addition of a stimulus in another sense. This means that when stimuli from different senses are combined, the enhancement in perception is greater when the individual sensory inputs are weak than when they are strong (Stein & Meredith, 1993; Spence, 2011). Let us say you are looking for your misplaced cellphone. If the ringer of your phone is set to a high volume and you call it, you can easily locate it just by hearing. However, if the ringer volume is low (weak auditory input), you will benefit more from also looking for the light of the screen or the vibration on a surface (visual and tactile inputs).

When looking at *Bayesian integration*, the brain is thought to combine sensory inputs in a statistically optimal manner, weighing each input according to its reliability and prior knowledge. Imagine you are at a party in a crowded room, and you are trying to locate a friend whose voice you hear, but you cannot see them. You have two sources of information: the sound of your friend's voice (auditory information) and the visual information from scanning the room. Each of these sources of information is uncertain to some degree: the voice could be drowned out in the crowded room, making it difficult to pinpoint its exact location, and your visual scan of the room could be impeded by the crowd and poor lighting.

According to *Bayesian integration*, one's brain takes both sources of information and weighs them according to their reliability or certainty. If the auditory information is more reliable, it will have a greater influence on your perception of where your friend is located, and vice versa. In this way, *Bayesian integration* allows us to combine different senses to form the most reliable perception possible (Friston, 2005; Marr, 1982).

Another common example is the *ventriloquism effect,* where visual information (seeing the ventriloquist's puppet seeming to talk) overrides auditory information (the ventriloquist's voice actually coming from the ventriloquist's mouth, not the puppet), leading us to perceive the puppet as the source of the voice (Alais & Burr, 2004).

Bayesian integration is thought to play a role in many multisensory phenomena and is a central idea in current theories of perception. In other words, *Bayesian integration* can be used to explain how the brain combines information from different senses to form a coherent and unified perception of the world.

Notes

1. Anne Treisman's attenuation model refines Broadbent's filter theory by using an attenuator rather than a complete filter, allowing unattended information to be processed at a weaker level. A second stage then analyzes

meaning, enabling personally relevant stimuli (like your name) to break through, illustrating how attention is more flexible than once thought.

2. Deutsch and Deutsch's *late selection model* (1963) proposes that all incoming stimuli undergo *both* physical and semantic analysis *before* attention is selectively allocated. In this view, the filter (or selection mechanism) operates *after* meaning is evaluated, allowing for more flexible and context-dependent attention. This helps explain findings such as the *cocktail party effect*, where unattended information can still receive some level of processing. In addition to Treisman's attenuation model, Deutsch and Deutsch's framework broadened our understanding of selective attention by incorporating elements of both early and late selection theories.

References

Alais, D., & Burr, D. (2004). The ventriloquist effect results from near-optimal bimodal integration. *Current Biology, 14*(3), 257–262. https://doi.org/10.1016/j.cub.2004.01.029

Biederman, I. (1987). Recognition-by-components: A theory of human image understanding. *Psychological Review, 94*(2), 115–147. https://doi.org/10.1037/0033-295X.94.2.115

Broadbent, D. E. (1958). *Perception and communication.* Pergamon Press.

Cain, M. S., Leonard, J. A., Gabrieli, J. D. E., & Finn, A. S. (2016). Media multitasking in adolescence. *Psychonomic Bulletin & Review, 23*(6), 1884–1891. https://doi.org/10.3758/s13423-016-1036-3

Chater, N. (2018). *The mind is flat: The illusion of mental depth and the improvised mind.* Allen Lane.

Deutsch, J. A., & Deutsch, D. (1963). Attention: Some theoretical considerations. *Psychological Review, 70*(1), 80–90. https://doi.org/10.1037/h0039515

Eysenck, M. W., & Keane, M. T. (2020). *Cognitive psychology: A student's handbook* (8th ed.). Psychology Press.

Fischler, M. A., & Elschlager, R. A. (1973). The representation and matching of pictorial structures. *IEEE Transactions on Computers, C-22*(1), 67–92. https://doi.org/10.1109/T-C.1973.223602

Freeman, J. B., & Ambady, N. (2011). A dynamic interactive theory of person construal. *Psychological Review, 118*(2), 247–279. https://doi.org/10.1037/a0022327

Friston, K. (2005). A theory of cortical responses. *Philosophical Transactions of the Royal Society B: Biological Sciences, 360*(1456), 815–836. https://doi.org/10.1098/rstb.2005.1622

Gauthier, I., & Tarr, M. J. (1997). Becoming a "Greeble" expert: Exploring mechanisms for face recognition. *Vision Research, 37*(12), 1673–1682. https://doi.org/10.1016/S0042-6989(96)00286-6

Marciano, L., Ostroumova, M., Schulz, P. J., & Camerini, A. L. (2022). Digital media use and adolescents' mental health during the COVID-19 pandemic: A systematic review and meta-analysis. *Frontiers in Public Health, 9*, 793868. https://doi.org/10.3389/fpubh.2021.793868

Marr, D. (1982). *Vision: A computational investigation into the human representation and processing of visual information*. W. H. Freeman.

McGurk, H., & MacDonald, J. (1976). Hearing lips and seeing voices. *Nature, 264*, 746–748. https://doi.org/10.1038/264746a0

Newport, C. (2019). *Digital minimalism: Choosing a focused life in a noisy world*. Portfolio/Penguin.

Posner, M. I. (1980). Orienting of attention. *Quarterly Journal of Experimental Psychology, 32*(1), 3–25. https://doi.org/10.1080/00335558008248231

Posner, M. I., & Petersen, S. E. (1990). The attention system of the human brain. *Annual Review of Neuroscience, 13*(1), 25–42. https://doi.org/10.1146/annurev.ne.13.030190.000325

Powell, L., Parker, J., & Harpin, V. (2018). What is the level of evidence for the use of currently available technologies in facilitating the self-management of difficulties associated with ADHD in children and young people? A systematic review. *European Child & Adolescent Psychiatry, 27*, 1391–1412. https://doi.org/10.1007/s00787-017-1092-x

Rosen, L. D., Lim, A. F., Carrier, L. M., & Cheever, N. A. (2011). An empirical examination of the educational impact of text message-induced task switching in the classroom: Educational Implications and Strategies to Enhance Learning. *Educational Psychology, 17*(2), 163–177. https://doi.org/10.5093/ed2011v17n2a4

Simons, D. J., & Chabris, C. F. (1999). Gorillas in our midst: Sustained inattentional blindness for dynamic events. *Perception, 28*(9), 1059–1074. https://doi.org/10.1068/p281059

Spence, C. (2011). Crossmodal correspondences: A tutorial review. *Attention, Perception, & Psychophysics, 73*(4), 971–995. https://doi.org/10.3758/s13414-010-0073-7

Spence, C., & Driver, J. (2004). *Crossmodal space and crossmodal attention*. Oxford University Press.

Stein, B. E., & Meredith, M. A. (1993). *The merging of the senses*. MIT Press.

Swing, E. L., Gentile, D. A., Anderson, C. A., & Walsh, D. A. (2010). Television and video game exposure and the development of attention problems. *Pediatrics, 126*(2), 214–221. https://doi.org/10.1542/peds.2009-1508

Thompson, P. (1980). Margaret Thatcher: A new illusion. *Perception, 9*(4), 483–484. https://doi.org/10.1068/p090483

Treisman, A. (1964). Verbal cues, language, and meaning in selective attention. *American Journal of Psychology, 77*(2), 206–219. https://doi.org/10.2307/1420127

Treisman, A., & Gelade, G. (1980). A feature-integration theory of attention. *Cognitive Psychology, 12*(1), 97–136. https://doi.org/10.1016/0010-0285(80)90005-5

Vatakis, A., & Spence, C. (2007). Crossmodal binding: Evaluating the "unity assumption" using audiovisual speech stimuli. *Perception & Psychophysics, 69*(5), 744–756. https://doi.org/10.3758/BF03193776

Wallace, M. T., & Stevenson, R. A. (2014). The construct of the multisensory temporal binding window and its dysregulation in developmental disabilities. *Neuropsychologia, 64*, 105–123. https://doi.org/10.1016/j.neuropsychologia.2014.08.005

CHAPTER 4

Memory

Sensory Memory, Short-Term Memory, and Long-Term Memory

Memory is a fundamental component of human cognition, allowing us to recall past events, learn new skills, and perform countless other tasks (Squire & Dede, 2015). Neurobiology is deeply intricate and involves complex networks of *neurons* (nerve cells) in the brain. Let us focus on the three main types of memory: *sensory, short-term,* and *long-term.*

Sensory memory is the initial, brief storage of sensory information. It holds large amounts of incoming data for a very short period (less than a second for visual information and a few seconds for auditory information). It is often considered part of the perception process. For example, when you see a lightning bolt in the sky, even after the bolt is gone, a brief image of it stays in your mind. This brief retention of visual detail is an example of *visual sensory memory* or *iconic memory. Iconic memory* (visual) and *echoic memory* (auditory) are examples of *sensory memory* (Neisser, 1967; Baddeley, 2000).

Short-term memory (STM) is a temporary storage system that holds information for approximately 20–30 seconds; it is also referred to as *working memory* (Miller, 1956; Baddeley, 2012). The capacity of short-term memory is limited, typically holding approximately 7 ± 2 items (such as numbers, words, or other simple pieces of information) for no more than 20–30 seconds at a time. For example, when you are given a phone

H. Kankam, *A Brief Excursion into Human Cognition*,
https://doi.org/10.1007/978-3-031-89752-8_4

number, you might repeat it in your head for a few seconds until you dial it. Information in an STM can be lost through decay (if not rehearsed) or displacement (due to new information entering the STM).

Long-term memory (LTM) is the relatively permanent storage of information. It has a vast capacity and can store information for a lifetime. For example, your memory of your first day at school, a vacation you took a few years ago, or facts such as the capital of France, are stored in *long-term memory*. Information is transferred from the STM to the LTM through processes such as rehearsal, elaboration, and organization (Baddeley, 2000; Miller, 1956).

From a neurobiological standpoint, different types of memories are stored in different areas of the brain (Squire & Wixted, 2011). The very simplified view is as follows:

- the *hippocampus*, located in the medial temporal lobe, plays a crucial role in the formation of new long-term memories of experienced events (also known as episodic or autobiographical memories). It is like a gateway through which new memories must pass before reaching their permanent storage place in the brain;
- the *prefrontal cortex* is important for working memory;
- *procedural memory*, a type of long-term memory involving how to perform different actions and skills (such as riding a bike), is primarily stored in the *basal ganglia and cerebellum;*
- *semantic memory*, another type of long-term memory, represents our memory of facts, concepts, and knowledge about the external world. The *temporal lobe* is involved in storing these memories.

Memory storage and retrieval are made possible by the connections between neurons and synapses. The strengthening of these synapses is often referred to as *long-term potentiation* (LTP), and it is thought to be the primary mechanism by which memories are stored in the brain (Bliss & Collingridge, 2013). The saying "neurons that fire together wire together" summarizes this concept.

An example of memory in action can be learning to ride a bike. First, the procedural knowledge of balance, pedaling, and steering is consciously processed in *working memory*. Through practice and repetition, this knowledge becomes encoded within *long-term memory* and becomes automatic so that we are able to ride a bike without consciously thinking about the mechanics involved. This encoding process involves synaptic strengthening between neurons in areas such as the *basal ganglia* and *cerebellum*.

Working Memory and Its Models

Working memory is an extension of the concept of *short-term memory* and is responsible for the temporary storage and manipulation of information necessary for complex cognitive tasks, such as learning, reasoning, and problem-solving. Baddeley and Hitch suggested the *working memory model* in 1974. The model was revised in 2000 to include a fourth component, the *episodic buffer* (Baddeley & Hitch, 1974; Baddeley, 2000).

The initial model proposes that *working memory* consists of three components. The *central executive,* a supervisory system that controls and coordinates the activities of the other components, which are the *phonological loop,* responsible for the temporary storage and rehearsal of auditory and verbal information, and the *visuospatial sketchpad,* responsible for the temporary storage and manipulation of visual and spatial information. The fourth component, added in 2000, is the *episodic buffer,* which integrates information from the *phonological loop, visuospatial sketchpad,* and *long-term memory* to form coherent episodes or chunks.

Episodic and Semantic Memory

Episodic and *semantic memory* are two types of declarative (explicit) long-term memory that involve the conscious recollection of facts and events (Tulving, 1972; Schacter & Tulving, 1994).

Episodic memory refers to the ability to recall specific events or experiences that have occurred in the past. In other words, it allows us to mentally "travel" back in time and relive past experiences. It involves remembering the who, what, where, and when of a particular event. For example, remember the details of a vacation, a birthday party, or a conversation with a friend. *Episodic memory* is closely linked to the medial temporal lobe, particularly the hippocampus.

In contrast, *semantic memory* pertains to the recollection of general knowledge, concepts, and facts that are independent of any particular event or experience. It includes knowledge about language, history, science, and other domains of knowledge. *Semantic memory* is the memory system that underlies our ability to understand language, recognize objects and faces, and comprehend abstract concepts. *Semantic memory* relies on a distributed network of brain regions, including the medial temporal lobe and the neocortex.

Episodic and *semantic memory* differ in several ways. *Episodic memory* is autobiographical, meaning that it is tied to a specific individual's experiences, whereas *semantic memory* is more objective and shared among people. *Episodic memory* is time bound, meaning that it has a temporal dimension and is tied to specific moments in time, whereas *semantic memory* is timeless and not tied to a particular moment. Additionally, *episodic memory* is more vulnerable to forgetting over time, whereas *semantic memory* is more resistant to forgetting. Both *episodic* and *semantic memory* are important for everyday functioning, and they work together to allow us to navigate the world around us and make sense of our experiences. Groundbreaking research on *episodic* and *semantic memory* was carried out by Endel Tulving, which was initially introduced in his 1972 paper (Tulving, 1972) and was later expanded (Schacter & Tulving, 1994).

When individuals with neurogenerative diseases such as dementia are studied, episodic memory is significantly impaired, resulting in challenges with respect to remembering recent events and creating new memories. Difficulties in recalling conversations, appointments, or significant life events are frequently encountered. As the disease progresses, individuals may additionally face struggles in recollecting distant memories. Moreover, with the decline in cognitive abilities, *semantic memory* can also be impacted, although this tends to remain relatively intact during the early stages of the condition. With further progression of the disease, individuals may encounter difficulties in word finding, comprehension, and general knowledge.

Autobiographical Memory and False Memories

Autobiographical memory is a type of episodic memory that involves the recollection of personal life events and experiences and the development of one's concept of self (Conway & Pleydell-Pearce, 2000). *Autobiographical memory* is influenced by factors such as emotions, goals, and cultural expectations.

False memories are distortions or fabrications of events or experiences that did not actually occur. These can arise from several factors, for example, *misinformation* refers to exposure to misleading information after an event, which can lead to the incorporation of that information into memory. Then, there is *imagination inflation*, where the vivid imagining of an event can increase belief in its occurrence, leading to the formation of *false memories.*

False memories can also result through source-monitoring errors, meaning confusing the source of information, such as misattributing an event experienced by someone else, to oneself.

Elizabeth Loftus is a prominent American psychologist known for her extensive research on memory, particularly eyewitness testimony and false memories (Loftus, 1997). She has shown that false memories can be induced through suggestion and that they can be just as vivid and detailed as true memories. Loftus's research has shown that eyewitness testimony can be unreliable and subject to distortion. She has conducted numerous experiments in which participants are shown a video of a simulated event and later asked to recall details about it. She reported that the way questions are phrased can influence what people remember and that memories can be easily manipulated and distorted through *suggestion.*

One of Loftus's most famous experiments involved showing participants a video of a car accident and then asking them how fast the cars were going when they "smashed into each other" versus when they "contacted" each other. The participants who were asked the question with the word "smashed" were more likely to report a higher speed than those who were asked the question with the word "contacted," even though the video was exactly the same for both groups (Loftus & Palmer, 1974).

The implications of false memories can be significant and far-reaching, affecting various aspects of our lives.

There are legal implications in criminal cases where eyewitness testimonies are critical pieces of evidence. As described above, false memories can lead to inaccurate testimonies, resulting in wrongful convictions or acquittals. Factors that can contribute to false memories in eyewitnesses include suggestive questioning, exposure to misinformation, and stress experienced during the event.

False memories in therapeutic settings can be problematic, particularly when they involve the unintentional implantation—by therapists—of false memories of traumatic events, such as childhood abuse. This can lead to damaging consequences for patients and their families, including the erosion of trust, strained relationships, and unnecessary emotional distress.

False memories can result from various *cognitive biases* that shape how we process and recall information. For example, *confirmation bias* may lead us to selectively remember information that supports our beliefs, whereas the *availability heuristic* may cause us to overestimate the likelihood of events that are more easily brought to mind.

Our memories play a crucial role in shaping our *self-concept* and *personal identity. False memories* can distort our self-perception and influence our beliefs about our past experiences, values, and relationships.

False memories can affect *decision-making* by altering our perception of past events and influencing our judgments about future situations. For example, a false memory of a negative experience with a particular activity may lead us to avoid similar activities in the future, even if the actual experience was not as negative as the memory produced.

False memories can impact our social interactions and relationships, i.e., they have social implications. For example, a false memory about a past conflict with a friend may cause unnecessary tension and resentment. Additionally, the spread of false memories within a group or community can lead to the formation of shared false beliefs or collective memories, influencing group dynamics and decision-making.

In conclusion, the implications of false memories are vast, so it is essential to understand the factors that contribute to memory distortions and to develop strategies to minimize their occurrence and impact (Loftus, 2005).

References

Baddeley, A. D. (2000). The episodic buffer: A new component of working memory? *Trends in Cognitive Sciences, 4*(11), 417–423. https://doi.org/10.1016/S1364-6613(00)01538-2

Baddeley, A. D. (2012). Working memory: Theories, models, and controversies. *Annual Review of Psychology, 63*, 1–29. https://doi.org/10.1146/annurev-psych-120710-100422

Baddeley, A. D., & Hitch, G. (1974). Working memory. In G. Bower (Ed.), *The psychology of learning and motivation* (Vol. 8, pp. 47–89). Academic Press.

Bliss, T. V. P., & Collingridge, G. L. (2013). Expression of NMDA receptor-dependent LTP in the hippocampus: Bridging the divide. *Molecular Brain, 6*, 5. https://doi.org/10.1186/1756-6606-6-5

Conway, M. A., & Pleydell-Pearce, C. W. (2000). The construction of autobiographical memories in the self-memory system. *Psychological Review, 107*(2), 261–288. https://doi.org/10.1037/0033-295X.107.2.261

Loftus, E. F. (1997). Creating false memories. *Scientific American, 277*(3), 70–75. https://doi.org/10.1038/scientificamerican0997-70

Loftus, E. F. (2005). Planting misinformation in the human mind: A 30-year investigation of the malleability of memory. *Learning & Memory, 12*(4), 361–366. https://doi.org/10.1101/lm.94705

Loftus, E. F., & Palmer, J. C. (1974). Reconstruction of automobile destruction: An example of the interaction between language and memory. *Journal of Verbal Learning and Verbal Behavior, 13*(5), 585–589. https://doi.org/10.1016/S0022-5371(74)80011-3

Miller, G. A. (1956). The magical number seven, plus or minus two: Some limits on our capacity for processing information. *Psychological Review, 63*(2), 81–97. https://doi.org/10.1037/h0043158

Neisser, U. (1967). *Cognitive psychology*. Appleton-Century-Crofts.

Schacter, D. L., & Tulving, E. (1994). What are the memory systems? In D. L. Schacter & E. Tulving (Eds.), *Memory systems 1994* (pp. 1–38). MIT Press.

Squire, L. R., & Dede, A. J. O. (2015). Conscious and unconscious memory systems. *Cold Spring Harbor Perspectives in Biology, 7*(3), a021667. https://doi.org/10.1101/cshperspect.a021667

Squire, L. R., & Wixted, J. T. (2011). The cognitive neuroscience of human memory since H.M. *Annual Review of Neuroscience, 34*, 259–288. https://doi.org/10.1146/annurev-neuro-061010-113720

Tulving, E. (1972). Episodic and semantic memory. In E. Tulving & W. Donaldson (Eds.), *Organization of memory* (pp. 381–403). Academic Press.

CHAPTER 5

Language

Language Acquisition and Development

Language acquisition refers to the process by which humans learn to understand and use a language from infancy to adulthood. The process involves several stages:

- Prelinguistic stage (0–12 months): infants engage in vocalizations, such as cooing and babbling, and begin to understand simple words and phrases (Feldman, 2020);
- One-word stage (12–18 months): children start to use single words to convey meaning, such as "mama" or "dada" (Clark, 2016);
- Two-word stage (18–24 months): children begin to combine words to form simple phrases, such as "more milk" or "big dog" (Tomasello, 2003);
- Telegraphic stage (2–3 years): children start to produce more complex sentences but may still omit function words and use simplified grammar (Bruner, 1983);
- Later language development (3+ years): children continue to refine their vocabulary, grammar, and pragmatic skills throughout childhood and adolescence (Clark, 2016).

H. Kankam, *A Brief Excursion into Human Cognition*,
https://doi.org/10.1007/978-3-031-89752-8_5

There are various theories that consider the process of *language acquisition*. Some of these are interesting to look at, as they have very different approaches:

The two theories of *language acquisition* we consider here include *nativist theory* (Chomsky, 1965, 1986; Lenneberg, 1967), which emphasizes the role of innate and biological factors, and *social interactionist theory* (Vygotsky, 1978; Bruner, 1983; Tomasello, 2003), which highlights the importance of social and environmental influences, i.e., communication between children and their caregivers or peers in the process of acquiring language.

To approach the subject in some detail, it would be interesting to look at some key principles of *nativist theory,* as well as the arguments of its critics:

Innate Knowledge: Nativists believe that certain knowledge is hardwired into the human brain and not solely derived from experience. For example, some propose that humans possess an innate understanding of basic mathematical principles, as well as a predisposition to learn language (Chomsky, 1965, 1986);

Language Acquisition: *Nativist Theories* of language development posit that humans have a built-in "language acquisition device" (LAD) or "universal grammar" that enables them to acquire language rapidly and effortlessly. This innate capacity is believed to be unique to humans and is triggered by exposure to language during a critical period in early childhood (Lenneberg, 1967);

Modularity of Mind: Nativists often argue that the human mind is composed of distinct, specialized modules, each dedicated to processing specific types of information (Fodor, 1983). This view suggests that our cognitive abilities are dependent not only on general-purpose learning mechanisms but also upon specialized, innate mechanisms that have evolved for specific tasks;

Critical Periods: *Nativist Theories* propose that there are specific time windows during which certain cognitive and linguistic abilities can be acquired most easily. If these critical periods are missed, learning becomes more difficult or may not occur at all (Lenneberg, 1967).

The critics of *nativist theory* argue that it underestimates the role of environmental factors and learning in cognitive development. They point to evidence from various fields, including neuroscience, linguistics, and psychology, which suggests that human knowledge and abilities are shaped by a complex interplay between innate factors and environmental influences (Snow, 1999).

For a broader view, let us take a brief look at the key principles of *social interactionist theory* and the arguments of its critics:

Zone of Proximal Development (ZPD): Vygotsky's (1978) concept of the ZPD refers to the difference between a child's current developmental level and their potential developmental level when the child is supported by guidance or collaboration with a more knowledgeable individual, such as a parent, teacher, or peer. Social interaction within the ZPD enables children to advance their language and cognitive development by building on their existing abilities;

Scaffolding: Scaffolding, as posited by Bruner (1983), is the process through which caregivers or more knowledgeable peers provide support to help a child accomplish tasks they would not be able to perform independently. This support is gradually reduced as the child's competence increases. In the context of language development, *scaffolding* may involve adjusting the complexity of speech to match the child's level, providing feedback, or using gestures and body language to aid comprehension;

Joint Attention and Intention Reading: Social interactionist theories emphasize the importance of *joint attention*, the shared focus of a child, and their caregiver upon an object or event, with regard to language development. Joint attention facilitates the child's understanding of the social context and the meaning of words. *Intention reading* refers to the ability to infer the intentions and goals of others, which is critical for learning the communicative functions of language (Tomasello, 2003).

Usage-Based Learning: According to social interactionists, language learning is a *usage-based* process in which children acquire linguistic structures and rules by observing patterns in the language to which they are exposed. The frequency and consistency of these patterns play a significant role in language acquisition (Tomasello, 2003).

Social-cognitive skills: Social interactionist theories emphasize the role of *social-cognitive skills,* such as theory of mind, perspective-taking, and empathy, in language development. These skills enable children to understand and interpret the intentions and mental states of others, which is crucial for effective communication (Bruner, 1983).

Critics of *social interactionist theory* argue that it may not adequately explain the rapid rate of language development in young children or the ease with which they acquire complex grammatical structures (Pinker,

1994). Nevertheless, the social interactionist perspective highlights the importance of social and contextual factors in the process of language acquisition, providing a more comprehensive understanding of how children learn to communicate.

The assumption is, as with many other theories, that language acquisition is a mix of both of the stated theories (Snow, 1999).

Phonetics, Phonology, Morphology, Syntax, Semantics, and Pragmatics

Linguistics, the scientific study of language and its structure, is traditionally divided into several subdisciplines, which include *phonetics, phonology, morphology, syntax, semantics, and pragmatics.* The neurobiological processes involved in these linguistic components pertain to the field of neurolinguistics, which explores how the brain processes and comprehends language. A simplified breakdown for each component is as follows:

Phonetics delves into the attributes of speech sounds—the physical sounds of human speech—covering their production, transmission, and perception with regard to their physical qualities. It addresses the articulatory, acoustic, and auditory facets of speech sounds.

Neurobiologically, the auditory cortex in the superior temporal gyrus plays a crucial role in processing these sounds. The motor cortex, along with *Broca's area*, is involved in the production of speech sounds (Ladefoged & Johnson, 2014).

Phonology, on the other hand, is concerned with abstract, mental representations of speech sounds, and the regulations that dictate their arrangement and patterns within a language (Dehaene-Lambertz, 2017). In other words, this refers to the way sounds function within a particular language. *Phonology* investigates the "phoneme," which is the smallest sound unit that differentiates meaning in a language. While the exact neural correlates are still being explored, research suggests the involvement of the superior temporal gyrus, along with regions in the frontal and parietal lobes, in the processing of phonological information.

Morphology explores the formation and structure of words, including the guidelines for combining "morphemes," the smallest meaning-bearing units in a language (e.g., roots, prefixes and suffixes).[1] Morphological processing engages a network of regions, including the left inferior frontal gyrus part of the prefrontal cortex (part of *Broca's area*), the posterior superior temporal gyrus (part of *Wernicke's area*), and the angular and supramarginal gyri. This network is involved in analyzing word forms and accessing stored word meanings. Notably, Bozic et al. (2010) elaborated on a more expanded view of language processing.

Syntax examines the rules that dictate the organization of words and phrases to create grammatically correct sentences. It analyzes how words are assembled and structured to convey meaning through syntactic categories (e.g., nouns, verbs, adjectives) and principles (e.g., word order, agreement, constituency). Like *morphology*, syntactic processing engages a network involving *Broca's area* (particularly for understanding grammatical structure) and *Wernicke's area* (for comprehending sentence meaning) (Friederici, 2011).

Semantics, meanwhile, investigates the meaning of words, phrases, and sentences, as well as the relationships between words (e.g., synonymy, antonymy, and hyponymy) and the rules for interpreting sentence meaning on the basis of their syntactic structure. The comprehension of meaning involves a widespread network of regions, including the temporal lobes and inferior parietal lobule, which are involved in semantic memory, as well as the frontal lobes, which are important for semantic working memory and control processes (Humphries et al., 2006).

Pragmatics addresses the study of how context influences the interpretation of meaning in language. It focuses on the ways in which speakers use language to convey meaning beyond the literal or dictionary definitions of words and sentences. *Pragmatics* examines the social, cultural, and situational factors that shape language use and understanding (Levinson, 1983).

Some key concepts and areas of study within the area of *pragmatics* are as follows:

Pragmatics analyzes how utterances function as actions, such as making requests, giving commands, asking questions, and making promises. It examines how speakers use language to perform actions (speech acts) and how listeners understand and respond to these acts.

Pragmatics helps to recognize the importance of context in interpreting meaning.

Context includes the physical setting, social relationships, shared knowledge, and cultural norms that influence communication. Pragmatics analysis takes into account these contextual factors to understand how meaning is constructed.

Pragmatics also assists in exploring how listeners go beyond the literal meaning of words to make *inferences* and fill in gaps in meaning. Speakers often convey meaning indirectly or imply certain information, and listeners use contextual cues to infer the intended meaning. In this way, *pragmatics* investigates the implied meaning in utterances.

Presuppositions are assumptions that speakers make about what their listeners already know or believe. *Implicatures* refer to additional meanings conveyed indirectly by the speaker that go beyond the explicit content of these utterances.

Pragmatics examines the ways in which speakers use language to maintain social harmony and show *politeness*. It investigates politeness strategies, speech rituals, and cultural variations in politeness norms.

Pragmatics studies the use of deictic expressions (Deixis), such as pronouns (e.g., "I," "you") and demonstratives (e.g., "this," "that"), which depend upon the context of the speech act for their interpretation.

Pragmatics analyzes extended stretches of language, such as conversations and written texts, to uncover patterns of language use and the implicit meanings conveyed within them (Speech and Discourse Analysis).

Overall, *pragmatics* plays a crucial role in understanding how language is used in real-life communication and how meaning is negotiated between speakers and listeners. It bridges the gap between language structure and language use, highlighting the dynamic and context-dependent nature of linguistic meaning.

While *semantics* is concerned with the meaning of words and sentences, *pragmatics* goes beyond this to investigate how meaning is constructed and interpreted in real-life communication. It explores how speakers use language to achieve their communicative goals and how listeners interpret and respond to those linguistic cues.

The following is an example that illustrates the role of *pragmatics*: imagine that two friends, Sarah and John, are having a conversation.

> Sarah: "It's quite warm in here, isn't it?"
> John: "Yeah, I forgot to turn off the heater."

In this context, the pragmatic interpretation of John's response relies on the contextual cues provided by Sarah. While Sarah's statement appears to be a simple observation about the room temperature, it may also carry an implied request or suggestion to adjust the environment.

John's response acknowledges Sarah's observation, implying that he agrees with her and reveals that he is responsible for the warm temperature. By interpreting Sarah's remark pragmatically, John infers her intention and assumes that she wants him to turn off the heater.

The true meaning of John's response goes beyond the literal words he used, as he addresses the implied request and takes appropriate action based on the context (Levinson, 1983).

This example demonstrates how *pragmatics* help us understand that meaning in communication is not solely determined by the words themselves but also by the context, shared knowledge, and the speaker's intentions.

As mentioned, *pragmatics* examines the social, cultural, and situational factors that shape language use and understanding. One can easily understand how misunderstandings can be caused by *pragmatic* interpretations.

Scenario: Two friends from different cultural backgrounds, Alex (from the United States) and Maria (from Japan), are having a conversation.

> Alex: "Hey Maria, your outfit looks interesting today. Did you pick it out yourself?"
>
> Maria: "Yes, I did. Thank you!"

In this scenario, Alex's intention was to compliment Maria on her outfit. However, Maria's response might seem somewhat reserved to Alex, which could create a cultural misunderstanding.

In Japanese culture, it is often considered impolite to accept compliments directly or boast about one's own achievements. Instead, modesty and humility are highly valued. When someone receives a compliment, it is customary to downplay it or attribute it to others. In this case, Maria's response, "Yes, I did," might seem simple and reserved for Alex, who may have expected a more enthusiastic response such as "Thank you! I'm glad you think so!"

As a result, Alex may interpret Maria's response as indifferent or lacking appreciation for the compliment, leading to potential miscommunication or cultural misunderstanding (Wierzbicka, 2003).

Language Comprehension and Production

Language comprehension and production refer to the mental processes responsible for interpreting and creating spoken or written language. They involve understanding the language that we hear or read (comprehension) and constructing meaningful sentences to express our thoughts and ideas (production). These processes are essential for effective communication and involve various cognitive mechanisms and language-specific knowledge (Gaskell et al., 2018; Goldrick et al., 2014).

Language comprehension encompasses deciphering linguistic input (such as speech sounds or written text), determining the meaning of words and phrases, and merging this information with previous knowledge and context to grasp the intended message. Crucial processes in *language comprehension* include *word recognition*, *syntactic parsing*, and *semantic interpretation*. For example, when you're reading a book, you must decode the meaning of the words, understand the relationships between characters, and follow the plot. This requires the ability to understand language at multiple levels, from individual words and phrases to complex sentences and narratives. When someone tells a joke, you must understand not only the literal meanings of the words but also the implied meanings and the punchline. This involves understanding the nuances of language, including tone, context, and cultural references.

Language production entails the conceptualization of ideas and messages, the choice and arrangement of words and phrases, and the creation of suitable linguistic outputs (for example, speech or writing) (Goldrick et al., 2014). Vital processes in language production include lexical access, syntactic organization, and phonological and articulatory encoding. During a conversation, you need to listen to what the other person is saying (comprehension) and respond appropriately (production). Your responses require you to quickly form meaningful sentences, which may also involve adjusting your language on the basis of the context or the person you're talking to. If you are giving a speech, you need to organize your thoughts, construct sentences, modulate your tone of voice, and use body language to communicate effectively. Each of these aspects involves language production. With respect to these specific activities, the language-related regions of the brain (such as *Broca's area* for production and *Wernicke's area* for comprehension) work together to process and produce language. Importantly, language comprehension and production are highly interconnected, with effective communication often requiring a combination of both (Gaskell et al., 2018).

Bilingualism and Second Language Acquisition

Bilingualism refers to the ability to use two languages proficiently, whereas second language acquisition is the process of learning a nonnative language after the first language has been acquired. Several factors can influence the success of second language acquisition, including age, motivation, cognitive ability, learning strategies, and the linguistic environment (Grosjean, 1982; Van Hell & Tanner, 2012).

Bilingual language development: Bilingual children typically follow similar developmental stages to monolingual children but may exhibit unique patterns of language development depending on factors such as language exposure, language dominance, and the degree of similarity between the two languages (Bialystok, 2001; De Houwer, 2009; Genesee et al., 2004).

Simultaneous bilingualism occurs when a person, often a child, learns two languages at the same time. For example, a child may grow up in a home where one parent speaks English and the other parent speaks Spanish, resulting in the child learning both languages simultaneously from birth (De Houwer, 2009; Genesee & Nicoladis, 2007).

Sequential or consecutive bilingualism occurs when a person learns a second language after having acquired their first language. For example, a person who grows up speaking German at home and in their community may later learn English when they begin school or when they move to an English-speaking country (Grosjean, 2010; McLaughlin, 1984).

Cognitive and neural effects of bilingualism: Bilingualism has been associated with cognitive advantages, such as enhanced executive function, cognitive flexibility, and metalinguistic awareness. Studies have also revealed differences in the neural organization and activation patterns of bilingual individuals compared with those of monolingual individuals. Neuroimaging studies have shown that bilinguals have more gray matter in areas of the brain associated with language processing than monolinguals do (Bialystok et al., 2012; Mechelli et al., 2004). Studies have also revealed differences in the neural organization and activation patterns of bilingual individuals compared with those of monolingual individuals (Abutalebi & Green, 2016).

Bilingual language processing: Bilingual individuals often engage in simultaneous activation of both languages during language processing, even when only one language is used. This activation requires the management of potential crosslinguistic interference, which is thought to be a contributing factor with regard to the cognitive advantages associated with bilingualism (Kroll & Bialystok, 2013; Van Hell & Tanner, 2012).

Second language acquisition theories: Several theories have been proposed to explain the process of second language acquisition, including *the contrastive analysis hypothesis* (Lado, 1957),[2] *the interlanguage hypothesis* (Selinker, 1972),[3] and the *input hypothesis* (Krashen, 1985).[4] Various teaching methods and learning strategies have been developed to facilitate second language acquisition, such as the audio-lingual method, the communicative approach, and task-based language teaching. Effective language learning strategies include setting clear goals, engaging in active practice, using authentic materials, and focusing on both form and meaning (Ellis, 2008a, 2008b; Lightbown & Spada, 2013). Let us look at this example: a student from China moves to the United States for college and is an intermediate English speaker. To improve her English language skills, she takes English language courses at her university (formal instruction). At the same time, she lives in a dormitory with English-speaking students and frequently uses English for daily activities (immersion). Through this combination of instruction and immersion, she gradually improves her proficiency in English, eventually achieving fluency.

Theories of second language acquisition vary in their focus. Some emphasize the role of the linguistic environment and social interaction (as advocated in the sociocultural theory of Vygotsky, 1978; Lantolf, 2000), while others highlight cognitive processes and internal mental representations of language (as discussed in *cognitive linguistic theory*, Ellis, 2008a, 2008b; Langacker, 2008).

Notes

1. Roots are the core part of a word, usually derived from Latin or Greek, that carries the central meaning. Prefixes and suffixes are added to roots to create new words.

   Examples of roots:

   "bio" - life (e.g., biology, biography)

   "graph" - to write or draw (e.g., autograph, geography)

   "tele" - distance, far (e.g., telephone, television)

"aqua" - water (e.g., aquarium, aqueduct)

Examples of prefixes:

"un-" - not, opposite of (e.g., unhappy, undo)

"re-" - again, back (e.g., rewrite, reapply)

"pre-" - before (e.g., preheat, prehistoric)

"dis-" - apart, away (e.g., disappear, disconnect)

Examples of suffixes:

"-ed" - past tense for regular verbs (e.g., walked, talked)

"-ing" - present participle for verbs (e.g., walking, talking)

"-ly" - adverb form of adjectives (e.g., quickly, happily)

"-ness" - noun form of adjectives, indicating a state or quality (e.g., happiness, darkness)

2. Contrastive analysis hypothesis (CAH) asserts that differences between a learner's L1 and an L2 drive errors in language acquisition. By comparing both languages, instructors can anticipate learners' challenges and shape teaching strategies. While influential, critics say that CAH overlooks individual, cognitive, and social factors and that not all predicted errors occur in practice.
3. The Interlanguage Hypothesis, coined by Larry Selinker in 1972, proposes that second language learners develop a unique and evolving linguistic system influenced by their first language, the target language, and the learning context. This "interlanguage" follows systematic rules yet remains dynamic, showing variability over time. Key features include fossilization (persistent non-target-like forms), transfer (positive or negative influence from the native language), and progression through developmental stages common to most learners. Recognizing interlanguage as systematic and changeable helps educators address persistent errors, adapt instruction, and more effectively support ongoing language development.
4. Stephen Krashen's input hypothesis argues that second language acquisition (L2) occurs when learners receive comprehensible input slightly above their current proficiency ($i + 1$). Unlike conscious language learning (memorizing rules), acquisition is subconscious and relies on meaningful, engaging

input. Krashen also suggested a natural order of grammar acquisition and emphasized affective factors such as motivation and self-confidence in lowering the "affective filter," making learning smoother. Finally, his Monitor Hypothesis proposes that explicit knowledge can correct output, but overreliance on it may hinder natural acquisition. While critics note that output and explicit instruction also matter, Krashen's theory has profoundly influenced communicative teaching methods that prioritize rich, understandable input.

References

Abutalebi, J., & Green, D. W. (2016). Neuroimaging of language control in bilinguals: Neural adaptation and reserve. *Bilingualism: Language and Cognition, 19*(4), 689–698. https://doi.org/10.1017/S1366728916000225

Bialystok, E. (2001). *Bilingualism in development: Language, literacy, and cognition.* Cambridge University Press.

Bialystok, E., Craik, F. I. M., & Luk, G. (2012). Bilingualism: Consequences for mind and brain. *Trends in Cognitive Sciences, 16*(4), 240–250. https://doi.org/10.1016/j.tics.2012.03.001

Bozic, M., Tyler, L. K., Ives, D. T., Randall, B., & Marslen-Wilson, W. D. (2010). Bihemispheric foundations for human speech comprehension. *Proceedings of the National Academy of Sciences, 107*(40), 17439–17444. https://doi.org/10.1073/pnas.1000531107

Bruner, J. S. (1983). *Child's talk: Learning to use language.* W. W. Norton & Company.

Chomsky, N. (1965). *Aspects of the theory of syntax.* MIT Press.

Chomsky, N. (1986). *Knowledge of language: Its elements and origins.* Praeger.

Clark, E. V. (2016). *First language acquisition* (2nd ed.). Cambridge University Press.

De Houwer, A. (2009). *Bilingual first language acquisition.* Multilingual Matters.

Dehaene-Lambertz, G. (2017). The phonological brain. In G. Gaskell & J. Mirković (Eds.), *The Oxford handbook of psycholinguistics* (2nd ed.). Oxford University Press.

Ellis, N. C. (2008a). The dynamics of second language emergence: Cycles of language use, language change, and language acquisition. *Modern Language Journal, 92*(2), 232–249.

Ellis, R. (2008b). *The study of second language acquisition* (2nd ed.). Oxford University Press.

Feldman, H. (2020). Language development from 0–12 months. In P. K. Smith & C. Hart (Eds.), *The Wiley-Blackwell handbook of childhood social development* (3rd ed., pp. 61–82). Wiley-Blackwell.

Fodor, J. A. (1983). *The modularity of mind: An essay on faculty psychology.* MIT Press.
Friederici, A. D. (2011). The brain basis of language processing: From structure to function. *Physiological Reviews, 91*(4), 1357–1392. https://doi.org/10.1152/physrev.00006.2011
Gaskell, M. G., Mirković, J., & Hare, M. (2018). Language comprehension and production. In M. G. Gaskell (Ed.), *The Oxford handbook of psycholinguistics* (2nd ed., pp. 57–74). Oxford University Press.
Genesee, F., & Nicoladis, E. (2007). Bilingual first language acquisition. In E. Hoff & M. Shatz (Eds.), *Blackwell handbook of language development* (pp. 324–342). Blackwell. https://doi.org/10.1002/9780470757833.ch16
Genesee, F., Paradis, J., & Crago, M. (2004). *Dual language development and disorders: A handbook on bilingualism & second language learning.* Brookes.
Goldrick, M., Ferreira, V., & Miozzo, M. (Eds.). (2014). *The Oxford handbook of language production.* Oxford University Press.
Grosjean, F. (1982). *Life with two languages: An introduction to bilingualism.* Harvard University Press.
Grosjean, F. (2010). *Bilingual: Life and reality.* Harvard University Press.
Humphries, C., Binder, J. R., Medler, D. A., & Liebenthal, E. (2006). Syntactic and semantic modulation of neural activity during auditory sentence comprehension. *Journal of Cognitive Neuroscience, 18*(4), 665–679. https://doi.org/10.1162/jocn.2006.18.4.665
Krashen, S. D. (1985). *The input hypothesis: Issues and implications.* Longman.
Kroll, J. F., & Bialystok, E. (2013). Understanding the consequences of bilingualism for language processing and cognition. *Journal of Cognitive Psychology, 25*(5), 497–514. https://doi.org/10.1080/20445911.2013.799170
Ladefoged, P., & Johnson, K. (2014). *A course in phonetics* (7th ed.). Cengage Learning.
Lado, R. (1957). *Linguistics across cultures: Applied linguistics for language teachers.* University of Michigan Press.
Langacker, R. W. (2008). *Cognitive grammar: A basic introduction.* Oxford University Press.
Lantolf, J. P. (2000). *Sociocultural theory and second language learning.* Oxford University Press.
Lenneberg, E. H. (1967). *Biological foundations of language.* Wiley.
Levinson, S. C. (1983). *Pragmatics.* Cambridge University Press.
Lightbown, P. M., & Spada, N. (2013). *How languages are learned* (4th ed.). Oxford University Press.
McLaughlin, B. (1984). *Second-language acquisition in childhood: Vol. 2. School-age children.* Lawrence Erlbaum.

Mechelli, A., Crinion, J. T., Noppeney, U., O'Doherty, J., Ashburner, J., Frackowiak, R. S. J., & Price, C. J. (2004). Structural plasticity in the bilingual brain. *Nature, 431*, 757. https://doi.org/10.1038/431757a

Pinker, S. (1994). *The language instinct*. William Morrow and Company.

Selinker, L. (1972). Interlanguage. *International Review of Applied Linguistics, 10*(3), 209–241. https://doi.org/10.1515/iral.1972.10.1-4.209

Snow, C. E. (1999). Social perspectives on the emergence of language. In B. MacWhinney (Ed.), *The emergence of language* (pp. 257–276). Lawrence Erlbaum Associates.

Tomasello, M. (2003). *Constructing a language: A usage-based theory of language acquisition*. Harvard University Press.

Van Hell, J. G., & Tanner, D. (2012). Second language proficiency and cross-language lexical activation. *Language Learning, 62*(2), 148–171. https://doi.org/10.1111/j.1467-9922.2012.00710.x

Vygotsky, L. S. (1978). *Mind in society: The development of higher psychological processes*. Harvard University Press.

Wierzbicka, A. (2003). *Cross-cultural pragmatics: The semantics of human interaction* (2nd ed.). Walter de Gruyter.

CHAPTER 6

Reasoning and Problem-Solving

Reasoning and problem-solving are critical cognitive processes that allow individuals to make sense of the world, make decisions, and solve problems. It involves the ability to form conclusions, judgments, or inferences from facts or premises. It is generally classified into two categories: *deductive reasoning* and *inductive reasoning* (Evans, 2008; Johnson-Laird, 2008).

Deductive and Inductive Reasoning

Deductive reasoning is a top-down approach in which one starts with a general principle or set of rules and applies it to specific instances. *Deductive reasoning* entails deriving particular inferences from broad theories or assumptions. If the underlying assertions are correct and the reasoning follows logical principles, then the resultant conclusion is inevitably true. For example, given the premises "All humans are mortal" and "Socrates is human," one can deduce that "Socrates is mortal" (Johnson-Laird, 2008).

Inductive reasoning involves drawing general conclusions from specific observations or instances. Unlike *deductive reasoning, inductive reasoning* does not guarantee the truth of the conclusion but provides only a degree of probability. This is a bottom-up approach where one starts with specific instances and tries to develop a general principle or set of rules. For

H. Kankam, *A Brief Excursion into Human Cognition*,
https://doi.org/10.1007/978-3-031-89752-8_6

example, observing many white swans might lead one to conclude that "all swans are white," even though this conclusion may not be universally true (Evans, 2008).

Heuristics and Biases

Heuristics and *biases* are essential concepts in the fields of cognitive psychology and behavioral economics. They offer insights into how humans make decisions, often in ways that deviate from what might be considered rational or optimal.

The psychologists Daniel Kahneman and Amos Tversky are generally considered the founders of *heuristic and bias* research programs (Kahneman et al., 1982; Tversky & Kahneman, 1974). Their work in the 1970s and 1980s helped establish *cognitive biases* as a major area of study in psychology. Kahneman was awarded the Nobel Prize in Economic Sciences in 2002 for his work on judgment and decision-making, much of which was done in collaboration with Tversky.

The renowned German psychologist Gerd Gigerenzer, however, has been a prominent critic of the *heuristics* and *biases* tradition, arguing that heuristics can often lead to good decisions and that *biases* are sometimes better understood as adaptations to particular environments. Gigerenzer criticizes the *heuristics* and *biases* program for focusing too much on the negative, error-prone side of *heuristics* and not enough on their utility and effectiveness. His work has helped establish the "fast and frugal" school of thought (Gigerenzer, 2008; Gigerenzer et al., 1999) in decision-making research, which emphasizes the value of simple "rules of thumb." Here is a *recognition heuristics* example: suppose you are asked to determine which of two cities, San Diego or San Antonio, has a larger population. If you recognize the name "San Diego" but not "San Antonio," the *recognition heuristic* suggests that you should infer that San Diego has a larger population. This rule works under the assumption that larger, more significant entities are more likely to be recognized than smaller, less significant entities. Obviously, this *heuristic* does not guarantee a correct decision every time, but it provides a good enough answer quickly and with very little effort, demonstrating the practical value of simplicity in decision-making processes.

Richard H. Thaler is an economist and Noble Laureat who has drawn heavily on research in *heuristics* and *biases* to develop the field of *behavioral economics*. His work shows how *cognitive biases* can lead to anomalies in economic behavior that challenge traditional economic models. With Cass R. Sunstein, a legal scholar, the pair worked together to apply ideas from *heuristics* and *biases* research to public policy. Their work on the ***nudge theory***, which suggests that slight changes in the way choices are presented can have large effects on decisions, has been particularly influential. Thaler and Sunstein coauthored the book *Nudge: Improving Decisions About Health, Wealth, and Happiness* (Thaler & Sunstein, 2008).

However, what are *heuristics*? *Heuristics* are mental shortcuts that people use to find a quick solution or, in other words, to make decisions or judgments quickly. They are cognitive strategies or "rules of thumb" that significantly accelerate the process of finding a satisfactory solution, particularly when dealing with complex situations. However, these shortcuts may not always lead to the best or most accurate decision.

For example, the *availability heuristic* is our tendency to estimate the likelihood of an event on the basis of how easily examples or instances come to mind. In other words, we tend to think that events that happen more frequently around us are more likely to recur because we recall them with greater ease. This could lead us to overestimate the prevalence of certain events that are more memorable or dramatic. Here, is an example:

Suppose you watch the news and see a story about a plane crash. For the next few weeks, you are overly cautious about flying and believe it is exceedingly dangerous, even though, statistically, air travel is much safer than car travel. The plane crash story is easily recalled and readily "available" in one's memory owing to its recency and the emotional reaction it triggered, causing one to overestimate the risk of flying.

In this instance, the *availability heuristic* is at play. Because a vivid or dramatic event such as a plane crash is more memorable than countless plane journeys that occur safely every day, it can lead to an inaccurate perception of the likelihood of this type of event (Tversky & Kahneman, 1973).

The representativeness heuristic describes the tendency to judge the probability of an event, or the likelihood of a hypothesis, on the basis of how closely it resembles a known example or prototype. This can be shown by the following example, often known as the "Linda Problem," a classic illustration of the *representativeness heuristic* (as well as a *conjunction fallacy*).

Imagine that you meet a woman named Linda, who is single, outspoken, and very bright. She majored in philosophy and was deeply concerned with issues of discrimination and social justice, participating in antinuclear demonstrations during college.

Now, which of the following is more likely?

(A) Linda is a bank teller
(B) Linda is a bank teller and is active in the feminist movement

Many people might choose option B because it seems to represent more of the information given about Linda. However, statistically speaking, option A is more likely. This is because the set of all bank tellers (option A) is larger than the set of all feminist bank tellers (option B). Thus, there are simply more opportunities for Linda to be a bank teller than there are for her to be both a bank teller and a feminist.

People base their prediction on the degree to which Linda represents or matches their stereotypes or images of feminists, ignoring the base rates (i.e., the relative number of bank tellers and feminists) (Tversky & Kahneman, 1983).

Anchoring and adjustment heuristics refer to the tendency to rely heavily on an initial piece of information (the "anchor") and inadequately adjust one's estimate on the basis of subsequent information. Here, is an example:

Let us say you're buying a used car, and you have done some research and decided that $15,000 is a reasonable price to pay. When you get to the dealership, the salesperson tells you that the car you are interested in costs $18,000. Despite your research, you might end up negotiating from the $18,000 price (the "anchor"), rather than your initial estimate of $15,000. Therefore, you might end up paying something like $17,000 for the car, even though this is more than you originally thought the car was worth.

In this example, the salesman's initial price of $18,000 served as an "anchor" that influenced your final decision, even though you had other relevant information. The *anchoring* and *adjustment heuristic* can affect a wide range of decisions (Furnham & Boo, 2011; Tversky & Kahneman, 1974), from financial decisions such as this one to judgments about probability, length, and many others. The effect can be very influential, and it is often used strategically in situations such as negotiations or pricing strategies, where the first number that is introduced can set the stage for the rest of the discussion.

Now, let us look at *Biases*. *Biases* are systematic errors in thinking that influence the decisions and judgments that people make. Some of these *biases* may be a result of *heuristics*. *Biases* can lead to perceptual distortion, poor judgment, or irrational interpretation.

A prominent illustration of bias is *confirmation bias*. This refers to our inclination to seek out, understand, support, and remember details that reinforce our previously held beliefs or assumptions. Moreover, we often neglect or do not pay enough attention to other viewpoints or alternatives that might contradict our established perspectives. This can lead to skewed perspectives and decisions on the basis of incomplete or unbalanced information. The following is an example of *confirmation bias*:

Imagine you believe that eating many carrots greatly improves your eyesight because you once read it in a health magazine. Later, multiple articles on the internet were published: some state that carrots can contribute to eye health but do not significantly improve eyesight, whereas others support your belief that carrots greatly improve your eyesight.

Because of *confirmation bias*, you are more likely to focus on and remember the articles that confirm your existing belief about carrots and eyesight. You may ignore or forget about the articles suggesting otherwise or discredit their sources to keep your initial belief intact.

Confirmation bias can influence people's views in many areas, including social stereotypes, politics, and even scientific research, as people sometimes unintentionally cherry-pick data that support their stance (Nickerson, 1998).

Note that there are a multitude of biases (hindsight bias, self-serving bias, negativity bias, etc.) that can significantly impact our decisions and judgments in a variety of contexts.

While *heuristics* and *biases* can lead to errors, it is important to remember that they are not inherently bad. As described in the "fast and frugal" school of thought, heuristics can help us navigate complex environments that encompass an overwhelming amount of information, and biases can be adaptive under certain conditions by improving decision-making efficiency when speed is crucial and the available information is limited. An example of this is the *availability heuristic*, where people judge the frequency or probability of an event on the basis of how easily examples come to mind. However, being aware of these *heuristics* and *biases* can help us improve our decision-making processes, especially in situations where accuracy is more important than speed. This is particularly relevant in fields such as medicine, law, finance, and others, where decisions can have significant consequences.

In the age of artificial intelligence, an understanding of these cognitive processes is even more important. The main risk is that errors due to inherent ***human biases*** are transferred to AI systems, which are then utilized in the making of important decisions. Let us look at an inherent example:

Let us consider a scenario where a company is developing an AI system to review job applications and shortlist candidates for interviews. The company provides historical data of successful candidates as input to train the AI model. However, these historical data may contain inherent biases based on past hiring practices, such as gender or racial bias.

During the training process, if the AI system is exposed to a disproportionate number of successful applications from a particular gender or race, it may learn to associate those attributes with success. Consequently, when the AI system is deployed to review new job applications, it might unknowingly favor candidates who match the characteristics of historically successful applicants, perpetuating bias in the hiring process. In this case, the bias from the training data is transferred to the AI system, leading to discriminatory outcomes.

The AI system may unintentionally replicate and amplify existing societal biases, potentially exacerbating issues related to diversity and inclusion in hiring (Caliskan et al., 2017; Mehrabi et al., 2021).

It is crucial to address biases in AI systems by carefully curating training data, ensuring diversity and representation, and implementing bias mitigation techniques. Regular audits and ongoing monitoring of AI systems can help identify and rectify any unintended biases that may emerge during the deployment phase. Although we understand the origin of these potential problems, we must strive to implement designs and programs that mitigate these *biases*.

Problem-Solving Strategies

Problem-solving can be described as a cognitive process directed at achieving a goal when the solution is not immediately obvious. The process can be broken down into several steps:

Identifying the problem and ***defining the problem*** so that we can clearly understand it. The next step is to ***generate alternatives***, that is, consider workable solutions, followed by ***evaluating these alternatives*** as viable solutions. We act upon a chosen solution by ***implementing*** it and finally review the effectiveness of the chosen solution by ***evaluating*** the outcome. Consequently, the process is considered a learning process (Duncker,

1945; Ohlsson, 2011). We also tend to use strategies that can aid us in the problem-solving process. For example, using *trial and error in testing* different solutions until a successful one is found or using an existing *algorithm* so that we can systematically, step-by-step, come up with a solution. As already mentioned, mental shortcuts or "rules of the thumb"—*heuristics*—come into use by simplifying the problem-solving process but do not guarantee a solution. Another strategy would be to *work backward*, starting from the goal state and working in reverse to determine the steps needed to reach the initial state. By using *analogical reasoning*, the solution for a similar problem can be applied to a current problem to find a solution.

Insight, Creativity, and Expertise

Insight is the sudden realization or understanding of a solution to a problem, often described as an "aha!" moment. *Insight* problems typically involve restructuring the mental representation of the problem or overcoming a mental mind set (i.e., a tendency to approach a problem in a particular way on the basis of past experiences) (Ohlsson, 2011). Here, is an example:

Let us say you are a business owner, and you have two branches of your business in different locations. Branch A always performs better in sales than Branch B does. You have tried many things to improve the performance of Branch B, such as training the staff and improving the products, but nothing seems to work.

One day, you decide to spend some time at Branch B to observe. You notice that Branch B is located in a part of the town that is busy only in the mornings and afternoons but not in the evening. In contrast, Branch A is located in an area that remains busy even in the evening.

Your *insight* here is that the lower performance of Branch B is not primarily due to staff performance or product quality, but the specific business hours and location. People are not around to shop in the evening, which is when most sales take place at Branch A. This *insight* could lead you to adjust the business strategy of Branch B, such as focusing on morning and afternoon sales, or moving to a location that has more evening foot traffic.

Creativity is the ability to generate novel, original, and valuable ideas or solutions. *Divergent thinking*, which involves generating multiple viable solutions, is an essential aspect of creativity. Factors that can promote creativity include cognitive flexibility, openness to experience, and intrinsic motivation (Ward et al., 1997). We can look at *creativity* from different perspectives.

For example, *scientific creativity*, when a marine biologist studying coral reefs developed a new method for regenerating dying reefs, used a unique combination of genetic engineering and eco-friendly materials. This method not only revives reefs but also accelerates their growth, demonstrating an innovative approach to address global environmental problems.

Another perspective could be *literary creativity*, where a writer creates a novel with a nonlinear timeline, interweaving multiple characters' narratives across different time periods. The novel challenges conventional storytelling norms and engages readers in piecing together the complex narrative puzzle. An example of *literary creativity* involving a nonlinear timeline is found in the novel *Cloud Atlas* by David Mitchell. In this book, six different stories spanning several centuries and multiple genres are intricately woven together. Each narrative is interrupted and nested within the next narrative, only to return and conclude in the second half of the book. This structure challenges readers in connecting themes, characters, and plots across different eras and settings, effectively engaging them in a complex narrative puzzle. By deviating from traditional linear storytelling, Mitchell not only defies conventional norms but also enriches the reader's experience by offering a unique way to perceive the interconnectedness of humanity across time and space (Ward et al., 1997).

Expertise is the highest level of skill or knowledge in a particular domain and is achieved through extensive experience, practice or training. Experts possess superior problem-solving abilities in their domain of *expertise*, characterized by faster and more accurate performance, the use of domain-specific strategies, and greater pattern recognition and memory for domain-relevant information. For example, the "Shouldice Hospital" in Canada has been dedicated to the repair of hernias since 1945; this is the only surgical procedure performed by surgeons. The procedure has been continually refined over time such that the recurrence rate is less than 1%. Numerous research papers in peer-reviewed journals have been published on this institution and its expert staff and on qualified medical personnel from all over the world to share innovative surgical techniques (Simons et al., 1996).

Research into reasoning and problem-solving is ongoing. As our scientific and technological capabilities continue to advance, we can expect further breakthroughs in our understanding of these essential cognitive processes.

References

Caliskan, A., Bryson, J. J., & Narayanan, A. (2017). Semantics derived automatically from language corpora contain human-like biases. *Science, 356*(6334), 183–186. https://doi.org/10.1126/science.aal4230

Duncker, K. (1945). On problem-solving. *Psychological Monographs, 58*(5), i–113. https://doi.org/10.1037/h0093599

Evans, J. S. B. T. (2008). Dual-processing accounts of reasoning, judgment, and social cognition. *Annual Review of Psychology, 59*(1), 255–278. https://doi.org/10.1146/annurev.psych.59.103006.093629

Furnham, A., & Boo, H. C. (2011). A literature review of the anchoring effect. *The Journal of Socio-Economics, 40*(1), 35–42. https://doi.org/10.1016/j.socec.2010.10.008

Gigerenzer, G. (2008). *Rationality for mortals: How people cope with uncertainty.* Oxford University Press.

Gigerenzer, G., Todd, P. M., & The ABC Research Group. (1999). *Simple heuristics that make us smart.* Oxford University Press.

Johnson-Laird, P. N. (2008). *How we reason.* Oxford University Press.

Kahneman, D., Slovic, P., & Tversky, A. (Eds.). (1982). *Judgment under uncertainty: Heuristics and biases.* Cambridge University Press. https://doi.org/10.1017/CBO9780511809477

Mehrabi, N., Morstatter, F., Saxena, N., Lerman, K., & Galstyan, A. (2021). A survey on bias and fairness in machine learning. *ACM Computing Surveys, 54*(6), 1–35. https://doi.org/10.1145/3457607

Nickerson, R. S. (1998). Confirmation bias: A ubiquitous phenomenon in many guises. *Review of General Psychology, 2*(2), 175–220. https://doi.org/10.1037/1089-2680.2.2.175

Ohlsson, S. (2011). *Deep learning: How the mind overrides experience.* Cambridge University Press. https://doi.org/10.1017/CBO9780511780295

Simons, M. P., Kleijnen, J., van Geldere, D., Hoitsma, H. F. W., & Obertop, H. (1996). Role of the Shouldice technique in inguinal hernia repair: A systematic review of controlled trials and a meta-analysis. *British Journal of Surgery, 83*(6), 734–738. https://doi.org/10.1002/bjs.1800830606

Thaler, R. H., & Sunstein, C. R. (2008). *Nudge: Improving decisions about health, wealth, and happiness.* Yale University Press.

Tversky, A., & Kahneman, D. (1973). Availability: A heuristic for judging frequency and probability. *Cognitive Psychology, 5*(2), 207–232. https://doi.org/10.1016/0010-0285(73)90033-9

Tversky, A., & Kahneman, D. (1974). Judgment under uncertainty: Heuristics and biases. *Science, 185*(4157), 1124–1131. https://doi.org/10.1126/science.185.4157.1124

Tversky, A., & Kahneman, D. (1983). Extensional versus intuitive reasoning: The conjunction fallacy in probability judgment. *Psychological Review, 90*(4), 293–315. https://doi.org/10.1037/0033-295X.90.4.293

Ward, T. B., Smith, S. M., & Vaid, J. (Eds.). (1997). *Creative thought: An investigation of conceptual structures and processes.* American Psychological Association. https://doi.org/10.1037/10227-000

CHAPTER 7

Decision-Making and Judgment

Expected Utility Theory and Prospect Theory

Decision-making involves choosing between different options on the basis of the evaluation of their outcomes. *Expected utility theory* and *prospect theory* are both decision-making models, but they differ in several ways:

According to *expected utility theory* (Von Neumann & Morgenstern, 1944), individuals make decisions by considering the utility (i.e., value or satisfaction) of each possible outcome and the probability of its occurrence. They then choose the option with the highest *expected utility* or, in other words, what will benefit them most. This theory assumes that individuals are rational agents who make choices that maximize their expected benefits. The theory also assumes that people's preferences for outcomes are consistent (transitive) and independent of irrelevant alternatives. *Expected utility theory* posits that when faced with a series of choices, individuals will select the option that maximizes their *expected utility*, not necessarily their expected monetary value (Von Neumann & Morgenstern, 1944; Starmer, 2000). This idea often involves considering the level of risk associated with each choice. Here, is an example:

Let us say you are on a game show, and you're given two options:

Option 1: you receive $1000 guaranteed

Option 2: you have a 50% chance of winning $2500 and a 50% chance of winning nothing

H. Kankam, *A Brief Excursion into Human Cognition*,
https://doi.org/10.1007/978-3-031-89752-8_7

The expected monetary value of Option 2 is $1250 (0.5 * $2500 + 0.5 * $0), which is higher than the guaranteed $1000 from Option 1.

However, according to the *expected utility theory*, your *decision* will depend on your risk preference.

If you are risk averse (as many people are in regard to gains), you might opt for the sure $1000 because the guaranteed utility of that amount might be greater for you than the uncertain utility of possibly receiving $2500 or possibly receiving nothing. The fear of ending up with nothing could outweigh the possibility of gaining more.

On the other hand, if you are a risk-seeker, you might go for Option 2, because the utility of potentially winning $2500 is more attractive for you, despite the risk of ending up with nothing. This example illustrates how *expected utility theory* works. The *decision* that maximizes expected utility may differ from the *decision* that maximizes expected monetary value because of the individual's risk preferences.

Now, let us look at *prospect theory*, as proposed by Daniel Kahneman and Amos Tversky. *Prospect theory* challenges the assumptions of *expected utility theory* (Kahneman & Tversky, 1979; Barberis, 2013). It posits that people make decisions on the basis of potential gains and losses relative to a reference point rather than absolute outcomes, and it takes into account that people do not always behave rationally; people often do not weigh probabilities linearly in *decision*-making or in *judging* outcomes; they tend to overestimate small probabilities and underestimate large probabilities (*probability weighting*). The theory asserts that, in general, people feel the pain of a loss more acutely than the pleasure of a gain of the same size. This means that losses have a greater impact on people's decisions than do equivalent gains (*loss aversion*). Additionally, the impact of changes in wealth decreases as the size of the change increases. For example, the difference in satisfaction between gaining $100 and $200 is perceived as larger than the difference between gaining $1100 and $1200 (*diminishing sensitivity*).

Here, is an example:

Suppose you are given two scenarios:

Scenario 1: Guaranteed loss of $1000

Scenario 2: An 85% chance of losing $1200 but a 15% chance of losing nothing

In terms of the expected value, Scenario 1 is objectively better (as the expected loss is lower: $1000 vs. $1020). However, according to *prospect theory*, many people choose Scenario 2 because the chance of losing nothing (however, small) is more attractive, even though it comes with a risk of greater loss. Notably, the pain of losing is psychologically about twice as powerful as the pleasure of gaining.

Now, consider a different set of choices:

Scenario 1: Guaranteed gain of $1000

Scenario 2: An 85% chance of gaining $1200 but a 15% chance of gaining nothing

In this case, despite the higher expected value in Scenario 2, many people choose Scenario 1. This reflects the concept of risk aversion in the domain of gains—the certain outcome is more appealing than the gamble.

These examples highlight how people often overweigh potential losses compared with gains (*loss aversion*) and may not make decisions that align with the expected monetary value when faced with uncertainty.

Risk Perception and Risk-Taking Behavior

In the examples above, we have already introduced *risk* and its influence on *decision-making* and *judgment*. *Risk* refers to the potential for loss, damage, or negative outcomes that may result from external or internal vulnerabilities or from the occurrence of certain events. It equates with the possibility of something undesirable happening. *Risk* is usually considered the product of two factors: the probability of occurrence of an event and the impact or consequences of that event; it is characterized by uncertainty, as it involves future events that may or may not happen.

Our focus is on *risk perception* and *risk-taking behavior*. *Risk perception* defines the subjective *judgment* that people make about the probability and severity of a risk. It refers to people's beliefs, attitudes, judgments, and feelings, as well as the wider social and cultural values and dispositions that people adopt toward threats and hazards (Slovic, 1987).

This rightly indicates that *risk perception* can vary greatly among individuals and within specific communities, cultures, or societies. Various factors can influence how risk is perceived:

Probability and consequences/availability heuristic: People often assess risks on the basis of the perceived likelihood of the event occurring and the seriousness of the potential outcome. For example, people often perceive risks they can control (such as driving a car) as less threatening than risks they cannot control (such as riding in an airplane), even though statistically, the former is far riskier;

Familiarity and novelty: risks that are unfamiliar or novel are usually perceived as greater than familiar risks. This can explain why people are often more afraid of new diseases (such as COVID-19 when it first emerged) than of diseases they are familiar with (such as the flu), even though both may pose significant health risks;

Dread and catastrophic potential: risks that are seen as particularly dreadful or that could have catastrophic consequences tend to be perceived as higher. For example, the risk of nuclear accidents is often perceived as very high because of the *dread factor* and the potential for widespread harm;

Voluntary vs. involuntary exposure: Risks that are taken voluntarily, such as skydiving, are often perceived as less serious than risks to which individuals are exposed involuntarily, such as exposure to pollution;

Media influence: The way risks are portrayed in the media can have a significant effect on *risk perception*. For example, extensive media coverage of a natural disaster or a disease outbreak can heighten people's perception of these risks;

Personal experience: Past experiences with a hazard can greatly influence how a person perceives potential risk. If an individual or someone they know has been affected by a certain risk, they may perceive that risk as being higher.

Grasping the nuances of *risk perception* is pivotal across various domains, including health communication, environmental policymaking, and the establishment of public safety regulations. This understanding enables policymakers, scientists, and professionals specializing in risk communication to devise impactful strategies for risk communication. Additionally, it helps address public concerns and correct widespread misconceptions related to diverse risk types.

Risk-taking behavior refers to the inclination to engage in activities that have the potential for undesirable or harmful outcomes but are also often associated with potentially significant rewards. These actions can either be advantageous or detrimental, depending on the specific circumstances and outcomes. Individual differences in *risk-taking* can be influenced by personality traits, cognitive biases, and situational factors (Slovic, 1987; Weber et al., 2002; Loewenstein et al., 2001).

Some key elements of *risk-taking behavior are as follows*:

Uncertainty: Risk-taking inherently involves uncertainty about the outcome. This uncertainty can be about the likelihood of the outcome, the magnitude of the outcome, or both;

Rewards: Generally, *risk-taking* is associated with the potential for a reward. This reward could be financial, as in business or investing, but it could also be psychological, such as the thrill of an extreme sport, or social, such as the status gained from a risky but successful endeavor;

Loss Potential: *Risk-taking* also implies the possibility of loss. This could be a material loss, such as losing money in a bad investment, or it could be nonmaterial, such as losing face in a social context or experiencing psychological distress.

The perception and acceptance of risk can vary greatly among individuals due to factors such as personality traits, age, gender, and cultural background. For example, some people are inherently more risk averse and tend to avoid uncertain situations, whereas others are more risk tolerant or even risk seeking, actively pursuing uncertain situations for their potential rewards.

Obviously, *risk-taking behavior* can have significant impacts on various aspects of life, including health, finances, and relationships. In psychology, it is often studied in relation to impulsivity, sensation-seeking behavior, and decision-making under uncertainty. In economics, the concept of risk aversion is a key part of theories about decision-making and market behavior. In public health, understanding *risk-taking behaviors* is essential in devising strategies to prevent harmful behaviors such as unsafe sex, drug use, and reckless driving.

Social and Emotional Influences on Decision-Making

Social and emotional factors can significantly impact decision-making processes. Some key influences include the following:

Peer pressure is one of the most common social influences on decision-making. It refers to the pressure an individual may feel to conform to the norms or behaviors of their social group. This obviously can significantly impact decision-making, particularly among adolescents, who are more susceptible to peer pressure. For example, a teenager might decide to smoke cigarettes because they perceive it as a way to fit in with their friends, despite knowing the health risks associated with smoking.

The values, attitudes, and behaviors instilled by family (*family influence*) can greatly impact decision-making. For example, a person raised in a family that values frugality may be more likely to make conservative financial decisions, such as saving for retirement or avoiding unnecessary expenses.

Cultural norms and values can greatly influence an individual's decision-making. The unwritten rules and expectations within a social/cultural group can influence decision-making, as individuals often conform to these norms to gain social approval or avoid disapproval. For example, in cultures where collective decision-making is valued, an individual might be less likely to make a major decision, such as getting married or changing jobs, without seeking input or approval from their family or community.

Our current *emotional state* can also greatly affect our decision-making process. If you are in a happy mood, you might be more likely to make optimistic decisions or take on risks.

Conversely, if you're feeling down, you might lean toward more pessimistic decisions or shy away from risks.

Fear is a powerful emotion that can strongly influence decision-making. For example, a person might decide not to take a potential job opportunity because they fear the unknown or the possibility of failure.

Love and emotional attachment can greatly influence an individual's decisions. For example, a person might decide to move to a new city or even a new country to be with someone they love.

Empathy can influence decision-making, especially in social contexts. If someone feels *empathy* for another person, they might make decisions that benefit that person, even at their own expense. For example, they might decide to donate to a charity after feeling *empathy* for the individuals the charity assists.

When people are *angry* or *frustrated,* they can make hasty decisions without considering long-term consequences. These decisions are often reactive rather than reflective or thoughtful. It can influence decision-making both directly and indirectly. For example, experiencing fear or anxiety may lead to more risk-averse choices, whereas anger may increase *risk-taking behavior*. Emotions can also impact the way we evaluate and process information, potentially leading to biased judgments (Lerner et al., 2015; Van Kleef, 2016).

In the digital age, the *influence of social media* on decision-making cannot be ignored. People can be swayed by online trends, the number of "likes" or "shares," or the opinions of influencers, leading them to make decisions that they might not have otherwise made.

Each of these examples powerfully illustrates the profound influence of emotions and social context on decision-making and behavior. Understanding these dynamics is crucial, and they are at the forefront of research in psychology, behavioral economics, and neuroscience.

Group Decision-Making and Problem-Solving

Group decision-making denotes the method by which a collective of individuals jointly choose one option from a range of available alternatives presented to them. The advantages of group decision-making include a wider variety of perspectives, a more comprehensive understanding of the issues at hand, increased acceptance and commitment to decisions made collectively, and the potential for more creative solutions.

However, there are also disadvantages, such as the potential for *groupthink* (where the desire for harmony or conformity leads to dysfunctional decision-making outcomes) (Hirokawa & Gouran, 2006; Janis, 1982), *group polarization* (when group discussions lead to more extreme positions than those initially held by individual members, this can result from social comparison processes, persuasive arguments, and the confirmation of preexisting *beliefs—shared information bias*), domination by a few members, diffusion of responsibility, and a longer time to reach a decision (Kerr & Tindale, 2011).

A notable research framework for group decision-making is the *functional perspective on group decision-making* by Randy Hirokawa and Dennis Gouran (Hirokawa & Gouran, 2006).[1] This framework suggests that the quality of *group decision-making* largely depends on the functions or tasks the group performs, such as understanding the problem, identifying alternatives, evaluating the positive and negative characteristics of these alternatives, and selecting the best solution.

Group problem-solving is a situation that arises when trying to reach a goal or objective with others, and there is an obstacle or barrier (for example, complex or ill-defined problems) that prevents straightforward achievement of the goal.

Techniques commonly used for *group problem-solving* include brainstorming, the *nominal group technique* (NGT; Delbecq et al., 1975),[2] (individuals generate solutions independently and then combine and rank them), and *the Delphi method* (Dalkey & Helmer, 1963)[3] (a structured communication technique originally developed as a systematic, interactive forecasting method that relies on a panel of experts).

Research into *group problem-solving* often centers on the concept of collective intelligence. *A significant study* by Anita Woolley et al. (2010) revealed that collective intelligence in groups is not strongly correlated with the intelligence of a group's individual members. Instead, it is more closely linked to factors such as equal contributions among members, the group's social sensitivity, and the proportion of women in the group.

Notes

1. The functional perspective on group decision-making suggests that groups make better decisions when they effectively perform five key functions:

   Problem Analysis: Clearly, define the problem, identify its causes, and understand its context.

   Establishing evaluation criteria: Determine relevant standards (e.g., cost, feasibility, effectiveness) to judge potential solutions.

   Generating Solutions: Produce a diverse range of ideas or solutions.

   Evaluating Solutions: Assess each option on the basis of the established criteria.

   Implementing and Monitoring the Chosen Solution: Execute the selected solution and track its effectiveness.

   A supportive communication climate, constructive conflict, and shared leadership enhance these functions. According to Hirokawa and Gouran, groups fail when they neglect any of these crucial tasks. This perspective provides a practical framework for improving group decision-making processes. (Gouran & Hirokawa, 1996).
2. The Nominal Group Technique (NGT) is a structured brainstorming process that fosters balanced participation and minimizes groupthink. It moves from silent idea generation to round-robin sharing of ideas, followed by discussion. Finally, each member privately ranks the ideas, and the facilitator aggregates the results to identify the top solutions. NGT is highly effective but requires a capable facilitator to ensure fair and unbiased outcomes.
3. The Delphi method is a structured communication technique created by the RAND Corporation in the 1950s. Named after the Oracle of Delphi, it uses a panel of experts who anonymously provide insights over several rounds. After each round, the responses are compiled, summarized, and shared so that the experts can refine their answers in light of others' views. This iterative process continues until a consensus or stable result is reached. The method is particularly useful for tackling complex problems that lack a clear solution, as it reduces bias through anonymity and systematic feedback. However, this approach can be time-consuming and requires skilled facilitation for effective management.

References

Barberis, N. C. (2013). Thirty years of prospect theory in economics: A review and assessment. *Journal of Economic Perspectives, 27*(1), 173–196. https://doi.org/10.1257/jep.27.1.173

Dalkey, N., & Helmer, O. (1963). *An experimental application of the Delphi method to the use of experts*. RAND Corporation.

Delbecq, A. L., Van de Ven, A. H., & Gustafson, D. H. (1975). *Group techniques for program planning: A guide to nominal group and Delphi processes*. Scott, Foresman and Company.

Hirokawa, R. Y., & Gouran, D. S. (2006). The functional perspective on group decision making. In J. R. Baldwin, S. D. Perry, & M. D. Moffitt (Eds.), *Communication theories for everyday life* (pp. 249–261). Pearson/Allyn & Bacon.

Janis, I. L. (1982). *Groupthink: Psychological studies of policy decisions and fiascoes* (2nd ed.). Houghton Mifflin.

Kahneman, D., & Tversky, A. (1979). Prospect theory: An analysis of decision under risk. *Econometrica, 47*(2), 263–291. https://doi.org/10.2307/1914185

Kerr, N. L., & Tindale, R. S. (2011). Group-based forecasting?: A social psychological analysis. *International Journal of Forecasting, 27*(1), 14–40. https://doi.org/10.1016/j.ijforecast.2010.02.001

Lerner, J. S., Li, Y., Valdesolo, P., & Kassam, K. S. (2015). Emotion and decision making. *Annual Review of Psychology, 66*, 799–823. https://doi.org/10.1146/annurev-psych-010213-115043

Loewenstein, G. F., Weber, E. U., Hsee, C. K., & Welch, N. (2001). Risk as feelings. *Psychological Bulletin, 127*(2), 267–286. https://doi.org/10.1037/0033-2909.127.2.267

Slovic, P. (1987). Perception of risk. *Science, 236*(4799), 280–285. https://doi.org/10.1126/science.3563507

Starmer, C. (2000). Developments in non-expected utility theory: The hunt for a descriptive theory of choice under risk. *Journal of Economic Literature, 38*(2), 332–382. https://doi.org/10.1257/jel.38.2.332

Van Kleef, G. A. (2016). *The interpersonal dynamics of emotion: Toward an integrative theory of emotions as social information*. Cambridge University Press. https://doi.org/10.1017/CBO9781107261396

Von Neumann, J., & Morgenstern, O. (1944). *Theory of games and economic behavior*. Princeton University Press.

Weber, E. U., Blais, A.-R., & Betz, N. E. (2002). A domain-specific risk-attitude scale: Measuring risk perceptions and risk behaviors. *Journal of Behavioral Decision Making, 15*(4), 263–290. https://doi.org/10.1002/bdm.414

Woolley, A. W., Chabris, C. F., Pentland, A., Hashmi, N., & Malone, T. W. (2010). Evidence for a collective intelligence factor in the performance of human groups. *Science, 330*(6004), 686–688. https://doi.org/10.1126/science.1193147

CHAPTER 8

Learning and Skill Acquisition

Classical and Operant Conditioning

Learning is the process of acquiring new knowledge, behaviors, or skills through experience. The process is the same for both young children starting to walk and talk and adults acquiring new skills. Two fundamental types of associative learning are known as *classical and operant conditioning*.

Classical conditioning, first defined by Ivan Pavlov (1927; Bouton, 2016; Rescorla, 1988; Pearce, 2013; Domjan, 2018), is a form of learning in which a neutral stimulus comes to evoke a response after being paired with a stimulus that naturally evokes that response. For example, if a bell (neutral stimulus) is repeatedly paired with the presentation of food (unconditioned stimulus), a dog will eventually salivate (conditioned response) in response to the bell alone.

On the other hand, *operant conditioning*, first described by B.F. Skinner (1938) and discussed in later studies (e.g., Staddon, 2016; Domjan, 2018; Pearce, 2013), is a learning process by which the likelihood of a type of behavior is increased or decreased on the basis of its consequences; i.e., reinforcement (either positive or negative) increases the likelihood of a behavior, whereas punishment (either positive or negative) decreases its likelihood; (positive refers to adding a stimulus, while negative

H. Kankam, *A Brief Excursion into Human Cognition*,
https://doi.org/10.1007/978-3-031-89752-8_8

refers to removing one). For example, a child who receives praise (positive reinforcement) for completing homework is more likely to repeat this behavior in the future.

Observational Learning/Social Learning Theory/ Social Cognitive Theory

Observational learning, also known as *social learning theory*, is the process of acquiring new behaviors or knowledge through the observation of others. Albert Bandura's (1977, 1986, 2001; Bussey & Bandura, 1999) social learning theory posits that individuals learn not only through direct experience but also through observing the actions and consequences of others. The key aspects of *observational learning* include the following:

- *Attention*: observers must pay attention to the relevant aspects of the modeled behavior;
- *Retention*: observers must encode and store the observed behavior in memory;
- *Reproduction*: observers must be capable of reproducing the observed behavior accurately;
- *Motivation*: observers must be motivated to perform the learned behavior, which is influenced by the perceived rewards or punishments associated with the behavior.

For example, a child may learn to tie their shoelaces by watching a parent or sibling. They observe the actions of others and then imitate those actions. This type of learning can also affect attitudes and behaviors. For example, a child might observe a peer being praised for saying "please" and "thank you" and then begin to use polite language themselves to receive praise.

Bandura's social learning theory emphasizes the importance of cognitive processes, which he argued were overlooked in traditional behaviorism (e.g., B.F. Skinner's work). Bandura suggested that individuals are not passive recipients of information but actively process information from their environments (Bandura, 2001). This makes them agents in their own learning, not simply products of their environment. This is demonstrated in his concept of "reciprocal determinism," which suggests that behavior, personal factors and the environment continually influence each other.

Bandura's most famous experiment, the "Bobo doll" study, demonstrated that children can learn aggressive behaviors simply by observing an adult acting aggressively. The children who watched an adult behaving violently toward a "Bobo doll" were more likely to act aggressively toward the doll themselves.

One key element of Bandura's social learning theory is the concept of *self-efficacy*, which refers to an individual's belief in their capacity to execute behaviors necessary to attain specific performance. *Self-efficacy* can affect a person's choice of activities, how much effort they will invest in them, and how they will feel while performing them. While both Skinner's *operant conditioning* and Bandura's *social learning theory* involve learning from the environment, they focus on different processes. Skinner's theory is more focused on the relationship between behaviors and their consequences (rewards or punishments), such that learning is a result of direct experience. Bandura's theory, on the other hand, emphasizes learning through observation and cognitive processes, suggesting that people can learn from observing others' experiences and the consequences of their actions, even without experiencing those consequences themselves.

For example, when Skinner's *operant conditioning* is used, a rat in a Skinner box learns to press a lever to receive food (a rewarding consequence). In contrast, in the framework of Bandura's *social learning theory*, a person might learn to avoid touching a hot stove after observing someone else becoming burned (without needing to burn themselves).

Importantly, while both theories involve learning from the environment, Skinner emphasizes direct consequences, and Bandura focuses on learning through observation and cognitive processes.

Implicit and Explicit Learning

Implicit and *explicit learning* refer to different ways in which individuals acquire knowledge or skills.

Implicit learning is the unconscious or unintentional acquisition of knowledge or skills, often occurring without awareness of the learning process. This type of learning is typically involved in motor skill acquisition and the development of habits or perceptual abilities. Here is an example: if you have ever learned the lyrics of a song simply by hearing the song repeatedly (without making a conscious effort to memorize the lyrics), you have experienced *implicit learning*. Another example would be learning to ride a bike. At first, it requires a lot of conscious effort, but over time, the process becomes automatic, and you can ride without consciously thinking about how to do it.

Arthur Reber (1967, 1989) is one of the key researchers in this area (see also Frensch & Rünger, 2003; Cleeremans & Dienes, 2008). In the 1960s, he conducted a series of experiments showing that people could learn complex rules without any explicit awareness of the rules themselves.

Explicit learning is the conscious and intentional acquisition of knowledge or skills, often involving conscious awareness of the learning process. This type of learning is typically involved in the acquisition of factual knowledge, rules or strategies. Learning in a classroom is often explicit. For example, a math teacher might explicitly teach students the Pythagorean theorem. The students know that they are being taught this concept, and they thus make a conscious effort to understand and remember it.

A key researcher in *explicit learning* would be B.F. Skinner, who focused on the concept of *operant conditioning*, where behavior is learned through reinforcement or punishment (Frensch & Rünger, 2003). This can be seen as a form of *explicit learning* because the learner becomes aware of the relationship between their behavior and its consequences.

Additionally, much of the research on *explicit memory*, as shown in the preceding chapters (which are closely related to *explicit learning*), was conducted by Endel Tulving. He proposed that memory can be divided into two main types: *episodic* (personal experiences and specific events, time-related) and *semantic* (facts and general knowledge), both of which are part of *explicit memory*. Importantly, *implicit and explicit learning* often occur simultaneously and involve two different ways in which our brains process and store information.

Cognitive Skill Development and Expertise

Cognitive skill development (Ericsson et al., 1993; Van Merriënboer & Kirschner, 2018) refers to the process of acquiring and refining skills that involve mental processes, such as *problem-solving*, reasoning, and decision-making (Ericsson, 2008, 2020). Here is an example of evolving *problem-solving* skills: at the age of two, a child might encounter the problem of a toy being out of reach. Initially, the child might cry or show signs of frustration. With little guidance and encouragement, the child might be taught to use a tool such as a stick to retrieve the toy or to climb (safely) to reach it. Over time, the child begins to understand that they can use tools or their own actions to overcome obstacles.

As the child grows older, the problems it encounters become more complex. For example, a five-year-old individual might struggle with a more complex toy, such as a puzzle. At first, she/he might randomly try to fit the pieces together. A caregiver can guide the child to recognize patterns and match the pieces accordingly, for example, by looking at the colors or shapes on the pieces.

By the time children become teenagers, the problems become even more complex: they may struggle with a math problem at school. Initially, this problem could involve calculus or complex algebra that demands not only a strong grasp of mathematical concepts but also the ability to apply logical reasoning and problem-solving skills. Teenagers now have a repertoire of strategies at their disposal: breaking the problem down into smaller parts, using a process of elimination, making educated guesses and checking them, and so on. They also learn that they can seek out resources such as textbooks, online tutorials, and knowledgeable people to help them understand and solve problems.

At each stage of development, individuals refine their *problem-solving* capacity, a key cognitive skill. They learn to identify problems, generate possible solutions, evaluate and implement these solutions, and assess the outcomes. Each stage builds on the previous stage, as the individual encounters increasingly complex problems and develops increasingly sophisticated problem-solving skills.

Expertise, on the other hand, is the high level of skill or knowledge in a particular domain achieved through extensive experience, practice or training. Here, an example where we consider developing *expertise* in playing the piano is as follows:

Stage 1 - Beginner: a person decides to learn to play the piano. At this initial stage, they may start learning about the different parts of the piano, the layout of the keys, and simple music theories such as notes, scales, and chords. They start practicing basic finger exercises and simple melodies. The learner may initially struggle with coordinating their fingers and reading sheet music.

Stage 2 - Intermediate: After a year or two of consistent practice and lessons, the individual has learned to play more complex pieces of music, can sight-read basic sheet music, and has improved finger dexterity and independence. They understand and use proper fingering techniques and have a basic understanding of music theory. They start to practice regularly with a metronome to improve their timing.

Stage 3 - Advanced: With several more years of dedication and practice, the individual is able to play advanced compositions, possibly from different musical periods such as Baroque, Classical, Romantic, or Contemporary. They can interpret and play with different dynamics, articulations, and expressions and are able to learn new pieces on their own. They may start to perform in front of others and receive feedback.

Stage 4 - Expert: After many years of dedicated practice, study and performance, the individual has developed a deep understanding of music theory and piano technique. They are able to interpret and perform complex pieces of music expressively, conveying emotion and nuance. They may even compose their own pieces, improvise, capably teach others, or perform professionally. At this stage, they continue to refine their skills, constantly seek feedback, and engage in deliberate practice to improve specific aspects of their performance.

At each stage of this development, individuals deepen their knowledge, skills, and understanding, as well as their ability to apply these in different contexts, which is a key aspect of developing *expertise*. They also develop meta-skills such as perseverance, self-assessment, and continuous learning, which are important traits of experts in any field.

Here is a list of key aspects that are part of *cognitive skill development* and *expertise*, which are also contained in our "Piano" example:

- *Deliberate practice*, which is a structured and goal-directed form of practice that involves focused attention, immediate feedback, and the refinement of specific aspects of performance. It is considered an essential component of *expertise* development.
- As individuals become more skilled in a domain, their performance often becomes more *automatic*, requiring less conscious effort and attention. *Automaticity* allows experts to perform complex tasks more efficiently and effectively than novices do.
- Experts often possess superior *pattern recognition* abilities and *domain-specific memory*, enabling them to quickly identify relevant information, make accurate predictions, and solve problems more effectively.
- *Metacognition*, or the awareness and understanding of one's own cognitive processes, plays a crucial role in skill development and

expertise. Experts often possess superior *metacognitive abilities*, allowing them to monitor and regulate their performance more effectively and adapt their strategies as needed.

Transfer of learning is the application of knowledge or skills acquired in one context to new and different contexts. Transfer can be positive when learning from one situation facilitates performance in another situation or negative when learning from one situation hinders performance in another situation. Factors influencing the *transfer of learning* include the similarity between the learning and transfer contexts, the level of mastery of the initial learning, and the degree of cognitive flexibility.

Scaffolding is a teaching method by which an instructor or more knowledgeable peer provides support and guidance to a learner, allowing them to achieve goals that would otherwise be unattainable (Vygotsky, 1978; Wood et al., 1976; Reiser, 2004). *Scaffolding* typically involves breaking complex tasks into smaller steps, providing guidance and feedback, and gradually withdrawing support as the learner becomes more competent.

Guided learning, similar to scaffolding, involves an instructor or peer providing structured assistance, often through modeling, prompting, and feedback, to facilitate the learner's acquisition of skills or knowledge.

Individual differences, such as differences in cognitive ability, personality traits, *motivation*, and prior knowledge, can significantly impact the process of learning and *skill acquisition*. For example, individuals with higher levels of working memory capacity or intelligence may acquire new skills more quickly or efficiently than those with lower levels. Similarly, factors such as *motivation*, *self-efficacy*, and interest can influence the degree to which individuals engage in deliberate practice and persist in the face of challenges.

Advancements in technology have led to new approaches and tools for *learning and skill acquisition* (Clark & Mayer, 2016; Wang & Hannafin, 2005; Kizilcec et al., 2017). Examples include:

- Educational software and apps: These tools can provide individualized instruction, adaptive learning experiences, and immediate feedback, helping learners acquire knowledge and skills more efficiently;
- Online learning platforms and massive open online courses (MOOCs): These platforms offer a wide range of educational

resources and courses, enabling learners to access high-quality instruction and materials, regardless of their location or background;
- Virtual and augmented reality (VR and AR): These technologies can be used to create immersive learning environments, allowing learners to practice skills and acquire knowledge in realistic, context-rich settings;
- Artificial intelligence and machine learning: AI-driven tutoring systems and adaptive learning technologies can provide personalized instruction and feedback, tailoring the learning experience to each individual's needs and abilities.

References

Bandura, A. (1977). *Social learning theory.* Prentice-Hall.

Bandura, A. (1986). *Social foundations of thought and action: A social cognitive theory.* Prentice-Hall.

Bandura, A. (2001). Social cognitive theory: An agentic perspective. *Annual Review of Psychology, 52*, 1–26. https://doi.org/10.1146/annurev.psych.52.1.1

Bouton, M. E. (2016). *Learning and behavior: A contemporary synthesis* (2nd ed.). Sinauer.

Bussey, K., & Bandura, A. (1999). Social cognitive theory of gender development and differentiation. *Psychological Review, 106*(4), 676–713. https://doi.org/10.1037/0033-295X.106.4.676

Clark, R. C., & Mayer, R. E. (2016). *E-learning and the science of instruction: Proven guidelines for consumers and designers of multimedia learning* (4th ed.). Wiley. https://doi.org/10.1002/9781119239086

Cleeremans, A., & Dienes, Z. (2008). Computational models of implicit learning. In R. Sun (Ed.), *The Cambridge handbook of computational psychology* (pp. 396–421). Cambridge University Press. https://doi.org/10.1017/CBO9780511816772.018

Domjan, M. (2018). *The principles of learning and behavior* (7th ed.). Cengage.

Ericsson, K. A. (2008). Deliberate practice and acquisition of expert performance: A general overview. *Academic Emergency Medicine, 15*(11), 988–994. https://doi.org/10.1111/j.1553-2712.2008.00227.x

Ericsson, K. A. (2020). Towards a science of the acquisition of expert performance in sports: Clarifying the differences between deliberate practice and other types of practice. *Journal of Sports Sciences, 38*(2), 159–176. https://doi.org/10.1080/02640414.2019.1688618

Ericsson, K. A., Krampe, R. T., & Tesch-Römer, C. (1993). The role of deliberate practice in the acquisition of expert performance. *Psychological Review, 100*(3), 363–406. https://doi.org/10.1037/0033-295X.100.3.363

Frensch, P. A., & Rünger, D. (2003). Implicit learning. *Current Directions in Psychological Science, 12*(1), 13–18. https://doi.org/10.1111/1467-8721.01213

Kizilcec, R. F., Saltarelli, A. J., Reich, J., & Cohen, G. L. (2017). Closing global achievement gaps in MOOCs. *Science, 355*(6322), 251–252. https://doi.org/10.1126/science.aag2063

Pavlov, I. P. (1927). *Conditioned reflexes: An investigation of the physiological activity of the cerebral cortex.* Oxford University Press.

Pearce, J. M. (2013). *Animal learning and cognition: An introduction* (3rd ed.). Psychology Press. https://doi.org/10.4324/9781315782911

Reber, A. S. (1967). Implicit learning of artificial grammars. *Journal of Verbal Learning and Verbal Behavior, 6*(6), 855–863. https://doi.org/10.1016/S0022-5371(67)80149-X

Reber, A. S. (1989). Implicit learning and tacit knowledge: An essay on the cognitive unconscious. *Journal of Experimental Psychology: General, 118*(3), 219–235. https://doi.org/10.1037/0096-3445.118.3.219

Reiser, B. J. (2004). Scaffolding complex learning: The mechanisms of structuring and problematizing student work. *Journal of the Learning Sciences, 13*(3), 273–304. https://doi.org/10.1207/s15327809jls1303_2

Rescorla, R. A. (1988). Pavlovian conditioning: It's not what you think it is. *American Psychologist, 43*(3), 151–160. https://doi.org/10.1037/0003-066X.43.3.151

Skinner, B. F. (1938). *The behavior of organisms: An experimental analysis.* Appleton-Century.

Staddon, J. E. R. (2016). *Adaptive behavior and learning* (2nd ed.). Cambridge University Press. https://doi.org/10.1017/CBO9781139998369

Van Merriënboer, J. J. G., & Kirschner, P. A. (2018). *Ten steps to complex learning: A systematic approach to four-component instructional design* (3rd ed.). Routledge. https://doi.org/10.1007/s11528-018-0254-0

Vygotsky, L. S. (1978). *Mind in society: The development of higher psychological processes.* Harvard University Press.

Wang, F., & Hannafin, M. J. (2005). Design-based research and technology-enhanced learning environments. *Educational Technology Research and Development, 53*(4), 5–23. https://doi.org/10.1007/BF02504682

Wood, D., Bruner, J. S., & Ross, G. (1976). The role of tutoring in problem solving. *Journal of Child Psychology and Psychiatry, 17*(2), 89–100. https://doi.org/10.1111/j.1469-7610.1976.tb00381.x

CHAPTER 9

Emotion and Motivation

Theories of Emotion and Emotional Processing

Understanding and studying *emotions* and *emotional processing* in a "scientific" context can be very challenging. *Emotions* are judged as *subjective*, as personal experiences can differ significantly from person to person. What makes one person happy might not have the same effect on another, and what one person finds distressing might not bother someone else. This obviously makes it hard to develop "standardized measures of emotions" or, in other words, "observable measures" (unlike in physical processes). While we can "indirectly" measure physiological responses such as heart rate, skin conductivity, and brain activity, which provide some indications of emotional state, they do not capture the full range of emotional experiences.

Emotions are *complex* and *multifaceted*, encompassing a mix of physiological responses, subjective experiences, and expressive behaviors. This *complexity* adds to the difficulty in defining and studying *emotions* in a universal context. To add to the *complexity*, there are *cultural differences* in the way people experience and express *emotions*. A normal expression of anger, sadness, or happiness in one culture might be seen as inappropriate or unusual in another culture. One good example to demonstrate *cultural differences* in *emotions* is the *concept of happiness* in Western versus Eastern cultures (Uchida & Kitayama, 2009; Tsai et al., 2007).

H. Kankam, *A Brief Excursion into Human Cognition*,
https://doi.org/10.1007/978-3-031-89752-8_9

In many Western cultures, *happiness* is often tied to personal achievement and success. People often express *happiness* in an openly joyful, exuberant way. It is viewed as a high-arousal positive emotion that individuals seek to experience as frequently as possible. For example, in the United States, the pursuit of *happiness* is enshrined as an inalienable right in the Declaration of Independence. Here, the cultural emphasis is on individual self-fulfillment and personal choice.

On the other hand, in many Eastern cultures, *happiness* is often associated with social harmony and tranquility. Rather than seeking individualistic joy, *happiness* may be more connected with fulfilling social roles and contributing to the well-being of the group. For example, in Japan, the concept of "wa" or harmony is paramount in society. *Happiness* can be seen as maintaining a state of balance and avoiding conflict. The expression of *happiness* may be more subdued, emphasizing inner peace and contentedness over overt displays of joy. This could involve a serene smile, a gentle nod of appreciation, or quiet words of gratitude. These understated expressions are deeply rooted in the cultural value of maintaining social harmony and personal inner peace.

In other words, these cultural contexts shape not only how people experience and understand the emotion of *happiness* but also how they express and pursue it. Importantly, these are general cultural tendencies, and as mentioned before, there are individual differences within every culture. It is not possible to develop a universal understanding of emotions.

Additionally, our *language* limits how we understand and discuss emotions. Some emotions may not have words that adequately express them, and language can also influence how we experience emotions. Interestingly, research (Pavlenko, 2012; Harris, 2004) has suggested that bilingual people can experience emotions differently depending on the language they use. This is known as the "bilingual emotional advantage." For example, speaking about a traumatic event in a second language can sometimes be less emotional than speaking about it in one's first language. This is explained through the psychological distance a second language generates, as well as the increased cognitive load, through the cognitive effort in narrating in a second language. In addition, a second language might not resonate emotionally as much as a native language and can carry alternative emotional frameworks, which can alter the way the speaker experiences and expresses feelings. These factors combined can make discussing traumatic events in a second language feel less immediate and intense, which can sometimes aid in the therapeutic process by allowing the speaker to navigate painful memories more manageably.

Different languages have unique words for specific emotions that do not have direct equivalents in other languages. For example, the German word "Schadenfreude" refers to the feeling of joy one gets from seeing or hearing about another person's troubles. This nuanced emotional concept does not exist as a single term in English. A specific word for an emotion can significantly heighten an individual's awareness and recognition of that emotional state when it arises. This linguistic precision not only deepens our understanding of our own feelings but also enhances our ability to communicate them effectively to others.

It is crucial to acknowledge, however, that the interplay between language and emotion is intricate and multifaceted, shaped by a multitude of factors such as personal history and, as previously mentioned, the broader sociocultural environment. This complexity underscores the profound impact that language has on our emotional lives, revealing its role as a powerful tool in shaping human experience and interpersonal connections.

There is a tendency to think of emotions as uniquely human, but many animals also show signs of emotional behavior. This *anthropocentric perspective* can limit our understanding of emotions and their evolutionary origins. Research has revealed the following:

It has been well documented that primates, particularly our closest relatives, the great apes, exhibit behaviors and physiological responses indicative of emotion. Chimpanzees, for example, exhibit signs of grief, depression, joy, and even a sense of fairness. In studies, primates have been shown to experience stress, fear, and anxiety and have demonstrated the ability to comfort and console each other (de Waal, 2008).

Elephants are often cited as animals capable of profound emotions (Poole & Moss, 2008). They have been observed exhibiting behaviors indicative of grief, such as revisiting the bones of deceased herd members and showing signs of distress. They also show signs of joy, playfulness, and even empathy, exhibiting consolation behavior toward distressed companions. We observe similar behavior with dolphins and whales.

Birds, especially corvids such as crows, ravens, and parrots, show signs of complex emotions. They demonstrate problem-solving skills, play behavior, and even appear to have a concept of fairness. Grief-like behavior and pair bonding have also been observed (Emery, 2006).

One of our closest animal companions, the dog, is known to exhibit a range of emotions, including joy, fear, anger, disgust, excitement, contentment, distress, and even love. They are adept at reading human emotions and respond accordingly, which suggests a level of emotional understanding (Siniscalchi et al., 2018).

Of course, many of these conclusions are based on the interpretation of behaviors and physiological responses, so they come with the caveat that we cannot know for certain what an animal is "feeling" in the way humans understand it. However, these studies suggest that many animals have the capacity for a range of emotional experiences. The neurobiology of emotions, including the role of brain regions such as the amygdala and neurotransmitters such as dopamine and serotonin (e.g., mesolimbic dopamine activation), also shows commonalities across a variety of species, further supporting the idea that nonhuman animals experience emotions.

At this point, I would like to clarify the difference between *emotion* and *affect*. *Emotion* and *affect* are often used interchangeably in casual conversation, but they have distinct meanings both in psychology and in the context of this book.

Emotion generally refers to complex psychological states and involves a variety of components. *Emotions* are typically classified as brief, intense reactions to specific events or stimuli. They are usually more specific than *affect* and can be identified with labels such as joy, fear, anger, sadness, surprise, disgust, etc. They often involve physiological responses, expressive behaviors, and conscious experiences.

Affect is a broader term that expresses the underlying experience of feeling, *emotion,* or mood. It refers to the basic, raw "valenced" (positive or negative) experiences of *emotion*. It is often described in terms of *affective states* such as pleasure or discomfort, and these states can be short-lived (like a reaction to a specific event) or longer-term (like a general mood). *Affect* is typically less specific and less intense than what is commonly understood as *emotion* (Barrett, 2017).

The following is a simple analogy. Imagine you're in a movie theater. Your *affect* is the overall light level in the theater, which is the general mood or atmosphere. Meanwhile, your *emotions* may be likened to the individual frames of the film being shown: they are the specific, intense experiences you have in response to the stimuli on the screen.

While these definitions begin to provide us with a general idea, *emotion* and *affect* are complex constructs that are still the subject of ongoing research and discussion in the field of psychology. As such, the understanding and interpretation of these terms may vary.

Over time, various theories have been proposed to explain the nature of emotions and how they are processed. Some prominent theories include the "James–Lange theory" (James, 1884)[1] proposed in the nineteenth century, which posits that physiological arousal precedes the experience of *emotion*. In other words, we experience *emotions* as a result of our body's responses to stimuli. "The Cannon-Bard theory" (Cannon, 1927),[2] developed in the 1920s, suggests that physiological arousal and emotional experience occur simultaneously and independently. According to this view, the brain processes emotional information and generates physiological responses simultaneously. In the 1960s, the "Schachter-Singer Two-Factor theory" (Schachter & Singer, 1962)[3] evolved, which addressed some deficits in the existing theories. This theory proposes that emotion is the result of both physiological arousal and cognitive interpretation. An individual first experiences physiological arousal and then cognitively interprets this arousal on the basis of contextual information to determine the specific emotion being experienced. At around the same time, the "Cognitive Appraisal theory"[4] (also known as the "Lazarus theory of emotion" (Lazarus, 1991)[4]) was proposed. This theory emphasizes the role of cognitive processes in determining emotional experiences. According to this view, *emotions* result from an individual's appraisal of a situation, which influences both the physiological response and the subjective emotional experience.

Role of Emotion in Cognition

Obviously, *emotions* play crucial roles in various cognitive processes, such as attention, memory, decision-making, and problem-solving. In this way, emotionally charged stimuli often capture attention more effectively than neutral stimuli do. This phenomenon is known as the *emotional attentional blink* (Anderson, 2005), which suggests that emotional stimuli can disrupt the processing of subsequent neutral stimuli. Furthermore, emotionally charged events and information are typically remembered better than neutral events or information. Emotional arousal during encoding can enhance memory consolidation, whereas emotional states during retrieval can influence the accessibility of memories.

Emotions can influence decision-making by affecting risk perception, the evaluation of outcomes, and the cognitive processing of information. *Emotions* can lead to both adaptive and maladaptive decision-making, depending on the context and the individual's ability to regulate their *emotions*. The following is a hypothetical example to illustrate this point:

Let us say you are a manager at a technology company, and you are faced with a decision regarding which project your team should tackle next. There are two options on the table:

Project A is a high-risk, high-reward venture. If it works, it could revolutionize your industry and give your company a significant competitive advantage. However, it also has a significant chance of failure, which could cost your team valuable time and resources;

Project B is a safe bet. It is less likely to fail, but it also has less potential for an enormous payoff. This approach would likely provide steady but unspectacular results.

Recently, you have experienced a significant failure in a different high-risk project, which has negatively impacted the company and your professional standing. This negative experience has made you feel anxious and uncertain about taking on another risky project.

Even though you recognize that Project A could have immense benefits, your recent experience with failure (and the negative emotions associated with that experience) may push you toward choosing the safer Project B. This is a clear example of how emotions—in this case, anxiety and fear—can influence decision-making, potentially leading you to make more conservative choices.

Notably, *emotions* can sometimes aid in *decision-making* ("aid" in this context does not refer to making a right or wrong decision but only the *decision-making* itself). For example, if a certain choice makes you feel good or aligns with your values (an example of *confirmation bias*), you might be more likely to choose this, even if other options might be objectively better in terms of practicality or efficiency. In this context, *emotions* can influence problem-solving performance by affecting cognitive flexibility, creativity, and persistence. Positive *emotions* can facilitate problem-solving by promoting cognitive flexibility and creativity, whereas negative *emotions* can impair performance by reducing cognitive flexibility and increasing perseveration. Conclusively, *emotions* play a key role in our preferences and motivations and are thus integral to the decisions we make every day.

As we are aware of our daily interactions, *cognition* and *emotions* are both essential aspects of human psychology that play crucial roles in shaping our experiences, behaviors, and overall well-being. Although they are distinct concepts, they are also closely intertwined and often influence each other in many ways. To better understand their differences, similarities, and interactions, let us take a step back and examine each one separately and then discuss the relationships between them.

Cognition refers to the mental processes and functions associated with acquiring, processing, storing, and using knowledge. It encompasses a wide range of abilities, including perception, attention, memory, learning, problem-solving, decision-making, language, and reasoning. *Cognition* is generally considered a more conscious, deliberate, and logical aspect of human psychology.

However, *emotions* are complex psychological states that arise as a result of the interpretation and appraisal of a particular situation, event, or internal thought process. They involve various components, such as subjective experience (e.g., feeling happy or sad), physiological reactions (e.g., increased heart rate or sweating), and behavioral expressions (e.g., smiling or crying). *Emotions* are generally considered more automatic, unconscious, and affective in nature.

Let us now consider their differences:

- *Cognitive* processes are more focused on information processing and problem-solving, whereas *emotions* are related to subjective experiences, physiological reactions, and behavioral expressions;
- *Cognition* often involves conscious, deliberate, and logical thinking, whereas *emotions* tend to be more automatic, unconscious, and affective;
- *Cognitive* processes can be influenced by an individual's knowledge, beliefs, and past experiences, whereas *emotions* are typically triggered by the appraisal of a situation, event, or internal thought process;
- *Cognition* and *emotions* have different neural substrates, with cognitive processes primarily involving the prefrontal cortex and other higher-order brain areas, whereas emotions are more associated with limbic structures such as the amygdala, hippocampus, and insula.

Let us now look at some of the similarities:

- Both *cognition* and *emotions* contribute to human experiences, behavior, and well-being;
- They both have an adaptive function, with *cognition* allowing us to navigate the world, solve problems, and make decisions, whereas *emotions* help us evaluate situations, guide our responses and motivate action;

- Both *cognitive* processes and *emotions* can be influenced by individual differences, including genetic, biological, and environmental factors (e.g., sociocultural factors). Let us now consider how they interact:
- *Cognition and emotions* often interact in complex ways, influencing and being influenced by each other. Emotional states can impact cognitive processes. For example, anxiety or stress may impair memory, attention and decision-making, whereas positive emotions can enhance creativity and problem-solving.
- *Cognitive* processes can influence *emotions*. For example, how we appraise a situation (e.g., as a threat or an opportunity) can determine our emotional response (e.g., fear or excitement);
- *Emotions* can act as a source of information, guiding our *cognitive* processes and *decision-making*. For example, the *somatic marker hypothesis* (Damasio, 1996)[5] suggests that emotional signals help us make better decisions by providing a "gut feeling" about the potential consequences of our actions; our emotional responses from past experiences significantly influence our future *decision-making*. This also provides a potential explanation for why individuals might make decisions that seem irrational when viewed from a purely logical perspective. This theory is supported by observations of individuals with damage to the ventromedial prefrontal cortex (a brain region involved in processing emotions), who have difficulty making beneficial decisions despite retaining their logical reasoning abilities.

Emotional Regulation

Emotional regulation refers to the processes by which individuals influence their emotional experiences and expressions, including the intensity, duration, and type of emotions they *experience*. *Emotional regulation* strategies can be either adaptive or maladaptive, depending on the context and the individual's goals. Some common emotion regulation strategies include the following:

Cognitive reappraisal, which involves reinterpreting the meaning of a situation or event in a way that changes its emotional impact. For example, an individual might reframe a failure as a learning opportunity;

Expressive suppression involves inhibiting the outward expression of an emotion, such as hiding feelings of sadness or anger. While this strategy can be useful in some situations, it can also have negative consequences for well-being and social functioning;

Distraction requires us to direct attention away from emotionally arousing stimuli or situations, focusing instead on neutral or positive aspects of the environment;

Acceptance and mindfulness, which are also used in therapy, require nonjudgmentally observing and accepting emotions as they arise without trying to change or suppress them. Mindfulness practices, such as meditation, can help individuals develop greater awareness and acceptance of their emotions (Gross, 1998).

Motivation Theories and Goal Setting

Motivation is the driving force that influences individuals to initiate, direct, and maintain goal-directed behaviors. Some key theories of motivation include the following:

"Drive theory" (Hull, 1943)[6] asserts that motivation is driven by biological needs or drives that seek to maintain homeostasis. Homeostasis is a concept borrowed from biology that refers to the body's automatic efforts to maintain a constant, normal state of balance or equilibrium. In psychological terms, homeostasis often refers to a state of psychological equilibrium or stability. For example, if someone experiences a significant change in their life, they might initially feel unsettled or anxious. Over time, however, they usually adapt to this change and return to a state of psychological homeostasis.

"Maslow's hierarchy of needs" (Maslow, 1943)[7] proposes a hierarchy of human needs, ranging from basic physiological needs to higher-level psychological needs, such as self-esteem and self-actualization.

"Expectancy-value theory" (Eccles, 1983)[8] suggests that motivation is determined by an individual's expectancy of success and the value they place on the desired outcome.

"Goal-setting theory" (Locke & Latham, 1990)[9] posits that specific, challenging and attainable goals can increase motivation and enhance performance. Effective goal setting involves setting SMART goals (Specific, Measurable, Achievable, Relevant, Time-bound).

Intrinsic and Extrinsic Motivation

Motivation can be categorized as intrinsic or extrinsic.

Intrinsic motivation refers to the drive to engage in an activity for inherent satisfaction or enjoyment, rather than for external rewards or benefits, and is associated with increased engagement, persistence and overall well-being (Ryan & Deci, 2017). For example, consider a woman named Sarah, who is an avid reader. She spends a significant amount of her free time diving into books, exploring different genres and learning from diverse perspectives. Sarah does not read because it is required for her job or because she wants to impress people with her knowledge. She reads simply because she loves learning new things and becomes lost in different worlds and stories. The enjoyment, relaxation, and satisfaction of expanding her understanding of the world are rewards in themselves.

Extrinsic motivation refers to the drive to engage in an activity due to external rewards, such as money, praise, or recognition, or to avoid negative consequences, such as punishment or disapproval. While *extrinsic motivation* can be effective in promoting certain behaviors, it can also undermine *intrinsic motivation* and have negative effects on well-being (Deci et al., 1999; Kohn, 1993). Once again, let us look at an example of stress caused by *extrinsic motivation.* Consider a man named Mike who works long hours in a high-stress job as a lawyer. Mike does not actually enjoy his work; in fact, it causes him a great deal of stress and anxiety. However, he continues to put in the hours because of the high salary and prestige that come with his position.

This is an example of *extrinsic motivation* because Mike's behavior (working long hours in a stressful job) is motivated by external rewards (money and status).

Now, let us consider the potential negative effects on Mike's well-being: because Mike is motivated primarily by external rewards rather than internal satisfaction, he may find his work unfulfilling. This could lead to burnout, a state of emotional, physical, and mental exhaustion caused by excessive and prolonged stress.

Additionally, the high-stress nature of Mike's job could have a negative impact on his physical health over time, contributing to problems such as insomnia, high blood pressure, and heart disease (Maslach et al., 2001; Karasek & Theorell, 1990). His personal relationships might also suffer because of the long hours spend at work.

Furthermore, since Mike's motivation is tied to external rewards, he may experience a loss of self-esteem or increased anxiety if those rewards are threatened or removed. For example, if he was to lose his job or receive a pay cut, this could severely impact his self-worth and happiness, since so much of his motivation and perceived success are tied to these external factors.

Through this minor example, we see that while *extrinsic motivation* can be a powerful driver of behavior, it can also have negative effects on an individual's well-being when it leads to stress, health problems, strained relationships, or an overreliance on external rewards for self-worth and satisfaction (Deci & Ryan, 2000).

Achievement Motivation

Achievement motivation is the drive to pursue and attain goals related to competence, mastery, and success. This type of motivation is influenced by a range of factors, such as individual differences in personality, cognitive abilities, and beliefs about intelligence and ability. The key aspects of achievement motivation include the following:

Mastery vs. Performance Goals

When an individual has a *mastery goal (also known as a learning goal)*, their primary focus is on learning, understanding, and mastering a new skill or knowledge area. The main objective is personal growth and development. They are motivated by the inherent joy of learning or the satisfaction they receive from understanding something new or improving their skills. Their focus is on the process of learning rather than the end result.

For example, a student who has *mastery goals* in a math class is concerned primarily with truly understanding math concepts, regardless of the grades they receive. They study to deepen their knowledge and skills, not to simply perform well on tests.

The advantage of *mastery goals* is that they tend to promote long-term learning and skill development. Research suggests that they are generally more adaptive, promoting greater persistence, engagement, and intrinsic motivation (Ames & Archer, 1988; Harackiewicz et al., 2000).

Individuals with *performance goals (also known as outcome goals)* primarily aim to attain positive assessments of their competence while concurrently seeking to evade any negative judgment. They are concerned with proving their abilities to others and often equate their self-worth with their *performance*. They may be driven by grades, recognition, or other external markers of success.

For example, a student who has *performance goals* in a math class is concerned primarily with obtaining high grades or outperforming their classmates, regardless of whether they truly understand the math concepts.

They study to do well on tests and assignments, not necessarily to deepen their understanding of the material.

While *performance goals* can motivate individuals to work hard and achieve high levels of success, they can also lead to stress, fear of failure, and a tendency to avoid challenging tasks that might lead to failure or exposure of their limitations. If an individual does not perform well, they might perceive it as a failure, which can negatively impact their self-esteem.

In an optimal scenario, a balance of *mastery* and *performance goals* can be beneficial (Harackiewicz et al., 1998). It is advantageous to strive for competence and be driven by a desire to learn and grow while also seeking to achieve and be recognized for one's capabilities (Dweck, 1986).

Self-Efficacy

Self-efficacy is a term coined by psychologist Albert Bandura (Bandura, 1977), and it is a central concept in "social cognitive theory." It refers to an individual's belief in their capacity to execute behaviors necessary to produce specific performance attainments. In simpler terms, *self-efficacy* is all about your belief in your ability to succeed in specific situations or to accomplish a task. Higher levels of *self-efficacy* are associated with increased motivation, persistence, and performance (Bandura, 1997; Zimmerman, 2000).

Your sense of *self-efficacy* can play a major role in how you approach goals, tasks, and challenges. It influences one's thought patterns, behaviors, and emotions in various ways:

Cognition: High *self-efficacy* tends to lead to more optimistic thought patterns.

Individuals with high *self-efficacy* tend to perceive difficult tasks as something to be mastered rather than something to be feared.

Motivation: *Self-efficacy* impacts the goals you choose, the effort you put into achieving them, and the persistence you display in the face of adversity. People with a strong sense of *self-efficacy* are more likely to embrace challenging tasks and show resilience when facing obstacles.

Emotion: Self-efficacy can also influence emotional responses to situations. People with low *self-efficacy* may believe that difficult tasks are beyond their capabilities, leading to stress, anxiety, and a narrow vision of how best to solve a problem.

Importantly, *self-efficacy* is not just about one's actual ability to do something but also one's perception of that ability (Pajares, 1997). Two people with the same skills and abilities might perceive their *self-efficacy* differently, leading to different actions and outcomes.

Self-efficacy can be built in various ways:

Mastery experiences: Successfully handling a task or a challenge builds self-efficacy, while failing to adequately deal with a task or challenge can undermine it;

Vicarious experiences: When we observe someone similar to us who succeeds through sustained effort, this can increase our belief that we too possess the capabilities to master similar activities.

Verbal persuasion: Encouragement from others can increase *self-efficacy*, as can constructive feedback;

Physiological and emotional states: A positive mood and physical wellness can enhance *self-efficacy* beliefs, whereas stressful reactions and tension are likely to decrease them.

This powerful concept has been applied in various contexts, including education, health, behavior change, and organizational management. By understanding and enhancing *self-efficacy*, individuals can greatly improve their performance and overall well-being.

Attribution Theory

Attribution theory is a psychological concept that attempts to explain how individuals interpret events and how their successes and failures (*attributions*) influence their motivation and future behavior (Weiner, 1986; Malle, 2007). The term "attribution" refers to how people "attribute" causes to events and behaviors. "Attribution theory," introduced by psychologist Fritz Heider (1958) and further developed by others, such as Harold Kelley (1967) and Bernard Weiner (1974, 1985), remains a significant area of study in social psychology (Harvey & Martinko, 2009; Malle, 2022).

The main components of *attribution theory* are as follows:

Internal vs. External Attribution: This aspect of the theory considers whether we attribute the cause of behavior to factors within a person (internal) or to the situation (external). For example, if someone fails a test, we might attribute it internally ("He did not study enough") or externally ("The test was unfairly difficult").

Stability: This considers whether the causes of the behavior are stable (unchanging) or unstable (changing). For example, if a person is late in a meeting, a stable attribution might be "They are always disorganized," whereas an unstable attribution might be "They got stuck in unexpected traffic."

Controllability: This aspect considers whether a person has control over the causes of their behavior. For example, if someone scores poorly in a game, we might consider whether they had control over the situation (e.g., "They did not practice enough") or did not have control (e.g., "Their opponent was unusually strong").

Harold Kelley proposed two main types of *attributions*: *dispositional attribution* and *situational attribution*. *Dispositional attribution* (or internal attribution) refers to attributing a person's behavior to their personality or individual characteristics, whereas *situational attribution* (or external attribution) refers to attributing a person's behavior to their environment or the situation at hand.

Kelley also suggested the idea of "attributional biases." For instance, *fundamental attribution error* refers to the tendency for people to overemphasize *dispositional* (or personality-based) explanations for behaviors observed in others while underemphasizing *situational* explanations. In other words, people tend to assume that the behavior of others is due to personality rather than their situations, which can lead to misunderstandings or incorrect judgments (Gilbert & Malone, 1995).

Bernard Weiner developed the theory further by examining how different types of *attributions* can affect feelings of success and failure, especially in the context of education. He suggested that *attributions* can affect how students perceive their academic successes and failures, influencing their motivation and self-esteem (Weiner, 1985).

Attribution theory is essentially about how we explain behaviors, either our own or those of others, and how those explanations can significantly impact our perceptions, interactions, and reactions.

Social and Cultural Influences on Motivation

Motivation is influenced not only by individual factors but also by social and cultural contexts. Some key social and cultural influences on motivation include the following:

Social comparison was first proposed by the social psychologist Leon Festinger (Festinger, 1954). In this case, individuals often compare themselves to others to evaluate their abilities, performance, and progress, especially when they are uncertain about their own abilities or opinions. *Social comparison* can have both positive and negative effects on *motivation*, depending on the context and the individual's interpretation of the comparison.

This comparison process takes two forms:

Upward social comparison occurs when individuals compare themselves with others who are better off or superior to them in some way. This type of comparison could lead to feelings of inadequacy and decreased self-esteem, but it could also motivate people to improve their abilities or status.

In addition, *downward social comparison* takes place when individuals compare themselves with others who are worse off or inferior to them in some way. This type of comparison typically makes people feel better about themselves or their personal situation. Both *upward* and *downward social comparisons* are useful in certain situations. For example, an *upward comparison* might motivate an individual to work harder, whereas a *downward comparison* can offer comfort in challenging times. However, these comparisons can also lead to unhealthy competition, jealousy, and negative feelings about oneself.

There are several key aspects of social comparison theory that should be mentioned:

- the tendency to compare oneself to others increases when the person feels uncertain about themselves;
- the person who is chosen for comparison tends to be similar to the individual making the comparison;
- if objective, nonsocial means are available to evaluate oneself, the tendency to make social comparisons decreases.

These behaviors can be seen across a variety of areas, including academics, physical appearance, and wealth. With the advent of social media, these *comparisons* are becoming increasingly prevalent and can have significant impacts on mental health. Research indicates that *social comparisons* on social media, whether *upward* (comparing oneself to those perceived as better off) or *downward* (comparing oneself to those perceived as worse off), significantly impact mental health (Feinstein et al., 2013; Appel et al., 2016). Studies have shown that frequent *upward comparisons* on platforms such as Facebook and Instagram can lead to reduced positive feelings and decreased self-esteem, whereas *downward comparisons* might temporarily increase one's mood or self-esteem. For example, when individuals on social media engage in *upward comparisons*, they often feel worse about their own achievements and happiness, leading to feelings of inadequacy and reduced life satisfaction. Conversely, *downward comparisons* might serve as a psychological defense mechanism, helping individuals feel better about their own circumstances by observing those who are less fortunate or successful. Additionally, research conducted across various platforms revealed that these *comparison* habits can lead to complex emotional responses, further influencing users' mental health depending on their personal context and the frequency of such comparisons (Vogel et al., 2014).

Cultural values and *beliefs* refer to shared ideas and standards that are considered acceptable and obligatory by a particular group of people. These *values* and *beliefs* are integral aspects of our identity and shape our behavior, perceptions, and attitudes toward different aspects of life, such as family, religion, education, and work. They are typically passed down from generation to generation and influence social norms within a given culture. These cultural factors can strongly influence an individual's motivation and goal pursuits (Hofstede, 2001; Markus & Kitayama, 1991).

More specific details about cultural values and beliefs that are important in this context are as follows:

Family structure: In some cultures, the nuclear family (parents and children) is considered the core family unit, whereas in others, the extended family (including grandparents, aunts, uncles, and other relatives) is just as important. The role of different family members can also vary, with different expectations for men, women, and children, depending on culture.

Religious beliefs: Many cultures have specific religious beliefs that guide their worldview and behavior. These beliefs can influence everything from dietary practices to ethical standards to beliefs about life and death.

Education and knowledge: Cultures differ in the value they place on education and knowledge. Some cultures highly value academic learning and formal education, whereas others may place more emphasis on practical skills and experiential learning.

Work ethics and business practices: In some cultures, hard work and ambition may be highly valued, whereas in others, the balance between work and life or community contribution may be more important. Business practices can also vary, with different attitudes toward hierarchy, negotiation, and customer relationships.

Individualism vs. collectivism: Some cultures value the rights and freedoms of the individual, with an emphasis on personal achievement and independence (such as the United States), whereas others are more collectivist, valuing the societal or family group, cooperation and interdependence over individual achievement (such as many Asian cultures) (Hofstede, 2001; Markus & Kitayama, 1991; Triandis, 1995).

Communication styles: Cultures can differ significantly in their communication styles, with some preferring directness and clarity, whereas others prefer more indirect and subtle ways of conveying messages. For example, in American culture, communication tends to be direct and explicit. People are encouraged to express their thoughts, feelings, and opinions openly and clearly. In a business meeting, an American manager might directly say, "This project is not on track; we need to make changes immediately." In contrast, Japanese culture often favors more indirect communication. The emphasis is on maintaining harmony and avoiding conflict, so messages are conveyed in a less straightforward manner. In a similar business scenario, a Japanese manager might say, "Let us consider some possible improvements to enhance our project's progress," which subtly implies that changes are needed without direct criticism.

Nonverbal communication practices can also differ widely across cultures. Italians are known for using expressive gestures and facial expressions to accompany their verbal communication (Gudykunst & Ting-Toomey, 1988; Hall, 1989). A conversation might be full of hand gestures that emphasize points or express emotions, such as the classic pinched fingers to denote precision or frustration.

Conversely, Finns typically use minimal nonverbal communication. They value personal space and are more reserved, often maintaining a neutral facial expression and limited body movements during discussions.

These examples highlight how cultural backgrounds can influence not only what is communicated but also how it is expressed, both verbally and nonverbally.

Attitudes toward authority and hierarchy: Some cultures are more hierarchical, with clear distinctions between social and professional classes and a great deal of respect given to those in authority. Others are more egalitarian, emphasizing equal rights and opportunities for all.

Concepts of time: Cultures often differ in their orientation toward time. Some cultures are more future-oriented, planning and looking ahead, whereas others are more past-oriented, emphasizing tradition and history. There are also differences in the perceptions of punctuality and time management.

Food and cuisine: Culinary traditions and dietary habits are an integral part of cultural values and beliefs. What is considered edible, delicious, or taboo can vary significantly from one culture to another.

The specifics of these cultural values and beliefs can vary widely even within a single culture and can change over time. They are also influenced by other factors, such as socioeconomic status, education, and personal experience.

Social Support and Social Expectations

Social support and social expectations play a significant role in an individual's motivation, with impacts on various domains, such as academic achievement, work productivity, physical health and mental well-being. The support and expectations of significant others, such as parents, teachers, and peers, can influence an individual's motivation and beliefs about their abilities. High expectations and encouragement can foster *motivation* and *self-efficacy,* whereas negative feedback or low expectations can undermine *motivation* and self-belief.

Social support refers to the emotional, instrumental, or informational resources provided by a network of individuals—usually close friends, family, and community members—that help a person cope with stress and challenges. It comes in various forms:

Emotional support, which includes expressions of empathy, love, trust, and care;

Instrumental support, which refers to tangible aid and services, such as financial help or assistance with tasks;

Informational support consists of advice, suggestions, and information that a person might use to address problems;

Appraisal support refers to information useful for self-evaluation purposes, such as constructive feedback and affirmation.

The presence of *social support* can lead to increased motivation in several ways:

- Supportive networks often provide *encouragement*, which can motivate individuals to pursue their goals;
- When the individual and the supportive network *share common goals*, the motivation to achieve these goals can increase;
- People within the support network can act as *role models* (Cohen & Wills, 1985), providing tangible examples of what can be achieved;

- *Social support* can protect individuals from the potential negative effects of high stress (House, 1981) (*buffering effect*).

Social expectations refer to the beliefs and norms within a person's social network concerning what might be appropriate or expected behavior. These expectations can be powerful motivational forces (Cialdini & Trost, 1998).

Social norms can set standards for behavior, leading individuals to alter their behavior to conform to these norms, whether consciously or unconsciously.

Every *social role* comes with a set of expectations. These *role expectations* can motivate individuals to behave in a certain way to fulfill the responsibilities and duties associated with their roles.

In many social contexts, there are expectations about what a person should achieve (e.g., parents expecting their children to perform well in school). These *achievement expectations* can serve as motivational goals.

Sometimes, individuals *internalize* these social expectations, and they become self-expectations, further driving motivation.

While *social support and expectations* can greatly increase *motivation*, they can also cause pressure and stress if they are unrealistic or if the individual lacks the resources to meet them; it is crucial to balance *support and expectations* with an individual's ability and aspirations.

Emotions and Motivation in the Workplace

Emotions and motivation play important roles in workplace performance, satisfaction, and well-being.

Emotions play a pivotal role in shaping an individual's job performance and decision-making processes. They can be positive (such as happiness, satisfaction, and enthusiasm) or negative (such as fear, anger, and sadness). *Emotional intelligence*, which refers to the ability to understand and manage one's own emotions as well as those of others, is now recognized as a crucial soft skill in the workplace (Salovey & Mayer, 1990; Ashkanasy & Daus, 2005). In the mid-twentieth century, management styles often emphasized a hierarchical, top-down approach where leaders made decisions with little input from subordinates. The ideal employee was often seen as one who strictly followed instructions, maintained high productivity, and demonstrated strong technical or task-specific skills. Emotional aspects such as understanding a colleague's feelings, managing one's own emotional reactions, or fostering a supportive team environment were not typically seen as priorities. For example, in the automotive industry during the 1950s and 1960s, the emphasis was largely on production efficiency and technical expertise to maximize output. Leadership was more about command and control rather than collaboration and emotional understanding. Managers were valued more for their ability to enforce rules and meet production targets than for their ability to connect with employees or manage the emotional climate of their teams. This approach started to shift significantly with the introduction of concepts such as "Emotional Quotient" (EQ) and broader recognition of its impact on leadership effectiveness and organizational performance, a shift that gained momentum, particularly after the publication of Daniel Goleman's book *Emotional Intelligence* in 1995 (Goleman, 1995). Today, emotional intelligence is seen as a crucial component of professional development and leadership.

Positive emotions contribute to enhancing creativity, productivity, decision-making abilities, and interpersonal relationships in the workplace. When employees are happy and content, they are much more likely to perform better and show increased loyalty toward their organization. On the other hand, *negative emotions*, if persistent, can lead to job dissatisfaction, low productivity, high employee turnover, and even mental health issues. However, they are not always harmful; for example, fear or anxiety can sometimes drive employees to meet tight deadlines or achieve challenging targets (Fredrickson, 2001; Barsade & Gibson, 2007).

Motivation, in the context of the workplace, refers to the inner desire to achieve specific goals. This is a psychological process that fuels an individual to act in such a way that a desired objective is reached. In the workplace, *motivation* can be *intrinsic* or *extrinsic*. As mentioned earlier in this chapter, *emotions* and *motivation* are deeply intertwined. For example, positive emotional states can foster both *intrinsic* and *extrinsic motivation*, whereas negative emotions can diminish an employee's *motivation*. Cultivating a positive emotional climate in the workplace can thus enhance *motivation* and lead to better organizational outcomes (Fisher, 2010).

Different theories and models have been developed to better understand these two factors in a workplace setting, such as Maslow's "Hierarchy of Needs," Herzberg's "Two-Factor Theory" (Herzberg, 1968),[10] and "the Job Characteristics Model" (Hackman & Oldham, 1976).[11] These models offer valuable insights into employee behavior and can guide strategies to improve morale, productivity, and job retention.

The following are a few factors whose influences on *emotions* and *motivation* in the workplace have been confirmed:

Job satisfaction: employees who are satisfied with their job and find it meaningful are more likely to be *motivated* and *engaged*, leading to higher performance and lower turnover;

Organizational culture: values, norms, and practices within an organization can shape employees' *emotions* and *motivation*, either by promoting or hindering performance, creativity, and collaboration. A positive organizational culture that values employee well-being, open communication and inclusiveness can foster *motivation* and job satisfaction.

Leadership and motivation: Effective leadership plays a critical role in fostering *motivation* and *engagement* among team members. Leaders can influence *motivation* through various strategies (Bass & Riggio, 2006), such as the following:

- *Transformational leadership:* Transformational leaders inspire and motivate followers by articulating a compelling vision, fostering a sense of collective identity, and providing individualized support and encouragement. This leadership style has been associated with increased motivation, job satisfaction, and performance among followers
- *Goal setting and feedback:* Leaders can facilitate motivation by helping employees set specific, challenging, and achievable goals and providing regular feedback on progress and performance.
- *Recognition and rewards:* Acknowledging and rewarding employees' accomplishments can increase *motivation*, *self-efficacy*, and commitment to the organization. However, it is important to ensure that rewards are perceived as fair and are not solely based on *extrinsic* factors, which can undermine *intrinsic* motivation.

Notes

1. The James-Lange theory of emotion proposes that physiological reactions (such as an increased heart rate) occur first and lead to the experience of emotion. Developed independently by William James (U.S.) and Carl Lange (Denmark) in the nineteenth century, it suggests that noticing one's body's reactions—such as a racing pulse when encountering a bear—produces the feeling of fear. However, later theories (e.g., Cannon-Bard,

Schachter-Singer) challenge this by arguing that emotion may arise simultaneously with these bodily changes or be influenced by cognitive interpretation.

2. Developed by Walter Cannon and Philip Bard in the 1920s, the Cannon–Bard theory of emotion proposes that we experience emotional feelings and physiological responses (e.g., sweating, trembling) at the same time. When an emotionally charged event occurs, the thalamus relays signals to both the brain's cortex, which generates conscious awareness of emotion, and the autonomic nervous system, which triggers accompanying bodily reactions. This contrasts with the James-Lange theory, which posits that physiological changes occur first and are then interpreted as emotions. The Cannon–Bard theory helps explain why the same bodily responses (like a racing heart) can correspond to various emotional states and why emotions sometimes occur in the absence of clear physiological changes. However, critics note that it downplays the role of cognitive appraisal in emotional experiences. The Schachter–Singer two-factor theory, for instance, highlights both physiological arousal and the individual's interpretation (labeling) of that arousal in shaping emotion.
3. The Schachter–Singer two-factor theory holds that emotion depends on both physiological arousal and the context-based interpretation of that arousal. In their classic experiment, participants who were injected with adrenaline labeled their arousal as happiness or anger, depending on the mood of those around them. While influential, the theory has been critiqued for its assumption about the timing of cognitive labeling and its ability to explain emotions that emerge with minimal physiological arousal.
4. Cognitive appraisal theory (Lazarus) posits that emotions stem from how people evaluate events relative to their goals and well-being. First, they determine whether an event is positive, negative, or neutral (primary appraisal) and then assess their coping resources (secondary appraisal). These interpretations lead to specific emotions (e.g., harm/loss → sadness, threat → fear, challenge → excitement, benefit/gain → happiness). Changing appraisals can modify emotional responses, offering insight into stress, coping, and emotional health.
5. Neuroscientist Antonio Damasio's Somatic Marker Hypothesis (1994) proposes that emotions play a vital role in decision-making by creating "somatic markers." These markers are physiological responses (e.g., a smile when happy or a racing heartbeat when stressed) that become stored in the brain alongside memories of the events that triggered them. When facing a new decision, the brain unconsciously refers to these positive or negative markers to guide choices. For example, if you previously profited from investing in certain stocks, you may develop a favorable marker that nudges you to repeat similar investments—even if logical data suggest otherwise.

This explains why emotions can override purely rational thought, as seen in individuals with ventromedial prefrontal cortex damage: they retain logical skills but struggle to make advantageous decisions.

6. Drive theory, introduced in the 1940s, posits that biological needs create tension (a "drive"), motivating organisms to act. When a drive—such as hunger or thirst—is satisfied, the organism repeats the behavior that provides relief, aiming for homeostasis (balance). Drives can be primary (rooted in biology) or secondary (learned, like a desire for money). Clark Hull notably proposed that the strength of a behavior depends on both the drive level and the habitual response. Critics argue that drive theory fails to explain why people sometimes seek greater arousal or act without clear biological drive.

   Consequently, contemporary motivation research often references alternative frameworks such as Maslow's hierarchy of needs, self-determination theory, or intrinsic-extrinsic motivation theory.
7. Maslow's hierarchy of needs, developed by Abraham Maslow in the mid-twentieth century, is often represented as a five-tiered pyramid. The base consists of physiological needs (food, water, warmth, rest). Next are safety needs (security, health, protection), followed by belongingness and love needs (relationships, friendship, family), and then esteem needs (achievement, respect, recognition). At the peak lies self-actualization, where individuals pursue personal growth, fulfillment, and their full potential. Maslow proposed that lower-level needs must typically be met before higher needs significantly influence behavior. However, more recent views suggest that these categories can overlap and may not follow a strict sequence. Critics also note that this model may be culturally specific, reflecting primarily Western ideas of motivation and self-fulfillment.
8. Expectancy-value theory, pioneered by John William Atkinson and Martin Fishbein in the mid-twentieth century, explains how individuals decide whether to engage in a task on the basis of two main factors: expectancy (their belief in the likelihood of success) and value (the importance they place on the outcome). Higher expectancy and value lead to stronger motivation to undertake an activity. This theory has been broadly applied in education, health behavior, marketing, and career counseling. For example, a student who believes that they can do well (high expectancy) and see clear benefits in succeeding (high value) will be more motivated to study.
9. Goal-Setting Theory, developed by Edwin Locke, posits that setting specific and challenging goals leads to higher performance—provided that the individual is committed, has the ability to achieve the goal, and does not face conflicting objectives. The key components include:

   Goal specificity – Clearly defined goals focus on effort and clarify expectations.

Goal Difficulty – Harder goals motivate greater effort, assuming that they remain achievable.

Feedback – Ongoing progress updates help individuals adjust their strategies and maintain motivation. Goal Commitment – Commitment increases when goals are personally important, self-efficacy is high, and individuals believe that effort will lead to success.

Task Complexity – Complex tasks may require additional training or support, although specific, challenging goals remain beneficial.

Widely applied in workplaces, education, and personal development, goal-setting theory underscores the power of distinct, challenging goals supported by feedback and commitment to enhance performance and outcomes.

Goal-setting theory has been widely applied in many domains, including organizational and work settings, education, health behavior, and personal growth. This suggests that by setting specific and challenging goals, providing feedback on progress, and maintaining commitment to goals, individuals can improve their performance and achieve desired outcomes.

10. Herzberg's two-factor theory (motivation-hygiene theory), developed by Frederick Herzberg in the 1950s, explains employee satisfaction and motivation through two categories of factors:

Hygiene Factors (Extrinsic): Salary, company policy, supervision, working conditions, job security, relationships with colleagues, status, and personal life. Their presence prevents dissatisfaction but does not create true motivation.

Motivators (Intrinsic): Achievement, recognition, the work itself, responsibility, advancement, and opportunities for growth. These factors foster genuine satisfaction and motivate employees.

In practice, ensuring good hygiene practices avoids dissatisfaction but does not necessarily motivate individuals. For real engagement, organizations must also emphasize motivators—meaningful work, recognition, and growth opportunities—to inspire and retain satisfied employees.

11. Developed by J. Richard Hackman and Greg Oldham in the 1970s, the job characteristics model proposes that five core job features—skill variety, task identity, task significance, autonomy, and feedback—foster three key psychological states: experienced meaningfulness, experienced responsibility, and knowledge of results. These states lead to positive outcomes, including high job satisfaction, stronger performance, and reduced absenteeism and turnover. However, individual differences—particularly growth needs strength—can influence how strongly people respond to enriched jobs. Overall, the model highlights the value of job enrichment by designing roles that enhance these core characteristics to increase intrinsic motivation and job satisfaction.

References

Ames, C., & Archer, J. (1988). Achievement goals in the classroom: Students' learning strategies and motivation processes. *Journal of Educational Psychology, 80*(3), 260–267. https://doi.org/10.1037/0022-0663.80.3.260

Anderson, A. K. (2005). Affective influences on the attentional dynamics supporting awareness. *Journal of Experimental Psychology: General, 134*(2), 258–281. https://doi.org/10.1037/0096-3445.134.2.258

Appel, H., Gerlach, A. L., & Crusius, J. (2016). The interplay between Facebook use, social comparison, envy, and depression. *Current Opinion in Psychology, 9*, 44–49. https://doi.org/10.1016/j.copsyc.2015.10.006

Ashkanasy, N. M., & Daus, C. S. (2005). Rumors of the death of emotional intelligence in organizational behavior are vastly exaggerated. *Journal of Organizational Behavior, 26*(4), 441–452. https://doi.org/10.1002/job.320

Bandura, A. (1977). Self-efficacy: Toward a unifying theory of behavioral change. *Psychological Review, 84*(2), 191–215. https://doi.org/10.1037/0033-295X.84.2.191

Bandura, A. (1997). *Self-efficacy: The exercise of control*. W. H. Freeman.

Barrett, L. F. (2017). *How emotions are made: The secret life of the brain*. Houghton Mifflin Harcourt.

Barsade, S. G., & Gibson, D. E. (2007). Why does affect matter in organizations? *Academy of Management Perspectives, 21*(1), 36–59. https://doi.org/10.5465/AMP.2007.24286163

Bass, B. M., & Riggio, R. E. (2006). *Transformational leadership* (2nd ed.). Lawrence Erlbaum Associates. https://doi.org/10.4324/9781410617095

Cannon, W. B. (1927). The James-Lange theory of emotion: A critical examination and an alternative theory. *The American Journal of Psychology, 39*(1/4), 106–124. https://doi.org/10.2307/1415404

Cialdini, R. B., & Trost, M. R. (1998). Social influence: Social norms, conformity, and compliance. In D. T. Gilbert, S. T. Fiske, & G. Lindzey (Eds.), *The handbook of social psychology* (Vol. 2, pp. 151–192). McGraw-Hill.

Cohen, S., & Wills, T. A. (1985). Stress, social support, and the buffering hypothesis. *Psychological Bulletin, 98*(2), 310–357. https://doi.org/10.1037/0033-2909.98.2.310

Damasio, A. R. (1996). The somatic marker hypothesis and the possible functions of the prefrontal cortex. *Philosophical Transactions of the Royal Society B: Biological Sciences, 351*(1346), 1413–1420. https://doi.org/10.1098/rstb.1996.0125

de Waal, F. B. M. (2008). Putting the altruism back into altruism: The evolution of empathy. *Annual Review of Psychology, 59*, 279–300. https://doi.org/10.1146/annurev.psych.59.103006.093625

Deci, E. L., & Ryan, R. M. (2000). The "What" and "Why" of goal pursuits: Human needs and the self-determination of behavior. *Psychological Inquiry, 11*(4), 227–268. https://doi.org/10.1207/S15327965PLI1104_01
Deci, E. L., Koestner, R., & Ryan, R. M. (1999). A meta-analytic review of experiments examining the effects of extrinsic rewards on intrinsic motivation. *Psychological Bulletin, 125*(6), 627–668. https://doi.org/10.1037/0033-2909.125.6.627
Dweck, C. S. (1986). Motivational processes affecting learning. *American Psychologist, 41*(10), 1040–1048. https://doi.org/10.1037/0003-066X.41.10.1040
Eccles, J. (1983). Expectancies, values, and academic behaviors. In J. T. Spence (Ed.), *Achievement and achievement motives* (pp. 75–146). W. H. Freeman.
Emery, N. J. (2006). Cognitive ornithology: The evolution of avian intelligence. *Philosophical Transactions of the Royal Society B: Biological Sciences, 361*(1465), 23–43. https://doi.org/10.1098/rstb.2005.1736
Feinstein, B. A., Hershenberg, R., Bhatia, V., Latack, J. A., Meuwly, N., & Davila, J. (2013). Negative social comparison on Facebook and depressive symptoms: Rumination as a mechanism. *Psychology of Popular Media Culture, 2*(3), 161–170. https://doi.org/10.1037/a0033111
Festinger, L. (1954). A theory of social comparison processes. *Human Relations, 7*(2), 117–140. https://doi.org/10.1177/001872675400700202
Fisher, C. D. (2010). Happiness at work. *International Journal of Management Reviews, 12*(4), 384–412. https://doi.org/10.1111/j.1468-2370.2009.00270.x
Fredrickson, B. L. (2001). The role of positive emotions in positive psychology: The Broaden-and-Build Theory of positive emotions. *American Psychologist, 56*(3), 218–226. https://doi.org/10.1037/0003-066X.56.3.218
Gilbert, D. T., & Malone, P. S. (1995). The correspondence bias. *Psychological Bulletin, 117*(1), 21–38. https://doi.org/10.1037/0033-2909.117.1.21
Goleman, D. (1995). *Emotional intelligence: Why it can matter more than IQ.* Bantam Books.
Gross, J. J. (1998). The emerging field of emotion regulation: An integrative review. *Review of General Psychology, 2*(3), 271–299. https://doi.org/10.1037/1089-2680.2.3.271
Gudykunst, W. B., & Ting-Toomey, S. (1988). *Culture and interpersonal communication.* Sage.
Hackman, J. R., & Oldham, G. R. (1976). Motivation through the design of work: Test of a theory. *Organizational Behavior and Human Performance, 16*(2), 250–279. https://doi.org/10.1016/0030-5073(76)90016-7
Hall, E. T. (1989). *Beyond culture.* Anchor Books.
Harackiewicz, J. M., Barron, K. E., & Elliot, A. J. (1998). Rethinking achievement goals: When are they adaptive for college students and why? *Educational Psychologist, 33*(1), 1–21. https://doi.org/10.1207/s15326985ep3301_1

Harackiewicz, J. M., Barron, K. E., Tauer, J. M., Carter, S. M., & Elliot, A. J. (2000). Short-term and long-term consequences of achievement goals: Predicting interest and performance over time. *Journal of Educational Psychology, 92*(2), 316–330. https://doi.org/10.1037/0022-0663.92.2.316

Harris, C. L. (2004). Bilingual speakers in the lab: Psychophysiological measures of emotional reactivity. *Journal of Multilingual and Multicultural Development, 25*(2–3), 223–247. https://doi.org/10.1080/01434630408666530

Harvey, J. H., & Martinko, M. J. (2009). Attribution theory and research: Review and future prospects. In S. J. Lopez & C. R. Snyder (Eds.), *Oxford handbook of positive psychology* (2nd ed., pp. 477–485). Oxford University Press.

Heider, F. (1958). *The psychology of interpersonal relations.* Wiley. https://doi.org/10.1037/10628-000

Herzberg, F. (1968). One more time: How do you motivate employees? *Harvard Business Review, 46*(1), 53–62.

Hofstede, G. (2001). *Culture's consequences: Comparing values, behaviors, institutions and organizations across nations* (2nd ed.). Sage.

House, J. S. (1981). *Work stress and social support.* Addison-Wesley.

Hull, C. L. (1943). *Principles of behavior.* Appleton-Century.

James, W. (1884). What is an emotion? *Mind, 9*(34), 188–205.

Karasek, R., & Theorell, T. (1990). *Healthy work: Stress, productivity and the reconstruction of working life.* Basic Books.

Kelley, H. H. (1967). Attribution theory in social psychology. In D. Levine (Ed.), *Nebraska symposium on motivation* (Vol. 15, pp. 192–238). University of Nebraska Press.

Kohn, A. (1993). *Punished by rewards: The trouble with gold stars, incentive plans, A's, praise, and other bribes.* Houghton Mifflin.

Lazarus, R. S. (1991). *Emotion and adaptation.* Oxford University Press.

Locke, E. A., & Latham, G. P. (1990). *A theory of goal setting & task performance.* Prentice Hall.

Malle, B. F. (2007). Attributions as behavior explanations: Toward a new theory. In D. Chadee & J. Hunter (Eds.), *Current themes and perspectives in social psychology* (pp. 3–26). St. Augustine, Trinidad: SOCS, The University of the West Indies.

Malle, B. F. (2022). Attribution theories: How people make sense of behavior. In *Theories in social psychology* (2nd ed., pp. 93–120).

Markus, H. R., & Kitayama, S. (1991). Culture and the self: Implications for cognition, emotion, and motivation. *Psychological Review, 98*(2), 224–253. https://doi.org/10.1037/0033-295X.98.2.224

Maslach, C., Schaufeli, W. B., & Leiter, M. P. (2001). Job burnout. *Annual Review of Psychology, 52*, 397–422. https://doi.org/10.1146/annurev.psych.52.1.397

Maslow, A. H. (1943). A theory of human motivation. *Psychological Review, 50*(4), 370–396. https://doi.org/10.1037/h0054346

Pajares, F. (1997). Current directions in self-efficacy research. In M. Maehr & P. R. Pintrich (Eds.), *Advances in motivation and achievement* (Vol. 10, pp. 1–49). JAI Press.

Pavlenko, A. (2012). Affective processing in bilingual speakers: Disembodied cognition? *International Journal of Psychology, 47*(6), 405–428. https://doi.org/10.1080/00207594.2012.743665

Poole, J. H., & Moss, C. J. (2008). Elephant sociality and complexity: The scientific evidence. In C. Wemmer & C. A. Christen (Eds.), *Elephants and ethics: Toward a morality of coexistence* (pp. 69–98). Johns Hopkins University Press.

Ryan, R. M., & Deci, E. L. (2017). *Self-determination theory: Basic psychological needs in motivation, development, and wellness.* The Guilford Press. https://doi.org/10.1521/978.14625/28806

Salovey, P., & Mayer, J. D. (1990). Emotional intelligence. *Imagination, Cognition and Personality, 9*(3), 185–211. https://doi.org/10.2190/DUGG-P24E-52WK-6CDG

Schachter, S., & Singer, J. E. (1962). Cognitive, social, and physiological determinants of emotional state. *Psychological Review, 69*(5), 379–399. https://doi.org/10.1037/h0046234

Siniscalchi, M., D'Ingeo, S., & Quaranta, A. (2018). Emotional communication in the domestic dog (Canis familiaris): The effect of valence and intensity on vocalizations. *Animal Cognition, 21*(1), 1–11. https://doi.org/10.3390/ani8080131

Triandis, H. C. (1995). *Individualism & collectivism.* Westview Press.

Tsai, J. L., Louie, J. Y., Chen, E. E., & Uchida, Y. (2007). Learning what feelings to desire: Socialization of ideal affect through children's storybooks. *Personality and Social Psychology Bulletin, 33*(1), 17–30. https://doi.org/10.1177/0146167206292749

Uchida, Y., & Kitayama, S. (2009). Happiness and unhappiness in East and West: Themes and variations. *Emotion, 9*(4), 441–456. https://doi.org/10.1037/a0015634

Vogel, E. A., Rose, J. P., Roberts, L. R., & Eckles, K. (2014). Social comparison, social media, and self-esteem. *Psychology of Popular Media Culture, 3*(4), 206–222. https://doi.org/10.1037/ppm0000047

Weiner, B. (1974). *Achievement motivation and attribution theory.* General Learning Press.

Weiner, B. (1985). An attributional theory of achievement motivation and emotion. *Psychological Review, 92*(4), 548–573. https://doi.org/10.1037/0033-295X.92.4.548

Weiner, B. (1986). *An attributional theory of motivation and emotion.* Springer-Verlag.

Zimmerman, B. J. (2000). Self-efficacy: An essential motive to learn. *Contemporary Educational Psychology, 25*(1), 82–91. https://doi.org/10.1006/ceps.1999.1016

CHAPTER 10

Cognitive Neuroscience and Neuropsychology

Brain Regions and Networks That Are Involved in Cognition

Cognitive neuroscience is the interdisciplinary study of the neural basis of cognitive processes (Gazzaniga et al., 2019; Ward, 2015)

Cognitive processes, such as *perception, memory, decision-making,* and *language*, are considered the fundamental aspects of *human consciousness* and are thought to arise from complex interactions (mainly through "transmitters") between neurons in various parts of the brain (Bear et al., 2016).

Perception involves the interpretation of sensory inputs by the brain. Different modalities of perception are processed in different areas. For example, visual perception is primarily processed in the occipital lobe, which is a region known as the primary visual cortex (Grill-Spector & Weiner, 2014). Auditory perception takes place in the primary auditory cortex of the temporal lobe, whereas touch, temperature, and body position (somatosensory perception) are processed in the parietal lobe (Halgren et al., 1998).

Memory involves the hippocampus (Scoville & Milner, 1957; Squire & Wixted, 2011). Located in the medial temporal lobe, the hippocampus is crucial for the formation of new autobiographical and spatial memories. The surrounding cortex, known as the entorhinal cortex, also plays a key

H. Kankam, *A Brief Excursion into Human Cognition*,
https://doi.org/10.1007/978-3-031-89752-8_10

role in memory. Working memory is thought to involve the prefrontal cortex, particularly the dorsolateral prefrontal cortex (Fuster, 2015).

Attention is controlled by a network of regions, including the parietal cortex, the prefrontal cortex, and the cingulate cortex (Corbetta & Shulman, 2002). The lateral prefrontal cortex helps maintain focus upon specific information while allowing one to ignore distractions, and the anterior cingulate cortex monitors for errors and conflicts between tasks.

Decision-making involves numerous brain regions, particularly the prefrontal cortex (especially the ventromedial prefrontal cortex), which is thought to be involved in evaluating outcomes and making choices. Other regions, such as the amygdala, may be involved when decisions involve emotional considerations (Bechara et al., 2000; Rolls, 2015).

Language processing involves the coordinated activity of several brain regions. "Broca's area" (located in the left frontal lobe) and "Wernicke's area" (located in the left temporal lobe) are particularly important for producing speech and understanding language, respectively (Geschwind, 1972).

Emotional processing of fear- and threat-related stimuli involves the amygdala in the limbic system (LeDoux, 2014; Fanselow & Pennington, 2018). It plays a significant role in emotion and social behavior, fear conditioning, and the association of emotional value with experiences and memories. The amygdala is often associated with the "Four Fs" of survival: "*Fight, Flight, Freeze, and Fornicate.*"

Fight: When a threat is perceived, the amygdala, via its connections with other brain regions, can trigger a *fight* response. This reaction is characterized by behaviors aimed at confronting and dealing with the threat.

Flight: Similarly, the amygdala can initiate a *flight* response, which manifests as behaviors designed to escape from the threat. Both *fight* and *flight* responses are often triggered by fear, which is closely tied to the function of the amygdala.

Fawn/Freeze: The amygdala can also induce a *fawn/freeze* response, which is a sort of "on the spot" immobilization or "placating" in the face of danger, where neither fighting nor fleeing seems to be an appropriate reaction. In some cases, this is a way of avoiding detection by predators (Fanselow & Pennington, 2018).

Fornicate (Reproduction)/Feed: Here, the amygdala plays a role in reproductive behaviors by processing social and sexual cues and contributing to the emotional responses associated with reproduction. It also plays a role in feeding behavior, interpreting hunger signals, reward anticipation, and food-related cues essential for securing nourishment, maintaining energy and ensuring species survival.

These descriptions simplify complex processes that are in part not fully understood and are still the subject of active research. In truth, reality is much more complicated, with many cognitive processes involving intricate networks of brain regions and not solely a particular area (Ward, 2015). A dense network of interconnections exists between the amygdala, the ventromedial prefrontal cortex (vmPFC), and the dorsolateral prefrontal cortex (dlPFC) (Rolls, 2015). These three regions work together to help us navigate our emotional and social worlds. The amygdala provides the emotional context or significance of a situation, after which this emotional information is integrated into the vmPFC, which can influence decision-making processes. Owing to its role in executive functions, the dlPFC consequently takes these emotions and decisions into account to guide our actions and behavior in a goal-directed manner. Neuroplasticity, or the ability of the brain to reorganize itself by forming new neural connections, also plays a key role in these processes. Neuroplasticity is a topic we will examine in due course.

The network of the brain, often referred to as the *connectome*, is an intricate web of neurons and their interconnections (Sporns, 2011). This network allows different brain regions to communicate with each other, coordinating everything from basic bodily functions to complex cognitive processes. Neurotransmitters are chemical messengers used by neurons to communicate with each other. They are released from the axon terminals of a neuron (the presynaptic neuron) in response to an electrical signal, and they bind to specific receptors on another neuron (the postsynaptic neuron), influencing the likelihood that the second neuron will fire an action potential. The following are some of the most studied neurotransmitters (Bear et al., 2016):

- *Glutamate* is the most common neurotransmitter and is excitatory, which means that it increases the likelihood that a neuron will fire an action potential;
- *GABA* (gamma-aminobutyric acid) is the primary inhibitory neurotransmitter, meaning that it reduces the likelihood that a neuron will fire an action potential (thereby making it less likely to excite nearby neurons). Imbalances in GABA are thought to play a role in anxiety and epilepsy;
- *Dopamine* is involved in reward, motivation, and addiction (overly complex interactions). It is also important for motor control and is depleted in Parkinson's disease patients (Poewe et al., 2017);

- *Serotonin* plays a key role in mood regulation, appetite, sleep, and some cognitive functions, including memory and learning (Cowen & Browning, 2015). Imbalances in serotonin are associated with depression and obsessive–compulsive disorder;
- *Acetylcholine* is involved in memory and learning and plays a key role in stimulating muscle contraction (Fuster, 2015);
- *Norepinephrine,* also known as *noradrenaline,* influences attention and responding actions in the brain. It is also involved in fight or flight responses;
- *Endorphins* are the body's natural painkillers. They are released in response to stress or discomfort and produce a feeling of well-being.

Obviously, the list of neurotransmitters does not end here; this is a partial list.

Nevertheless, these neurotransmitters work together along intricate networks and pathways to enable complex behaviors and cognitive processes. The balance and interaction between these neurotransmitters are essential for maintaining normal brain function (Nestler et al., 2015). Any imbalance is likely to give rise to many known psychiatric and neurological disorders.

When neurotransmitters are mentioned, it is important to consider hormones and growth factors (often referred to as promoters in this context), as these also play crucial roles in neuron function and brain communication (Dechant & Neumann, 2002). Compared with neurotransmitters, they often act over longer timescales and distances.

Hormones are chemical messengers produced by glands in the endocrine system that travel through the bloodstream to various parts of the body, including the brain, where they can influence neuron function. For example:

Cortisol, a glucocorticoid, is released in response to stress. It can affect mood, motivation, and fear responses. Chronic elevated levels of cortisol are linked to mental health disorders such as depression and anxiety (Lupien et al., 2009).

Oxytocin is often referred to as the "love hormone" or "bonding hormone," as it plays a key role in social bonding, sexual reproduction, childbirth, and the period after childbirth (Meyer-Lindenberg & Tost, 2012).

Estrogen and testosterone are considered sex hormones but can secondarily influence mood, memory, and even spatial navigation. Their levels fluctuate throughout life and can impact brain function and disease risk

(Gillies & McArthur, 2010). It is relevant to look at these hormones outside their primary function as female or male sex hormones;

Growth factors/promoters are proteins that can stimulate cellular growth, proliferation, healing, and differentiation. They are particularly important in the nervous system because of their roles in development, maintenance, and repair. Here are a few examples of these important proteins and how they are involved in maintaining stasis in neural regulation:

- *BDNF (brain-derived neurotrophic factor)* supports the survival of existing neurons and encourages the growth and differentiation of new neurons and synapses. It is active in the hippocampus, cortex, and basal forebrain—areas vital to learning, memory, and higher thinking (Kowiański et al., 2018);
- *NGF (nerve growth factor)* promotes the growth, maintenance, and survival of certain target neurons. It is important in the development and survival of sympathetic and sensory neurons;
- *Insulin-like growth factor 1 (IGF-1)* is crucial for brain development and plasticity, promotes both neuron proliferation and differentiation, and serves to increase synaptic strength (Trejo et al., 2001).

Like neurotransmitters, the balance and interaction of hormones and growth factors are crucial for maintaining brain health and function. Dysregulation of these substances can also contribute to a variety of neurological and psychiatric disorders.

Methods in Cognitive Neuroscience

The technologies and methods used to investigate the relationship between brain activity and cognitive function have become more sophisticated and refined over the past decades (Cacioppo et al., 2008).

The first human *electroencephalography (EEG)* recording was made by Hans Berger, a German psychiatrist, in 1924 (Haas, 2003). He published his findings on the electrical activity of the human brain in 1929. EEG allows noninvasive recording of electrical activity from the human brain and has since become an essential tool in both clinical neurology and neuroscience research. Berger's discovery of the alpha wave, a particular type of brain wave, was one of the first notable findings using this technology (Berger, 1929). While the exact role of alpha oscillations in cognitive processes is still under investigation, studies have associated changes in alpha rhythms with various cognitive functions, including attention, memory, and information processing. The alpha rhythm is most prominently observed when an individual is awake but in a relaxed state with closed eyes. It diminishes or disappears when the eyes are opened or when the individual is actively processing information (Klimesch, 2012). As a result, the presence of the alpha rhythm became an early hallmark for the state of relaxed alertness. This has contributed to the alpha wave becoming a focal point in neurofeedback training and meditation research.

Functional magnetic resonance imaging (fMRI) is a technique that measures and maps the brain's activity. Unlike standard *magnetic resonance imaging (MRI)*, which creates images of structures, fMRI looks at blood flow in the brain to detect areas of activity (Logothetis, 2008). The foundational concept for fMRI is based on the observation that cerebral blood flow and neuronal activation are closely linked. When a brain region is more active, it consumes more oxygen, and to meet this increased demand, blood flow increases to that region. The initial experiments demonstrating the feasibility of fMRI were conducted in the early 1990s, and seminal papers that first described this technique were published around 1992. The specific methods used to detect *blood-oxygen-level-dependent (BOLD)* contrast, which most fMRI studies rely on today, were developed around this time. Seiji Ogawa (Ogawa et al., 1990) is often credited with pioneering work on BOLD contrast.

Since its introduction, fMRI has become a fundamental tool in neuroscience and cognitive psychology, allowing researchers to noninvasively explore the functional organization of the human brain by providing high spatial resolution in identifying specific brain regions involved in cognitive processes (Gazzaniga et al., 2019; Ward, 2015).

Magnetoencephalography (MEG) is a technique that measures the magnetic fields produced by neuronal activity in the brain. The first human MEG measurements were carried out in the early 1960s. Seminal work in the field was conducted by David Cohen at the Massachusetts Institute of Technology (MIT) in 1968 when he successfully detected the magnetic fields produced by the human heart and brain (Cohen, 1968). The actual development and refinement of MEG technology, however, took several more decades, with the introduction of superconducting quantum interference device (SQUID) magnetometers in the 1970s, thereby greatly increasing its sensitivity. An MEG provides both high spatial and temporal resolution, making it a valuable tool for studying the dynamics of cognitive processes (Hari & Parkkonen, 2015).

Transcranial magnetic stimulation (TMS) was invented in 1985 (Barker et al., 1985). The development of TMS was facilitated by Anthony Barker and colleagues in Sheffield, UK. TMS is used as a noninvasive tool in neuroscience research to study the functions of various brain regions. By applying TMS to specific areas of the brain, researchers can temporarily disrupt or enhance the function of that area and observe the resulting changes in behavior or cognition (Pascual-Leone et al., 2000). Furthermore, in clinical settings, TMS has been approved in the US by the Food and Drug Administration (FDA) for the treatment of major depressive disorder (MDD), migraine, and obsessive–compulsive disorder (OCD) (Perera et al., 2016).

Lesion studies, in the context of neuroscience and psychology, refer to the study of the function of specific brain regions by observing the effects of damage or lesions to those regions. The concept of studying the effects of brain damage to understand brain function dates back many centuries. One could argue that ancient Egyptians had some understanding of the relationship between brain damage and changes in function, as evidenced by the "Edwin Smith Papyrus" (circa 1600 BCE), which is one of the oldest surgical texts. It describes various cases of traumatic brain injuries and their outcomes (Breasted, 1930).

However, systematic lesion studies began to emerge in the nineteenth century. One of the most famous cases from this era is that of Phineas Gage, a railroad worker who survived an accident in which an iron rod was driven through his skull in 1848. The changes in his personality and behavior following the accident were recorded, which provided early insights into the role of the frontal lobes in personality and behavior (Harlow, 1868). In the latter half of the nineteenth century, scientists such as Paul Broca and Carl Wernicke made significant contributions by linking specific brain lesions to deficits in language abilities, leading to the identification of Broca's area and Wernicke's area, respectively (Geschwind, 1972). With the advancement of technology and methodologies in the twentieth century, lesion studies became more refined, allowing for a better understanding of the roles of specific brain regions in various cognitive functions (Bear et al., 2016).

Neuropsychological Disorders and Their Impact on Cognition

Neuropsychological disorders are conditions that result from brain damage or dysfunction and can significantly impact cognitive function (Lezak et al., 2012). Examples are as follows:

Alzheimer's disease, the most common form of dementia, is a neurodegenerative disorder characterized by progressive memory loss, cognitive decline, and impaired daily functioning. Alzheimer's disease primarily affects the hippocampus and surrounding medial temporal lobe structures (Lane et al., 2018). Some of the core cognitive and functional deficits associated with Alzheimer's disease are as follows:

- *Memory loss* is the most well-known symptom; short-term memory decreases first, with patients forgetting recent conversations or events. As the disease progresses, long-term memory is also affected.
- *Aphasia* refers to language problems. People with Alzheimer's disease may forget simple words or substitute inappropriate words, making their sentences difficult to understand; they have difficulty comprehending and frequently repeat themselves.
- *Apraxia* is the inability to carry out common tasks. For example, a person might forget how to tie their shoes or button a shirt.
- *Agnosia* is the inability to recognize familiar objects, sounds, or people. A person with Alzheimer's disease might not recognize a family member or might place a pressing iron in the refrigerator.
- *Spatial and temporal disorientation* occurs such that people with Alzheimer's disease can lose track of dates, seasons, and the passage of time; they may even be lost in familiar places.
- Through *impaired judgement* the affected person might make poor decisions, such as giving away large sums of money to strangers.
- *Difficulties in planning and solving problems* occur such that tasks that require sequential steps, such as cooking a recipe or paying bills, become difficult.
- There is a *decreased ability to concentrate:* this might be observed as difficulties in maintaining a conversation or following a TV program.
- *Changes in Personality and Behavior:* Patients might experience mood swings and become anxious, suspicious, depressed, or fearful. They may also exhibit socially inappropriate behaviors.

- Some patients can become *impulsive*, making hasty decisions without thinking about the consequences.
- *Neuropsychiatric symptoms,* which can include hallucinations, delusions, and paranoia, are also observed.

As Alzheimer's disease progresses, cognitive deficits become more pronounced, and individuals eventually require full-time care. Notably, the presentation of Alzheimer's disease can vary from person to person, and not everyone will experience all the symptoms listed above.

Parkinson's disease (PD) is a neurodegenerative disorder characterized by motor symptoms (tremors, rigidity, bradykinesia) and cognitive deficits, such as executive dysfunction and memory impairment. Parkinson's disease primarily affects the basal ganglia and dopaminergic pathways (Poewe et al., 2017; Aarsland et al., 2017). The severity of cognitive symptoms can vary widely, ranging from mild impairments to more severe forms of dementia in advanced stages. Some of the cognitive deficits associated with Parkinson's disease include the following:

Attention and working memory deficits; patients with PD, may have difficulty sustaining attention over extended periods or may be easily distracted. They may also struggle to temporarily retain and manipulate information, a key function of working memory.

Executive dysfunction refers to problems with the skills required for goal-directed behavior. Deficits can include:

- difficulty in planning and organizing activities
- problems with task switching or multitasking
- trouble with problem-solving and decision-making
- impaired impulse control, which might manifest as difficulty waiting one's turn or interrupting others
- reduced ability to initiate activities (*abulia*)

While memory impairments are often less pronounced than the memory issues observed in Alzheimer's disease, individuals with PD may still have difficulty with the following:

- retrieving memories, even if the information is retained
- forming new long-term memories, particularly when it requires active organization or association

Visuospatial dysfunction involves difficulties interpreting and interacting with one's environment, including the following:

- trouble judging distances or spatial relationships
- difficulty understanding visual information, such as reading maps or recognizing familiar places

With a decrease in processing speed, people with PD often experience a general slowing of cognitive processing, meaning that they may take longer to understand information, make decisions, or respond to questions.

Language difficulties, though less common, may cause some people with PD trouble:

- finding the right words (*anomia*)
- following or participating in complex conversations

Mood and affective symptoms, while not purely cognitive, many individuals with PD experience depression, anxiety, apathy, or irritability, which can further impact their cognitive function. Over time, especially in the later stages of the disease, some individuals may develop Parkinson's disease dementia (PDD), which involves more pronounced and widespread cognitive deficits (Aarsland et al., 2017).

Traumatic brain injury (TBI) can result from a blow to the head or a penetrating injury, leading to various cognitive deficits, including memory, attention, and executive function impairments, depending on the location and severity of the injury (McAllister, 2011), as well as other individual factors, including age, overall health, and the quality of medical and rehabilitative care received. Some cognitive deficits associated with TBI include attention and concentration, memory, executive functions, speed of processing, language and communication, perception and spatial skills, judgment and insight, and learning.

A *stroke*, whether it results from an *ischemic event* (blockage of a blood vessel) or a *hemorrhagic event* (bleeding in or around the brain), can lead to a wide range of cognitive deficits. The specific deficits a person experiences depend on the location and extent of the brain damage (Feigin et al., 2021). Some common cognitive deficits associated with *stroke are as follows*:

Attention and concentration deficits as well as memory impairments, spatial cognition deficits, and executive function difficulties. In addition, we find the following deficits:

Aphasia, a language disorder that can manifest in various ways;

Expressive aphasia (Broca's aphasia), which manifests in trouble speaking or writing what one intends to communicate;

Receptive aphasia (Wernicke's aphasia), difficulty understanding spoken or written language;

Global aphasia, a severe impairment in both understanding and expressing language;

Anomic or amnestic aphasia, the difficulty of finding the right words, especially nouns and verbs;

Apraxia is the difficulty in planning and performing motor functions, despite the absence of significant muscle weakness. For example, a person might struggle with tasks such as tying shoes or buttoning a shirt;

Agnosia is the inability to recognize familiar objects, sounds, or people, even if the sensory organs (such as the eyes or ears) are functioning correctly;

Perseveration, continuously repeating a particular response, such as a word, phrase, or gesture, despite the absence or cessation of a stimulus;

Neglect or *inattention* are usually observed after *right hemisphere strokes,* which is a condition where the individual is unaware of or ignores the left side of their body or the left side of their environment;

Impaired comprehension, difficulty understanding abstract concepts or complex instructions;

Emotional and personality changes, while not strictly cognitive, can lead to changes in mood and personality. This can include depression, anxiety, irritability, reduced impulse control, and emotional lability (sudden and uncontrollable emotional outbursts).

Importantly, not all stroke survivors experience all these deficits. The type and severity of cognitive problems after a stroke depend upon the location and size of the stroke and individual differences in brain anatomy and resilience. Rehabilitation can often help improve or compensate for some of these deficits.

When we examine the prevalence and incidence of neuropsychological disorders, it is estimated that Alzheimer's disease is prevalent, with more than 50 million people (approximately twice the population of Texas) affected worldwide, and stroke/brain hemorrhage has the highest incidence, with nearly 14 million new cases each year (Lane et al., 2018; Feigin et al., 2021).

Neuroplasticity and Cognitive Rehabilitation

Neuroplasticity, also known simply as *brain plasticity* or *neural plasticity,* refers to the ability of the brain to change and adapt as a result of experience, learning, or environmental stimuli (Pascual-Leone et al., 2005). This change can occur in various ways, from the growth of new neural connections to the reorganization of neural networks. Neuroplasticity occurs on multiple levels, from cellular changes (such as the strengthening or weakening of synapses) to cortical remapping. This ability means that the brain can reorganize itself by forming new neural connections throughout life. Through the process of *adaptation,* in response to new information, sensory stimuli, or damage, the brain can rearrange itself, shift functions, and create new pathways.

There are two distinct types of *neuroplasticity. Structural plasticity* refers to the ability of the brain to change its physical structure in response to learning or experience. For example, learning a new musical instrument might lead to growth and strengthening of the neural connections associated with the skills needed for playing that instrument. *Functional plasticity* refers to the ability of the brain to move functions from a damaged area to undamaged areas (Kolb et al., 2003). If one part of the brain becomes damaged (e.g., after a *stroke*), another part of the brain may take over the function previously performed by the damaged area.

The mechanisms that underlie *neuroplasticity* are *synaptic plasticity* and *neurogenesis.* At the core of *neuroplasticity* is the synapse, the junction between two neurons. Changes in *synaptic plasticity* can result from increased or decreased activity. The principle of "Hebbian plasticity"[1] is often summarized as "cells that fire together wire together," indicating that the repeated activation of neurons strengthens their connections (Hebb, 1949). *Neurogenesis* is the process by which new neurons are formed in the brain. For a long time, neurogenesis was believed to have occurred only during development. However, it is now known that this can continue in certain parts of the adult brain, notably the *hippocampus* (Boldrini et al., 2018), a region vital for learning and memory.

Several factors influence *neuroplasticity*. *Age* is a key variable that has a direct influence. While plasticity occurs throughout life, the brain is especially plastic during certain developmental periods, often referred to as critical or sensitive periods. However, even in adulthood, the brain retains a significant degree of plasticity.

Learning and new *experiences* promote neuroplastic changes. This is evident in skill acquisition, where practice can lead to proficiency and corresponding brain changes.

As noted above, after brain *injury*, the brain can reorganize itself to compensate for lost functions or maximize remaining functions. *Environmental enrichment*, i.e., exposure to complex and stimulating environments, can lead to neuroplastic changes, improving cognitive and sensory processing (Nithianantharajah & Hannan, 2006).

Understanding *neuroplasticity* has revolutionized rehabilitation approaches, especially after the abovementioned major events, such as strokes. Tailored therapies can promote brain recovery by harnessing the plastic nature of the brain. Some key aspects of cognitive rehabilitation include the following:

Cognitive training (Cramer et al., 2011) involves engaging in targeted exercises designed to improve specific cognitive abilities, such as attention, memory, or executive function. *Cognitive training* can promote neural reorganization and compensate for cognitive deficits by strengthening existing neural connections or forming new connections.

Constraint-induced movement therapy (CIMT) is a rehabilitation approach commonly used for stroke patients with motor impairments. It involves limiting the use of the less affected limb, forcing the individual to use the affected limb more frequently. This approach can promote *neuroplasticity* and functional recovery in the affected limb.

Environmental enrichment, as mentioned above, involves providing a stimulating and enriched environment to promote neuroplasticity and cognitive recovery following brain injury. This may include engaging in mentally challenging activities, social interaction, and physical exercise.

Pharmacological interventions can enhance *neuroplasticity* and cognitive function by modulating neurotransmitter systems or promoting the growth and survival of neurons. For example, medications that increase dopamine levels, such as Levodopa, can improve motor and cognitive function in Parkinson's disease patients.

Brain–computer interfaces (BCIs) *and neuroprosthetics* involve direct interfaces between the brain and external devices, such as computers or robotic limbs. These technologies can help restore lost function by bypassing damaged neural pathways or providing real-time feedback to promote neuroplasticity. This was recently demonstrated through work performed at the University of California, San Francisco (UCSF), in 2023, where a female patient, severely paralyzed after suffering a brainstem stroke 18 years ago, was able to improve her communication through speech by interfacing with BCIs (https://www.ucsf.edu/news/2023/08/425986/how-artificial-intelligence-gave-paralyzed-woman-her-voice-back; Moses et al., 2021).

Cognitive rehabilitation strategies are tailored to an individual's specific needs and deficits and may involve a combination of approaches to optimize recovery and functional outcomes. Importantly, the success of cognitive rehabilitation depends on several factors, including the severity and location of brain injury, the individual's age and cognitive reserve, and the timing and intensity of intervention.

The Role of Sleep in Cognitive Function and Neuroplasticity

Sleep plays a crucial role in cognitive function and the consolidation of memories. Different stages of sleep, such as slow-wave sleep and rapid eye movement (REM) sleep, are associated with various cognitive processes (Rasch & Born, 2013). Sleep is essential for the consolidation of newly acquired information, particularly during slow-wave sleep. This process involves the strengthening of neural connections and the integration of new information into existing memory networks. REM sleep is implicated in the processing and regulation of emotions. During REM sleep, the brain reactivates emotional experiences, helping individuals process and regulate their emotions more effectively (Rasch & Born, 2013; Xie et al., 2013). Importantly, sleep has been shown to enhance creativity and problem-solving abilities. The ability of the brain to form new connections and integrate seemingly unrelated information during sleep may facilitate the generation of novel ideas and solutions (Cai et al., 2009). Adequate sleep is critical for maintaining optimal attention and cognitive performance. Sleep deprivation can lead to impairments in attention, working memory, and executive function, negatively affecting overall cognitive performance (Killgore, 2010).

Note

1. Hebbian plasticity is the principle that when two neurons fire together, the connection (synapse) between them strengthens ("cells that fire together, wire together"). Conversely, if they fire out of sync, the synapse weakens ("cells out of sync, lose their link"). This concept, introduced by Donald Hebb in 1949, underlies how neural circuits adapt and learn. It forms the basis for long-term potentiation (LTP)—the persistent strengthening of synapses—and long-term depression (LTD)—the long-lasting weakening of synapses. Further refinements include spike-dependent plasticity (STDP) (where precise spike timing dictates whether synapses strengthen or weaken), homeostatic plasticity (which keeps overall activity levels in check), metaplasticity (how past activity influences future plasticity), and the modulatory effects of neurotransmitters such as dopamine and acetylcholine. While more complex mechanisms extend beyond pure Hebbian rules, Hebb's principle remains foundational in neuroscience and has significantly influenced both our understanding of learning and memory and the design of artificial neural networks.

References

Aarsland, D., Creese, B., Politis, M., Chaudhuri, K. R., Fagerström, C., Chan, P., et al. (2017). Cognitive decline in Parkinson disease. *Nature Reviews Neurology, 13*(4), 217–231. https://doi.org/10.1038/nrneurol.2017.27

Barker, A. T., Jalinous, R., & Freeston, I. L. (1985). Non-invasive magnetic stimulation of human motor cortex. *The Lancet, 1*(8437), 1106–1107. https://doi.org/10.1016/S0140-6736(85)92413-4

Bear, M. F., Connors, B. W., & Paradiso, M. A. (2016). *Neuroscience: Exploring the brain* (4th ed.). Wolters Kluwer.

Bechara, A., Damasio, H., & Damasio, A. R. (2000). Emotion, decision making and the orbitofrontal cortex. *Cerebral Cortex, 10*(3), 295–307. https://doi.org/10.1093/cercor/10.3.295

Berger, H. (1929). Über das Elektrenkephalogramm des Menschen. *Archiv für Psychiatrie und Nervenkrankheiten, 87*, 527–570. https://doi.org/10.1007/BF01797193

Boldrini, M., Fulmore, C. A., Tartt, A. N., Simeon, L. R., Pavlova, I., Poposka, V., et al. (2018). Human hippocampal neurogenesis persists throughout aging. *Cell Stem Cell, 22*(4), 589–599. https://doi.org/10.1016/j.stem.2018.03.015

Breasted, J. H. (1930). *The Edwin Smith Surgical Papyrus: Published in facsimile and hieroglyphic transliteration*. The University of Chicago Press.

Cacioppo, J. T., Berntson, G. G., & Nusbaum, H. C. (2008). Neuroimaging as a new tool in the toolbox of psychological science. *Current Directions in Psychological Science, 17*, 62–67. https://doi.org/10.1111/j.1467-8721.2008.005

Cai, D. J., Mednick, S. A., Harrison, E. M., Kanady, J. C., & Mednick, S. C. (2009). REM, not incubation, improves creativity by priming associative networks. *Proceedings of the National Academy of Sciences of the United States of America, 106*(25), 10130–10134. https://doi.org/10.1073/pnas.0900271106

Cohen, D. (1968). Magnetoencephalography: Evidence of magnetic fields produced by alpha-rhythm currents. *Science, 161*(3843), 784–786. https://doi.org/10.1126/science.161.3843.784

Corbetta, M., & Shulman, G. L. (2002). Control of goal-directed and stimulus-driven attention in the brain. *Nature Reviews Neuroscience, 3*(3), 201–215. https://doi.org/10.1038/nrn755

Cowen, P. J., & Browning, M. (2015). What has serotonin to do with depression? *World Psychiatry, 14*(2), 158–160. https://doi.org/10.1002/wps.20229

Cramer, S. C., Sur, M., Dobkin, B. H., O'Brien, C., Sanger, T. D., Trojanowski, J. Q., et al. (2011). Harnessing neuroplasticity for clinical applications. *Brain, 134*(Pt 6), 1591–1609. https://doi.org/10.1093/brain/awr039

Dechant, G., & Neumann, H. (2002). Neurotrophins. *Advances in Experimental Medicine and Biology, 513*, 303–334.

Fanselow, M. S., & Pennington, Z. T. (2018). A return to the psychiatric dark ages with a two-system framework of Fear. *Behaviour Research and Therapy, 100*, 24–29. https://doi.org/10.1016/j.brat.2017.10.012

Feigin, V. L., Stark, B. A., Johnson, C. O., Roth, G. A., Bisignano, C., Abady, G. G., et al. (2021). Global, regional, and national burden of stroke, 1990–2019: A systematic analysis for the Global Burden of Disease Study 2019. *The Lancet Neurology, 20*(10), 795–820. https://www.thelancet.com/journals/laneur/article/PIIS1474-4422(21)00252-0/fulltext

Fuster, J. M. (2015). *The prefrontal cortex* (5th ed.). Academic Press.

Gazzaniga, M. S., Ivry, R. B., & Mangun, G. R. (2019). *Cognitive neuroscience: The biology of the mind* (5th ed.). W. W. Norton & Company.

Geschwind, N. (1972). Language and the brain. *Scientific American, 226*(4), 76–83.

Gillies, G. E., & McArthur, S. (2010). Estrogen actions in the brain and the basis for differential action in men and women: A case for sex-specific medicines. *Pharmacological Reviews, 62*(2), 155–198. https://doi.org/10.1124/pr.109.002071

Grill-Spector, K., & Weiner, K. S. (2014). The functional architecture of the ventral temporal cortex and its role in categorization. *Nature Reviews Neuroscience, 15*(8), 536–548. https://doi.org/10.1038/nrn3747

Haas, L. F. (2003). Hans Berger (1873–1941), Richard Caton (1842–1926), and electroencephalography. *Journal of Neurology, Neurosurgery & Psychiatry, 74*(1), 9. https://doi.org/10.1136/jnnp.74.1.9

Halgren, E., Marinkovic, K., & Chauvel, P. (1998). Generators of the late cognitive potentials in auditory and visual oddball tasks. *Electroencephalography and Clinical Neurophysiology. Supplement, 44*, 211–221. https://stbil.sdsu.edu/pdfs/Halgren-1998.pdf

Hari, R., & Parkkonen, L. (2015). The brain timewise: How timing shapes and supports brain function. *Philosophical Transactions of the Royal Society B: Biological Sciences, 370*(1668), 20140170. https://doi.org/10.1098/rstb.2014.0170

Harlow, J. M. (1868). Recovery after severe injury to the head. *Publications of the Massachusetts Medical Society, 2*, 327–346. http://resource.nlm.nih.gov/66210360R

Hebb, D. O. (1949). *The organization of behavior: A neuropsychological theory*. Wiley. https://doi.org/10.1002/sce.37303405110

Killgore, W. D. S. (2010). Effects of sleep deprivation on cognition. *Progress in Brain Research, 185*, 105–129. https://doi.org/10.1016/B978-0-444-53702-7.00007-5

Klimesch, W. (2012). Alpha-band oscillations, attention, and controlled access to stored information. *Trends in Cognitive Sciences, 16*(12), 606–617. https://doi.org/10.1016/j.tics.2012.10.007

Kolb, B., Gibb, R., & Robinson, T. E. (2003). Brain plasticity and behavior. *Current Directions in Psychological Science, 12*(1), 1–5. https://doi.org/10.1111/1467-8721.01210

Kowiański, P., Lietzau, G., Czuba, E., et al. (2018). BDNF: A key factor with multipotent impact on brain signaling and synaptic plasticity. *Cellular and Molecular Neurobiology, 38*, 579–593. https://doi.org/10.1007/s10571-017-0510-4

Lane, C. A., Hardy, J., & Schott, J. M. (2018). Alzheimer's disease. *European Journal of Neurology, 25*(1), 59–70. https://doi.org/10.1111/ene.13439

LeDoux, J. E. (2014). Coming to terms with fear. *Proceedings of the National Academy of Sciences of the United States of America, 111*(8), 2871–2878. https://doi.org/10.1073/pnas.1400335111

Lezak, M. D., Howieson, D. B., & Loring, D. W. (2012). *Neuropsychological assessment* (5th ed.). Oxford University Press.

Logothetis, N. K. (2008). What we can do and what we cannot do with fMRI. *Nature, 453*(7197), 869–878. https://doi.org/10.1038/nature06976

Lupien, S. J., McEwen, B. S., Gunnar, M. R., & Heim, C. (2009). Effects of stress throughout the lifespan on the brain, behaviour and cognition. *Nature Reviews Neuroscience, 10*(6), 434–445. https://doi.org/10.1038/nrn2639

McAllister, T. W. (2011). Neurobiological consequences of traumatic brain injury. *Dialogues in Clinical Neuroscience, 13*(3), 287–300. https://doi.org/10.31887/DCNS.2011.13.2/tmcallister

Meyer-Lindenberg, A., & Tost, H. (2012). Neural mechanisms of social risk for psychiatric disorders. *Nature Neuroscience, 15*(5), 663–668. https://doi.org/10.1038/nn.3083

Moses, D. A., Metzger, S. L., Liu, J. R., Anumanchipalli, G. K., Makin, J. G., & Chang, E. F. (2021). Neuroprosthesis for decoding speech in a paralyzed person with anarthria. *The New England Journal of Medicine, 385*(3), 217–227. https://doi.org/10.1056/NEJMoa2027540

Nestler, E. J., Hyman, S. E., Holtzman, D. M., & Malenka, R. C. (2015). *Molecular neuropharmacology: A foundation for clinical neuroscience* (3rd ed.). McGraw-Hill.

Nithianantharajah, J., & Hannan, A. J. (2006). Enriched environments, experience-dependent plasticity and disorders of the nervous system. *Nature Reviews Neuroscience, 7*(9), 697–709. https://doi.org/10.1038/nrn1970

Ogawa, S., Lee, T. M., Kay, A. R., & Tank, D. W. (1990). Brain magnetic resonance imaging with contrast dependent on blood oxygenation. *Proceedings of the National Academy of Sciences of the United States of America, 87*(24), 9868–9872. https://doi.org/10.1073/pnas.87.24.9868

Pascual-Leone, A., Walsh, V., & Rothwell, J. (2000). Transcranial magnetic stimulation in cognitive neuroscience—Virtual lesion, chronometry, and functional connectivity. *Current Opinion in Neurobiology, 10*(2), 232–237. https://doi.org/10.1016/S0959-4388(00)00081-7

Pascual-Leone, A., Amedi, A., Fregni, F., & Merabet, L. B. (2005). The plastic human brain cortex. *Annual Review of Neuroscience, 28*, 377–401. https://doi.org/10.1146/annurev.neuro.27.070203.144216

Perera, T., George, M. S., Grammer, G., Janicak, P. G., Pascual-Leone, A., & Wirecki, T. S. (2016). The Clinical TMS Society consensus review and treatment recommendations for TMS therapy for major depressive disorder. *Brain Stimulation, 9*(3), 336–346. https://doi.org/10.1016/j.brs.2016.03.010

Poewe, W., Stott, S. R. W., Ledent, C., LeWitt, P. A., & Chaudhuri, K. R. (2017). Parkinson disease. *Nature Reviews Disease Primers, 3*, 17013. https://doi.org/10.1038/nrdp.2017.13

Rasch, B., & Born, J. (2013). About sleep's role in memory. *Physiological Reviews, 93*(2), 681–766. https://doi.org/10.1152/physrev.00032.2012

Rolls, E. T. (2015). Limbic systems for emotion and for memory, but no single limbic system. *Cortex, 62*, 119–157. https://doi.org/10.1016/j.cortex.2013.12.005

Scoville, W. B., & Milner, B. (1957). Loss of recent memory after bilateral hippocampal lesions. *Journal of Neurology, Neurosurgery & Psychiatry, 20*(1), 11–21. https://doi.org/10.1136/jnnp.20.1.11

Sporns, O. (2011). The human connectome: A complex network. *Annals of the New York Academy of Sciences, 1224*, 109–125. https://doi.org/10.1111/j.1749-6632.2010.05888.x

Squire, L. R., & Wixted, J. T. (2011). The cognitive neuroscience of human memory since H.M. *Annual Review of Neuroscience, 34*, 259–288. https://doi.org/10.1146/annurev-neuro-061010-113720

Trejo, J. L., Carro, E., & Torres-Aleman, I. (2001). Circulating insulin-like growth factor I mediates the protective effects of physical exercise against brain insults of different etiology and anatomy. *The Journal of Neuroscience, 21*(15), 5678–5684. https://doi.org/10.1523/JNEUROSCI.21-15-05678.2001

Ward, J. (2015). *The student's guide to cognitive neuroscience* (3rd ed.). Psychology Press.

Xie, L., Kang, H., Xu, Q., Chen, M. J., Liao, Y., Thiyagarajan, M., et al. (2013). Sleep drives metabolite clearance from the adult brain. *Science, 342*(6156), 373–377. https://doi.org/10.1126/science.1241224

CHAPTER 11

Social Cognition

Social Perception and Attribution

When referring to *social perception,* we consider a complex process that involves interpreting social cues, forming impressions, attributing behaviors, and understanding the intentions and emotions of others (Fiske & Taylor, 2013; Kunda, 1999). It plays a crucial role in our interactions, relationships, and overall understanding of the social world. It involves the cognitive and emotional mechanisms that allow us to form judgments and impressions about others to enable us to anticipate their actions and reactions (Aronson et al., 2019).

In Chap. 9, we discussed *attribution* in the forms of *internal attribution* (such as personality traits or intentions) and *external attribution* (such as situational influences) and described the theory (i.e., *attribution theory*) developed by the psychologist F. Heider, which suggests that people tend to make attributions on the basis of three factors, namely, consensus, distinctiveness, and consistency (Heider, 1958). In summary, *attribution* is a key component of *social perception*, involving the assignment of causes or reasons for observed behavior (Jones & Davis, 1965; Kelley, 1973).

There are additional components that help us understand *social perception:*

Theory of mind and empathy: Theory of mind is the ability to understand that others have mental states, such as beliefs, desires, and intentions,

H. Kankam, *A Brief Excursion into Human Cognition*,
https://doi.org/10.1007/978-3-031-89752-8_11

which may differ from our own (Premack & Woodruff, 1978). This cognitive capacity enables us to predict and explain the behavior of others and is essential for successful social interactions (Baron-Cohen, 1995; Frith & Frith, 2003). *Theory of mind* is often impaired in people with autism spectrum disorder, leading to difficulty in social interactions (Happé, 1994). It has been suggested that *theory of mind* can be improved with practice and training (Kovács et al., 2010). Similarly, *empathy* involves understanding and sharing others' emotions (Batson, 2011). There are two main types of *empathy*: *cognitive empathy,* which involves understanding another person's perspective and emotions without necessarily sharing their emotional state (Decety & Jackson, 2004), and *affective empathy,* which involves feeling the same emotions as the person we are empathizing with, often leading to a sense of compassion or concern for their well-being (Eisenberg et al., 2014).

Stereotyping, prejudice, and discrimination: Associating generalized traits with a group of individuals on the basis of shared characteristics, such as race, gender, or nationality, is called *stereotyping* (Macrae & Bodenhausen, 2000). While *stereotyping* can be a natural and efficient way of organizing social information, it can also lead to biased judgments and perpetuate harmful *stereotypes* (Fiske, 2018).

Prejudice, on the other hand, refers to negative attitudes or beliefs about a particular group, often based on *stereotypes* (Allport, 1954). *Discrimination* involves treating individuals unfairly or unequally on the basis of their membership in a particular group (Dovidio et al., 2010). *Stereotyping, prejudice, and discrimination* can have significant social and psychological consequences for both the targets and the perpetrators. These consequences can, in some cases, include feelings of isolation, anxiety, and low self-esteem (see Crocker & Major, 1989). *Prejudice* and *discrimination* can also lead to social inequality and the denial of basic rights and opportunities to certain groups (Sidanius & Pratto, 1999).

Group dynamics and collective cognition: In the study of *group dynamics,* the focus is on deciphering the intricate interactions and processes that unfold within social groups (Forsyth, 2019). These dynamics profoundly influence both individual behavior and the collective actions of the group. One critical element is group cohesion, which encapsulates the feelings of unity, belonging and commitment among members (Carron & Brawley, 2000). This sense of collective identity, often referred to as the "us" feeling, typically correlates with heightened satisfaction, performance, and adherence to group norms.

Social influence is another key factor that shapes how individuals modify their attitudes, beliefs, or behaviors in response to the actual or perceived presence of others (Cialdini & Goldstein, 2004). This influence manifests in diverse ways, including conformity, compliance, and obedience (Asch, 1956; Milgram, 1974). However, *social influence* can also act as a catalyst for *groupthink*—a psychological pattern in which the quest for group harmony or conformity leads to poor or irrational decision-making (Janis, 1972). Within this context, group members might suppress dissent, overlook critical evaluations of options, and prioritize unanimity over sound judgment. Various elements, such as group polarization, social reinforcement, confirmation bias, and pressures to conform, as well as the sway of authority figures, further modulate this *groupthink* phenomenon (Isenberg, 1986).

The concept of *collective cognition* involves the shared cognitive processes and mental frameworks that exist within a group. These collective cognitive structures significantly affect a group's problem-solving skills, creative potential, and decision-making capabilities (Kerr & Tindale, 2004). Researchers specializing in social cognition aim to unravel the complex relationship between individual cognitive processes and social contexts. This understanding can then inform strategies designed to mitigate bias, foster cooperation, and improve the quality of collective decisions.

Nonverbal communication and social cues: Nonverbal communication serves as a critical channel for transmitting information and emotions in social exchanges, using elements such as facial expressions, gestures, body language, and other nonlinguistic cues (Knapp et al., 2013). Mastery of nonverbal cues is integral to social cognition, offering key insights into others' thoughts, emotions, and intentions. Some pivotal components of nonverbal communication are as follows:

- *Facial expressions* serve as reliable barometers of an individual's emotional state, signaling emotions such as happiness, sadness, anger, or surprise. The skillful interpretation of these expressions is vital for effective social engagement and emotional comprehension (Ekman & Friesen, 1975).
- *Gestures*, encompassing hand and body movements, can relay information, accentuate spoken words or manifest emotions. The meaning of gestures often hinges on the cultural context, requiring an understanding of the norms and traditions specific to different cultures (Argyle, 1988).

- The field of *proxemics* delves into how people utilize space in social interactions, exploring dimensions such as personal distance and territorial behavior. Cultural variations in these norms can greatly influence social perceptions and the nature of interactions (Hall, 1966).
- The dynamics of *eye contact and gaze,* including their direction and duration, yield important social cues (Kleinke, 1986). These cues can signify diverse states or intentions, ranging from interest and emotional connection to signals of dominance or submission.

Social identity and self-categorization: Social identity refers to an individual's sense of self derived from their membership in social groups, such as nationalities, religions, or occupations (Tajfel & Turner, 1979).[1] *Social identity theory*, proposed by Henri Tajfel and John Turner, suggests that individuals strive to maintain a positive self-concept by identifying with and favoring their "in-groups over out-groups" (Hogg, 2016). To provide an example:

- *College Sports Fans:* Imagine a university where sports, particularly college football, are a significant part of campus life. Students, faculty, and alumni passionately support their teams and wear school colors with pride.
- *Social Identity:* Here, being a fan of the university's football team becomes part of an individual's social identity. Students identify as part of this larger group, experiencing a sense of belonging and community.
- *In-Group and Out-Group:* Those who support the team (wear the school colors, attend games, etc.) are considered the "in-group," whereas fans of rival teams or those indifferent to sports are the "out-group."
- *Categorization:* Students quickly categorize people as either supporters or nonsupporters of the team, simplifying complex social interactions and settings.
- *Identification*: The students start to align their behavior and attitudes with what is perceived to be the norm of this sports-loving community. They may start following the team's progress, discussing recent games, and even organizing social events around game schedules.
- *Comparison and Positive Distinctiveness:* Students may start to compare their team favorably against others, particularly rival schools.

Chants, songs, and slogans that put their team in a favorable light become common. This boosts collective self-esteem and helps establish positive distinctiveness for their group.

- *Conformity and Cohesion:* The more individuals identify with this group, the more they conform to the behaviors and attitudes commonly associated with being fans. This increases cohesion among members of the "in-group" (Brown, 2000).
- Impact *on Behavior and Attitudes:* Over time, this identification might even impact other behaviors and attitudes. For example, strong identification with a sports team can even influence academic pursuits, social activities, and long-lasting friendships.

This example shows how *social identity theory* can be applied to understand real-world phenomena, helping to explain how identification with a group can shape individual and collective behavior.

Self-Categorization Theory (SCT),[2] an extension of *social identity theory*, proposes that individuals classify themselves and others into various social categories on the basis of their shared characteristics (Turner et al., 1987). This process of *self-categorization* can lead to depersonalization, where individuals perceive themselves and others in terms of group membership rather than as unique individuals (Turner & Reynolds, 2012).

As an example, let us explore how *self-categorization theory* applies to fans of a college football team (Hogg & Reid, 2006).

Context: Imagine a large university where college football is a cultural cornerstone. Just as in our *social identity theory* example, students, faculty, and alumni passionately support the school team and attend games, even traveling for away matches. They proudly wear merchandise featuring the school logo and color.

Levels of Self-Categorization

Personal level: At this level, an individual might identify as a "die-hard fan," focusing on their personalized engagement with the team, such as personal rituals before a game.

Subgroup level: Among sports enthusiasts at the university, the individual may categorize themselves as a "Student Fan," distinguishing themselves from "Alumni Fans" or "Faculty Fans."

Organizational level: During a big game against a rival school, self-categorization might expand to be a "University X Fan," uniting all subgroups (students, faculty, alumni) against the common opponent.

Context-Dependent Identity

During Classes, while discussing the upcoming game in a classroom, students may categorize themselves on the basis of their faculty or major (e.g., fans who are Engineering students vs. Humanities students).

Game Day: On the day of a significant match, particularly against a fierce rival, the broader identity of being a "University X Fan" becomes most salient, overshadowing other identities.

Prototypicality

In the context of being a "Student Fan," someone who never misses a game and knows all the players' stats might be seen as a prototypical fan.

On a broader scale, a "die-hard fan" who has been attending games for years and embodies the spirit of the school might be considered the prototypical "University X Fan."

Depersonalization: As the game day approaches, individual achievements or interests may take a back seat as people begin to think in terms of "we" rather than "I." For example, "We have to beat the rival school" instead of "I want to see a win."

Accentuation: If there is a debate about which sport is the most important at the university, differences between football fans and basketball fans may be accentuated. Football fans may stress how football is more deeply embedded in the school's culture.

Consequences: How fans interact with each other, engage in rituals, or even treat fans of rival teams can be significantly influenced by the level of self-categorization. This also impacts the sense of belonging and community, shaping both individual and collective behaviors and emotions.

In this example, *self-categorization theory* can provide a nuanced understanding of the dynamic identities and behaviors among college football fans, depending on various factors such as context, competition, and social identification.

Intergroup Relations and Conflict

Intergroup relations involve the interactions and relationships between different social groups. *Intergroup conflict* can arise when groups compete for limited resources, have incompatible goals, or experience perceived threats to their social identity or status (Dovidio et al., 2010; Fiske & Taylor, 2013). Some key theories and concepts related to *intergroup relations* and *conflict* include the following:

- The *realistic conflict theory*,[3] initially developed by social psychologist Muzafer Sherif, proposes that intergroup conflict arises from competition for scarce resources, such as territory, power, or economic opportunities (Sherif, 1966; Sherif et al., 1961).
- As mentioned earlier, *social identity theory* suggests that individuals derive self-esteem from their group memberships and are motivated to favor their "in-group" over "out-groups," which can contribute to *intergroup conflict* (Tajfel & Turner, 1979). "The Contact Hypothesis,"[4] proposed by Gordon Allport, suggests that positive intergroup contact can reduce prejudice and improve intergroup relations. The key conditions for successful contact include equal status, cooperation, common goals, and institutional support (Allport, 1954; Pettigrew & Tropp, 2006).

By examining the cognitive processes underlying social perception, attribution, theory of mind, empathy, stereotyping, prejudice, discrimination, group dynamics, and collective cognition, researchers in the field of social cognition aim to better understand the complex interplay between individual cognition and the social context (Crisp, 2010; Fiske, 2018). This knowledge can inform interventions to promote positive *intergroup* relationships, reduce bias and discrimination, and foster more effective communication and collaboration within diverse groups (Crisp, 2010; Pettigrew, 1998).

Culture and Cognition

Culture plays a significant role in shaping cognition and social behavior. The study of cultural influences on *cognition* can help us better understand the variations in social cognitive processes across different populations

(Heine, 2016; Markus & Kitayama, 1991; Nisbett et al., 2001). There are several key aspects of *culture* and *cognition* that should be mentioned.

Different cultures may exhibit distinct cognitive styles, such as *analytic thinking* (focusing on objects and their properties) or *holistic thinking* (focusing on relationships and contexts). These differences in cognitive styles can affect various aspects of social cognition, such as perception, attribution, and decision-making (Nisbett et al., 2001). Now, let us look at these differences in detail.

Analytic thinking is common in Western cultures, particularly in the United States and Western Europe. This cognitive style focuses on objects in isolation from their contexts and prefers to use rules and logic to explain events (Nisbett, 2003). In contrast, *holistic thinking,* which is predominant in many East Asian cultures, emphasizes a *holistic thinking* context and the relationships between objects, leaning toward explanations on the basis of interconnectedness, and balance (Nisbett et al., 2001). Individuals from *collectivist cultures*, such as many Asian and Latin American cultures, also tend to be more *field dependent*, meaning that they are more likely to view objects as part of a larger field or context. In contrast, people from individualistic cultures such as the United States are more likely to be *field independent*, focusing on individual objects that are distinct from the surrounding field. In *high-context* cultures, which are often found in Asia and the Middle East, much of the information in communication is understood through context, nonverbal cues, and between-the-lines interpretation. Within *low-context* cultures such as the United States and Germany, communication is generally more explicit, and the message contains most of the information, reducing the need for contextual understanding (Hall, 1976).

Cultures also differ in their categorization styles. Rule-based categorization, which is predominant in Western cultures, focuses on categorizing objects on the basis of a set of *formal rules* or *attributes.* In contrast, some non-Western cultures prefer to categorize objects on the basis of *thematic* or *functional* relationships between them (Chiu, 1972; Norenzayan et al., 2002). Below are several real-world examples to illustrate the difference between *rule-based categorization* and categorization on the basis of *functional or thematic* relationships.

Rule-based Categorization: In a rule-based approach, objects are categorized on the basis of a set of formal rules or defining features. For example, consider the category "mammals." In *rule-based categorization*, an animal is classified as a mammal if it has the defining features of mammals—such as being warm-blooded, having a backbone, and nursing its young with milk. Whether we are discussing a whale, a dog, or a human, the category remains consistent on the basis of these specific, rule-based criteria.

Functional relationship-based categorization: Functional relationship-based categorization organizes objects on the basis of their utility or purpose. For example, you might categorize a knife, a cutting board, and vegetables together because they all have a functional relationship in the task of preparing food. Here, the categorization is not based on what these objects inherently are (i.e., a tool, a surface, and food) but rather on how they function together in a particular context.

Thematic relationship-based categorization: In *thematic categorization*, objects are grouped on the basis of a common theme or narrative, even if they are different in terms of function or form. For example, you might categorize a beach ball, sunscreen, and a swimsuit together because they all relate to the theme of going to the beach. These objects serve different functions and are categorized differently in a rule-based system (e.g., a beach ball might be categorized as a "toy," sunscreen as a "skincare product," and a swimsuit as "clothing").

Summary

Rule-based: warm-blooded + backbone + nursing young with milk = mammals

Functional: knife + cutting board + vegetables = preparing food

Thematic: beach ball + sunscreen + swimsuit = going to the beach

These different *categorization styles* can lead to misunderstandings or difficulty in communication when people from different cultural or cognitive backgrounds interact. Understanding these differences can provide valuable insights into how people think and approach the world.

In this context, it is important to emphasize that *individualism* is prominent in Western cultures; this cognitive style prioritizes personal goals over group goals and values individual autonomy. Whereas *collectivism* is more common in East Asian, African, and Latin American cultures, this cognitive style prioritizes group goals over individual goals (Markus & Kitayama, 1991; Triandis, 1995).

One may observe that studying the cognitive complexity observed in cultures is highly important. In some cultures, people are more comfortable holding multiple, contradictory viewpoints simultaneously, whereas in other cultures, individuals prefer more unambiguous perspectives. When studying risk tolerance, it has been noted that different cultures have differing attitudes toward uncertainty and risk, which can influence their cognitive styles. Some cultures are more risk averse, whereas others are more open to taking risks.

Cultural norms and values can influence social cognitive processes, such as conformity, altruism, and moral reasoning. Understanding these variations can provide insights into the cultural specificity of certain social cognitive processes and the universality of others.

It is essential to remember that these are generalizations and do not capture the cognitive style of every individual within a given culture. Moreover, globalization and cross-cultural interactions are continually reshaping and streamlining these cognitive styles.

Morality and Moral Reasoning

Morality and moral reasoning are essential aspects of social cognition, as they involve making judgments about what is right or wrong and thus guiding our behavior in our social interactions (Haidt, 2012). Over time, theories and concepts have been created, providing frameworks for understanding morality, ethical behavior, and the processes underlying moral judgments (Mikhail, 2011). Different theories might resonate more with different individuals, cultures, or situations, and the study of morality remains a dynamic field with ongoing debates and developments. The study of morality and moral reasoning clearly encompasses a vast range of theories and concepts from various disciplines, including philosophy, psychology, and anthropology. Some of the key theories and concepts are as follows:

"Deontological ethics (*Duty-Based Ethics*)"[5] was proposed by thinkers such as Immanuel Kant. This theory posits that certain actions are inherently right or wrong, irrespective of their outcomes (Korsgaard, 1996). Actions should be undertaken out of duty and in accordance with a set of moral rules or imperatives.

"Utilitarianism (*Consequence-Based Ethics*)"[6] is rooted in the works of Jeremy Bentham and John Stuart Mill; this theory argues that the best action is the one that maximizes overall happiness or pleasure for the greatest number of people (Mill, 1863).

"Virtue ethics"[7] was championed by ancient philosophers such as Aristotle; this approach emphasizes the role of character and virtue in ethical decision-making. It focuses on what kind of person we should be, rather than upon which rules to follow, or the consequences of our actions (Aristotle, trans. 2009).

"Moral relativism" is a perspective that argues that moral principles are not universal and are instead shaped by cultural, historical, and individual factors (Prinz, 2007).

"Social contract theory"[8] is based on the ideas of thinkers such as Jean-Jacques Rousseau and John Locke; this theory posits that people live together in society in accordance with an agreement that establishes moral and ethical norms (Locke, 1690/1980; Rousseau, 1762/1978).

"Moral-Realism vs. Anti-Realism"[9] describes a debate that pertains to whether there are objective moral facts. *Realists* believe in the existence of objective moral truths, *whereas antirealists* deny such existence, viewing morality as more subjective (Sayre-McCord, 1988).

"Care Ethics"[10] was proposed by Carol Gilligan and others. This perspective emphasizes the importance of care, empathy and relationships in moral decision-making (Gilligan, 1982).

"Moral Intuitionism and Dual Process Theories"[11] suggest that when focusing on *moral intuition*, people have intuitive feelings or beliefs about what is right or wrong, and this plays a crucial role in moral judgments rather than conscious reasoning. "Dual-process theory" proposes that both intuitive (automatic, emotional) and deliberative (conscious, rational) processes contribute to moral decision-making (Haidt, 2001; Greene et al., 2001).

"Moral development theory(ies)" was proposed by Lawrence Kohlberg (1969)[12] and Carol Gilligan (1982)[13] and is based on how morality develops in individuals as they grow. Kohlberg outlined a three-level, six-stage process of moral development, whereas Gilligan emphasized the difference in moral development between genders.

"Evolutionary Ethics"[14] examines morality through the lens of evolutionary biology, suggesting that certain moral behaviors might have been advantageous for our ancestors and thus became favored through natural selection (Joyce, 2006).

"Moral disengagement"[15] is a concept introduced by Albert Bandura (1986). It describes the cognitive processes through which individuals rationalize immoral behavior, distancing themselves from the consequences of their actions.

Researchers often use hypothetical scenarios to explore moral intuitions and principles. The "trolley problem" is a famous thought experiment that delves into the conflicts between *utilitarian* and *deontological* reasoning and was introduced by British philosopher Philippa Foot (1967) and expanded in several variations by others (Thomson, 1976). It is designed to probe our intuitions about moral decision-making. Its simplicity has led to its prominence in philosophical discourse, such that it is now a staple in discussions about ethics, especially in relation to the conflict between *utilitarian* and *deontological* principles (Greene et al., 2001).

The Classic Trolley Problem: Imagine a trolley on train tracks. Ahead on the tracks are five people tied up and unable to move. The trolley is headed straight for them. You are standing next to a lever. If you pull the lever, the trolley will divert onto a sidetrack. However, on this sidetrack, one person is tied. You face a dilemma:

- Do nothing, and the trolley kills the five people on the main track
- Pull the lever, diverting the trolley onto the sidetrack, where it will kill one person. The question is as follows: What is the most morally appropriate action? Different philosophical perspectives provide different answers:

A *utilitarian* might argue that you should pull the lever because this maximizes overall happiness or well-being by minimizing the number of deaths (one death instead of five);

A *deontologist* might argue that one should not intervene, as actively pulling the lever constitutes a direct action that causes harm, even if it leads to a better overall outcome. *The trolley problem* has many variations that further complicate the moral quandary:

The Fat Man Variant: instead of a lever, you're on a bridge over the tracks with a large man. If you push him off the bridge, his weight will stop the trolley, saving the five people but killing him. Would you push the man? Here, moral action becomes more direct and personal.

Loop Variant: the sidetrack loops back to the main track. If you divert the trolley, it will kill one person but then continue on and still kill the original five people unless that person's body stops the trolley. This introduces a further complexity of the value of one versus many.

The Trolley Problem is not just a philosophical exercise. It has practical implications, especially in the age of technology. For example, how should self-driving cars be programmed to respond in scenarios where they might have to choose between different harmful outcomes?

Although experiments such as the *Trolley problem* are crucial because they allow us to provide clear, albeit sometimes extreme, scenarios to help us examine our moral intuitions without real-world consequences, they test our intuitions. They also help to isolate and clarify particular moral concepts, making abstract ideas more concrete. By presenting variations of a scenario, they can challenge us to be consistent in our moral judgments and reveal potential contradictions in our beliefs.

While the *Trolley* problem does not provide definitive answers, it serves as a powerful tool for sparking debate, reflecting on our own values, and understanding the complexities of moral decision-making.

Finally, we look at *neuroethics*, an interdisciplinary field that addresses the ethical, legal, and societal implications of neuroscience (Illes & Racine, 2005). It seeks to understand the implications of our increasing ability to monitor, manipulate, and modify the brain.

Neuroethics can be divided into two main branches, which are brilliantly described as the *ethics of neuroscience* and the *neuroscience of ethics.*

The *ethics of neuroscience* are concerned with the ethical implications of methodologies and technologies in neuroscientific research. This encompasses the ethical conduct of research, the use of animals, the implications of brain imaging, and the clinical application of neurotechnologies. We then turn to the *neuroscience of ethics,* which investigates the neural foundations of moral cognition, emotion, and behavior. This asks questions such as the following: How do our brains make moral judgments? Can brain scans reveal truths about our moral intuitions? (Roskies, 2002).

To clarify, here is an example of *neuroethics,* (which is remarkably close to reality):

Imagine a scenario in which there is a pill developed from advances in neuroscience that can enhance cognitive abilities, effectively making anyone who takes it smarter, more focused, and more alert (Farah, 2015).

There are several *neuroethical* concerns related to this scenario:

Fairness: Is it fair for students to take this pill during exams? Does it provide an unfair advantage akin to doping in sports?

Coercion: If some employees start using the pill to improve performance at work, might there be pressure for all employees to take it to keep up, even if they have concerns about the long-term effects involved?

Health: What are the long-term effects of the pill? If these are unknown, is it ethical to market the pill without a comprehensive understanding of the possible effects?

Identity and *Authenticity*: Does enhancing one's cognitive abilities alter one's "true self"? Does it make achievements unauthentic?

Social Implications: If only wealthy people have access to this pill, will it exacerbate existing societal inequalities?

Another aspect of *neuroethics* might involve investigating what brain scans reveal about the decision-making process in individuals while considering whether to take the pill. If certain areas of the brain are active when making such a decision, does that imply a biological basis for risk aversion or an attraction to cognitive enhancement?

In essence, *neuroethics* grapples with the profound questions and dilemmas arising from our growing understanding of the brain and our ability to influence it. As *neuroscience* continues to advance, the relevance and importance of *neuroethics* will steadily grow.

Social Cognitive Neuroscience

Social cognitive neuroscience (SCN) is an interdisciplinary field that seeks to understand how brain processes give rise to social cognitive functions, which in turn enable us to interpret, navigate, and respond to the social world (Cacioppo & Decety, 2011). In essence, it combines approaches and methodologies from *social psychology* and *cognitive neuroscience* to investigate how brain structures and functions support our understanding of and interactions with others.

Some key topics in *social cognitive neuroscience* include *neural correlates of social cognitive processes*, where researchers use neuroimaging techniques, such as functional magnetic resonance imaging (fMRI), to identify brain regions and networks involved in various social cognitive processes, such as theory of mind, empathy, and moral reasoning (Frith & Frith, 2006). In addition, studies of social influences on neural processing have shown that the presence of others, or the perception of being observed, can influence neural activity and cognitive performance. Understanding these *social influences* on brain function can provide insights into the neural mechanisms underlying social behavior and cognition.

For a better understanding, I would like to explain the core areas of study in *social cognitive neuroscience in more detail*:

The theory of mind, often referred to as "mentalizing," is the ability to attribute mental states (such as beliefs, desires, and intentions) to oneself and others and to understand that others have beliefs, desires, and intentions that may differ from one's own.

Empathy is understood as the ability to understand and share the feelings of another. It involves both cognitive components (understanding someone else's perspective) and emotional components (feeling what someone else feels, e.g., pain; often activating the anterior insula and the anterior cingulate cortex, regions also implicated in firsthand experiences of pain) (Singer et al., 2004).

Moral cognition is the area that investigates the neural underpinnings of our judgments about what is right or wrong, exploring how different brain regions are involved in making moral decisions.

Self-awareness and self-knowledge examine the neural basis of self-concept, self-reflection, and other aspects of self-awareness.

Social perception investigates how we perceive and evaluate others, including processes related to face recognition, interpretation of facial expressions, and understanding social cues.

To provide some examples of *Theory of Mind:*

Research Question: How does the brain represent other people's beliefs or intentions?

Approach: Functional magnetic resonance imaging (fMRI) might be used to scan participants' brains while they read stories requiring them to infer a character's intentions or beliefs.

Findings: Studies have shown that a region called the temporoparietal junction (TPJ) is often activated during tasks requiring *theory of mind* (Saxe & Kanwisher, 2003).

Empathy example:

Research Question: How does the brain respond to the pain of others?

Approach: Researchers might use fMRI to monitor brain activity while participants watch videos of people experiencing pain or distress.

Findings: The anterior insula and anterior cingulate cortex, areas that are also activated when one experiences pain firsthand, are activated when one observes others in pain, indicating neural mechanisms of empathy (Singer et al., 2004).

Moral cognition example:

Research Question: How does the brain differentiate between morally acceptable and unacceptable actions?

Approach: Participants might be asked to make moral judgments about different scenarios (e.g., the *Trolley Problem*), while their brain activity is monitored via fMRI.

Findings: The ventromedial prefrontal cortex and the dorsolateral prefrontal cortex have been implicated in moral decision-making, with the former associated with emotion-driven judgments and the latter with more analytical reasoning (Greene et al., 2001).

These examples illustrate how *social cognitive neuroscience* combines experimental paradigms from social psychology with neuroimaging and other neurological methods to delve deeply into the brain mechanisms underlying our social interactions and understanding (Lieberman, 2007). This further illustrates the breadth and complexity of *social cognition* as a research area.

Notes

1. Henri Tajfel and John Turner developed social identity theory to explain how people's self-concepts derive from their group memberships and how these affiliations influence behavior and attitudes. The theory centers on a few key ideas:

    1. Social Identity – Individuals define themselves through group membership, which can enhance belonging and self-esteem.
    2. In-Group vs. Out-Group – People show favoritism toward their own group and may discriminate against those outside it.
    3. Categorization – Humans instinctively categorize others (e.g., by nationality, race, gender), simplifying the social world but also fostering stereotypes.
    4. Identification – Individuals adopt group norms and behaviors, shaping their perspectives and actions.
    5. Comparison and Positive Distinctiveness – Groups seek favorable comparisons with others, often leading to prejudices against out-groups.

    Social identity theory has broad applications, helping explain intergroup conflicts, racism, and nationalism. It also informs interventions aimed at reducing prejudice and fostering inclusivity by highlighting the arbitrary nature of many social distinctions.
2. Self-Categorization Theory (SCT), developed by John Turner and colleagues as an extension of social identity theory, examines the cognitive

processes behind how individuals classify themselves in various social contexts, influencing their attitudes, beliefs, and actions. It emphasizes multiple levels of self-categorization (ranging from personal to superordinate identities), context-driven shifts in identity (e.g., from "engineer" at work to "parent" at home), and the role of group prototypes in shaping influence. SCT also explains depersonalization (the temporary shift from personal to social identity), distinguishes intragroup behavior from intergroup behavior, and highlights "accentuation" or exaggerates within-group similarities and between-group differences. By clarifying how people self-categorize, SCT offers insights into group cohesion, leadership, stereotyping, and discrimination in areas such as organizational behavior and politics. It thus provides a strategic framework for fostering positive group dynamics, reducing prejudice, and enhancing collaboration.

3. Realistic conflict theory, developed by social psychologist Muzafer Sherif, explains how conflict, prejudice, and discrimination arise when groups compete for limited resources—whether tangible (e.g., food, territory, jobs) or intangible (e.g., prestige). This competition fosters in-group formation and out-group hostility, often driven by a zero-sum perception that one group's gain is another's loss. As tensions increase, negative stereotypes and discrimination can escalate. However, conflict can be reduced by introducing cooperative tasks that require both groups to work together toward shared objectives (superordinate goals).

   Key Points

   Competition for Resources: Central driver of intergroup conflict.

   In-Group vs. Out-Group: Competition encourages solidarity within one's group and prejudice toward outsiders.

   Zero-Sum Outlook: One side's gain is seen as another's loss, intensifying hostilities.

   Escalation: Negative stereotypes and discriminatory actions grow as competition continues. Conflict Reduction: Collaboration on mutual goals can ease hostilities.

   Examples

   Robbers Cave Experiment: Demonstrated how intergroup competition spurs hostility and how shared goals can reduce it.

   Ethnic Conflicts/Workplace Rivalries/Political Divides: Show similar patterns where resource scarcity and competition breed tension.

   Criticisms

   Oversimplification: Does not fully address ideological, historical, or religious underpinnings. Prejudice Without Competition: Fails to explain prejudices that arise without clear resource conflict. Power Dynamics: Insufficiently considers how power imbalances affect intergroup conflict.

Despite these critiques, realistic conflict theory remains influential in understanding social discord and offers strategies—particularly fostering cooperation—to mitigate conflict.

4. Proposed by Gordon Allport in 1954, the Contact Hypothesis (or Intergroup Contact Theory) argues that under certain conditions, direct interaction between members of different social, ethnic, or racial groups can significantly reduce prejudice. The key conditions include:

   Equal Status: Both groups must engage as equals.

   Common goals: Shared objectives achievable only through cooperation foster mutual respect. Intergroup Cooperation: Joint efforts diminish competition and encourage unity.

   Institutional Support: Authorities or societal norms must endorse and reinforce positive contact. Personal interaction: Close, meaningful contact helps challenge and replace stereotypes.

   Applications span schools, workplaces, community initiatives, and team sports, all aiming to create cooperative experiences that lower prejudice. Criticisms note that superficial contact may not change deeper biases, implementing ideal conditions can be difficult, and poorly managed interactions might worsen stereotypes. Despite these challenges, the contact hypothesis remains influential in designing interventions to improve intergroup relationships.

5. Deontological ethics (from the Greek *deon*, meaning "duty") evaluates actions by adhering to moral rules or duties rather than their consequences. It holds that certain actions are inherently right or wrong, regardless of outcomes.

   Rule-based: Actions are right or wrong and are based solely on moral rules.

   Moral Absolutism: Some deontologists claim that certain actions (e.g., lying, killing) are always wrong, irrespective of potential benefits.

   Intrinsic Value: Actions such as honesty are considered inherently good, whereas deception is inherently bad, regardless of consequences.

   Duties and Obligations: These can stem from reason, divine commands, rights, or social contracts. Kantian Deontology

   Categorical Imperative: Act only on maxims that can be universalized without contradiction.

   Respect for Persons: Treat humanity (in oneself or others) never merely as a means but always as an end.

   Autonomy and Rationality: Individuals have a duty to respect and preserve each person's rational agency.

   Challenges

   Rigidity: Strict adherence to rules may seem unreasonable when breaking them leads to better outcomes.

Moral Conflicts: Deontological duties can clash (e.g., telling the truth vs. protecting life).

Intuition: Some deontological principles (e.g., never lying) may conflict with common moral intuitions. Despite criticisms, deontological ethics remains influential in rights-based legal systems and many religious frameworks, emphasizing duty and inherent moral principles as distinct from consequences.

6. Utilitarianism is a consequentialist theory evaluating morality by outcomes, aiming to maximize overall happiness (or minimize suffering). It treats everyone's happiness equally and judges their actions on the basis of their results rather than their motives. Variants include:

   Act Utilitarianism: Judges each act by how much happiness it produces.

   Rule Utilitarianism: This focuses on the following rules that maximize happiness if applied universally.

   Preference Utilitarianism: Prioritizes satisfying individuals' preferences.

   Negative Utilitarianism: Emphasizing reducing suffering above increasing happiness.

   Key Thinkers

   Jeremy Bentham: Developed the "felicific calculus" to measure pleasure and pain.

   John Stuart Mill: Differentiated between higher (intellectual) and lower (bodily) pleasure, asserting that some pleasure has greater value.

   Criticisms include the difficulty of predicting consequences, its demanding nature, the risk of justifying unjust actions, oversimplification of moral situations, and challenges in comparing happiness across individuals. Despite these, utilitarianism remains influential, particularly in policy-making, where promoting overall well-being is a guiding principle.

7. Virtue ethics, rooted in Aristotle's ancient Greek philosophy, emphasizes character and the cultivation of virtues—such as courage, wisdom, and justice—rather than strict rules or the outcomes of actions. A key idea is Aristotle's golden mean, where virtue lies between two extremes (e.g., courage between recklessness and cowardice). Living virtuously fosters eudaimonia (flourishing), the ultimate goal of human life.

   Moral education through habituation (forming good habits) and practical wisdom (knowing how to act rightly in specific situations) are central to developing virtues. Unlike deontological ethics, which focuses on rules and duties, or consequentialism, which looks at outcomes, virtue ethics centers on who a person is rather than what they do. Critics note its lack of clear guidance for specific actions, potential cultural relativism, and risk of circular reasoning (defining virtue by the virtuous person). However, modern thinkers such as Alasdair MacIntyre, Elizabeth Anscombe, and Martha Nussbaum continue to shape and expand this tradition.

8. Social contract theory explains the origin of societal authority and individuals' obligation to obey it. It holds that people collectively form a society through an agreement—explicit or implicit—that sets moral and political rules, granting certain authorities the power to maintain order and protect rights in exchange for individuals giving up some freedoms.

   State of Nature

   (a) Thomas Hobbes viewed it as dangerous and chaotic: life was "solitary, poor, nasty, brutish, and short."
   (b) John Locke saw it as relatively peaceful but lacking security for natural rights (life, liberty, property).

   Formation of the Social Contract

   (c) Individuals agree to form a society, sacrificing certain freedoms in return for protection and the benefits of communal life.

   Legitimate Authority

   (d) Governments gain legitimacy from this agreement: they protect citizens and maintain order as part of their mandate.

   Revocation of Authority

   (e) If a government fails to protect citizens' rights, people are entitled to revolt or demand change.

   Notable Philosophers

   (f) Thomas Hobbes (1588–1679): Advocated absolute sovereignty for peace and security.
   (g) John Locke (1632–1704): Emphasized natural rights and the right to overthrow unjust governments.
   (h) Jean-Jacques Rousseau (1712–1778): Believed in society guided by the "general will," with collective participation in lawmaking.

   Modern Implications

   Social contract theory underpins modern democratic thought by highlighting the consent of the governed, the responsibilities of government, and the protection of individual rights. It remains a foundational concept in understanding how governments derive their authority and why citizens choose to follow them.

9. Moral realism and moral anti-realism are opposing views in metaethics. Realists maintain that there are objective moral facts—true regardless of anyone's beliefs—much like physical facts about the world. Ethical naturalists reduce these facts to observable phenomena, whereas ethical nonnaturalists treat them as unique, irreducible properties.

   On the other hand, antirealists deny the existence of objective moral truths. They view moral judgments as stemming from subjective attitudes, cultural norms, or social constructions. Error theorists claim that all moral discourse is mistaken because moral objectivity does not exist; subjectivists believe that moral truths depend on individual or societal attitudes; and constructivists argue that moral truths arise through shared rational or social processes.

   The main difference is that realists assert mind-independent moral facts and objective truth values, whereas antirealists consider moral truth to be either nonexistent, subjective, or collectively constructed. The debate continues, with each side offering detailed arguments for its stance.
10. Care ethics (or the ethics of care) is a moral theory emphasizing interpersonal relationships, empathy, and context over abstract principles and strict autonomy. It views people as inherently interdependent and highlights the moral importance of caring for others—especially those who are vulnerable or dependent—and caring about broader social well-being. Emotions such as empathy, compassion, and love are seen as crucial to ethical decision-making rather than as irrational forces to be set aside.

    Key Figures and Origins

    Carol Gilligan (In a Different Voice, 1982) argued that women often prioritize relationships and responsibility over abstract justice-based approaches.

    Nel Noddings expanded on the concept of caring relationships by examining the roles of the one-caring (caregiver) and the cared for.

    Applications

    Education: Focuses on understanding students holistically, not just their academic performance. Healthcare: Emphasizes the relational and emotional aspects of patient care.

    Policy and Social Justice: Suggests supporting caregiving, communal responsibilities, and social interconnectedness.

    Critiques

    Lack of Universal Principles: Skeptics claim that it provides insufficient guidance on complex or large-scale ethical problems.

    Gendered Assumptions: Some worry it reinforces stereotypical gender roles and portrays caring as inherently "feminine."

In sum, care ethics underscores the relational, context-sensitive, and empathetic dimensions of moral life, challenging traditional rule-centered ethics by focusing on the tangible responsibilities we have to one another.

11. Moral intuition is the fast, automatic "gut feeling" that arises in response to moral situations and is influenced by factors such as evolution, culture, and personal experience. Dual-process theories suggest that we have two systems for making moral judgments:

    System 1 (Intuitive) – rapid, emotionally charged, and largely unconscious. System 2 (Deliberative) – slower, analytical, and reflective.

    These two systems can conflict. A classic example is the *Trolley problem*: System 1 may produce a strong emotional response against pushing someone to save others (deontological view), whereas System 2 can support a more utilitarian rationale after careful thought.

    Significance

    Moral Education: Tailoring teaching methods to foster both intuitive and reflective moral development. Policy/Law: Guiding decisions where instincts and reasons may clash.

    Technology/AI: Informing the design of ethical decision-making systems (e.g., self-driving cars).

    Self-awareness: Helping individuals understand how emotions and reasoning shape their moral choices.

    Psychologist Jonathan Haidt highlights that much of our moral reasoning justifies intuitions post hoc, underscoring the powerful role that intuition plays in ethical decision-making.

12. Lawrence Kohlberg, influenced by Jean Piaget, proposed a stage-based theory of moral development extending throughout the lifespan. He identified three main levels—each containing two stages: Preconventional Morality (Stages 1 & 2):

    (i) Focuses on external rewards and punishments ("I don't steal to avoid punishment" or "I do good if there's something in it for me").

    Conventional Morality (Stages 3 & 4):

    (j) It emphasizes social approval and maintaining order ("I do good to be seen as a good person" and "I follow rules to keep society functioning").

    Postconventional Morality (Stages 5 & 6):

    (k) Relies on personal ethical principles and social contracts ("Laws can be changed if they violate fundamental rights" and "I follow universal ethical values even if they conflict with the law").

    Not everyone has reached the postconventional level, and Carol Gilligan critiqued Kohlberg's approach for favoring male-oriented perspectives, proposing an alternative emphasis on care and relationships. Despite criticisms, Kohlberg's model remains central to understanding how moral reasoning evolves over time.

13. Carol Gilligan criticized Lawrence Kohlberg's male-centric research on moral development, proposing that women often focus on care and relational concerns. In her three-level model—Orientation to Individual Survival, Goodness as Self-Sacrifice, and Morality of Nonviolence—Gilligan shows how moral understanding progresses from self-interest to a balanced concern for both self and others. She did not claim that only women use an ethic of care but highlighted the importance of recognizing multiple perspectives (justice vs. care) within moral development. Her work broadened discussions on gender and morality across different cultural and social settings.
14. Evolutionary ethics explores how human moral instincts and behaviors may have developed as adaptive traits. This suggests that emotions such as empathy, guilt, and shame—as well as actions such as altruism and cooperation—could have helped our ancestors survive and reproduce. Mechanisms such as kin selection (aiding relatives who share genes) and reciprocal altruism (expecting future help in return) help explain otherwise selfless behaviors. Some theorists also propose group selection, arguing that cooperative groups might outcompete less cohesive groups. However, critics emphasize that while these theories describe how morality might have evolved, they do not prescribe what is ethically right or wrong (guarding against the naturalistic fallacy). Additionally, cultural and rational factors contribute significantly to morality, challenging purely evolutionary explanations and raising questions about moral progress beyond survival or reproductive success.
15. Moral disengagement is the cognitive process of rationalizing or justifying unethical behavior so that individuals can avoid guilt or distress. The psychologist Albert Bandura identified several mechanisms within social cognitive theory that enable people to distance themselves from the harm of their actions, including moral justification ("it's for a greater good"), euphemistic labeling ("collateral damage"), advantageous comparison ("it's not as bad as…"), and shifting or diffusing responsibility ("just following orders" or "everyone else did it"). Additional mechanisms involve downplaying consequences, dehumanizing others, and blaming victims. On a societal scale, these processes can normalize harmful practices and justify systemic injustices. Individually, ongoing moral disengagement weakens personal moral standards and fosters repeated unethical behavior. Recognizing these mechanisms is crucial for educators, policymakers, and leaders to promote ethical decision-making and reduce harmful practices.

References

Allport, G. W. (1954). *The nature of prejudice*. Addison-Wesley.

Argyle, M. (1988). *Bodily communication* (2nd ed.). Methuen.

Aristotle. (2009). *Nicomachean ethics* (D. Ross, Trans.). Oxford University Press. (Original work written ca. 350 B.C.E.).

Aronson, E., Wilson, T. D., & Akert, R. M. (2019). *Social psychology* (10th ed.). Pearson.

Asch, S. E. (1956). Studies of independence and conformity: A minority of one against a unanimous majority. *Psychological Monographs, 70*(9), 1–70. https://doi.org/10.1037/h0093718

Bandura, A. (1986). *Social foundations of thought and action: A social cognitive theory*. Prentice-Hall.

Baron-Cohen, S. (1995). *Mindblindness: An essay on autism and theory of mind*. MIT Press. https://doi.org/10.7551/mitpress/4635.001.0001

Batson, C. D. (2011). *Altruism in humans*. Oxford University Press.

Brown, R. (2000). Social identity theory: Past achievements, current problems, and future challenges. *European Journal of Social Psychology, 30*(6), 745–778. https://doi.org/10.1002/1099-0992(200011/12)30:6<745::AID-EJSP24>3.0.CO;2-O

Cacioppo, J. T., & Decety, J. (2011). Social neuroscience: Challenges and opportunities in the study of complex behavior. *Annals of the New York Academy of Sciences, 1224*, 162–173. https://doi.org/10.1111/j.1749-6632.2010.05858.x

Carron, A. V., & Brawley, L. R. (2000). Cohesion: Conceptual and measurement issues. *Small Group Research, 31*(1), 89–106. https://doi.org/10.1177/104649640003100105

Chiu, L. (1972). A cross-cultural comparison of cognitive styles in Chinese and American children. *International Journal of Psychology, 7*(4), 235–242. https://doi.org/10.1080/00207597208246604

Cialdini, R. B., & Goldstein, N. J. (2004). Social influence: Compliance and conformity. *Annual Review of Psychology, 55*, 591–621. https://doi.org/10.1146/annurev.psych.55.090902.142015

Crisp, R. J. (Ed.). (2010). *The psychology of social and cultural diversity*. Wiley-Blackwell. https://doi.org/10.1002/9781444325447

Crocker, J., & Major, B. (1989). Social stigma and self-esteem: The self-protective properties of stigma. *Psychological Review, 96*(4), 608–630. https://doi.org/10.1037/0033-295X.96.4.608

Decety, J., & Jackson, P. L. (2004). The functional architecture of human empathy. *Behavioral and Cognitive Neuroscience Reviews, 3*(2), 71–100. https://doi.org/10.1177/1534582304267187

Dovidio, J. F., Hewstone, M., Glick, P., & Esses, V. (2010). Prejudice, stereotyping, and discrimination: Theoretical and empirical overview. In *The SAGE handbook of prejudice, stereotyping and discrimination* (pp. 3–28). https://doi.org/10.4135/9781446200919.n1

Eisenberg, N., Spinrad, T. L., & Knafo-Noam, A. (2014). Prosocial development. In M. Lamb & R. Lerner (Eds.), *Handbook of child psychology and developmental science* (Vol. 3, 7th ed.). Wiley-Blackwell. https://doi.org/10.1002/9781118963418.childpsy315

Ekman, P., & Friesen, W. V. (1975). *Unmasking the face: A guide to recognizing emotions from facial clues*. Prentice Hall.

Farah, M. J. (2015). The unknowns of cognitive enhancement. *Science, 350*(6259), 379–380. https://doi.org/10.1126/science.aad5893

Fiske, S. T. (2018). *Social beings: A core motives approach to social psychology* (4th ed.). Wiley.

Fiske, S. T., & Taylor, S. E. (2013). *Social cognition: From brains to culture* (2nd ed.). Sage.

Foot, P. (1967). The problem of abortion and the doctrine of double effect. *Oxford Review, 5*, 5–15.

Forsyth, D. R. (2019). *Group dynamics* (7th ed.). Cengage.

Frith, C. D., & Frith, U. (2003). Development and neurophysiology of mentalizing. *Philosophical Transactions of the Royal Society B: Biological Sciences, 358*(1431), 459–473. https://doi.org/10.1098/rstb.2002.1218

Frith, C. D., & Frith, U. (2006). The neural basis of mentalizing. *Neuron, 50*(4), 531–534. https://doi.org/10.1016/j.neuron.2006.05.001

Gilligan, C. (1982). *In a different voice: Psychological theory and women's development*. Harvard University Press.

Greene, J. D., Sommerville, R. B., Nystrom, L. E., Darley, J. M., & Cohen, J. D. (2001). An fMRI investigation of emotional engagement in moral judgment. *Science, 293*(5537), 2105–2108. https://doi.org/10.1126/science.1062872

Haidt, J. (2001). The emotional dog and its rational tail: A social intuitionist approach to moral judgment. *Psychological Review, 108*(4), 814–834. https://doi.org/10.1037/0033-295X.108.4.814

Haidt, J. (2012). *The righteous mind: Why good people are divided by politics and religion*. Pantheon Books.

Hall, E. T. (1966). *The hidden dimension*. Doubleday.

Hall, E. T. (1976). *Beyond culture*. Anchor Press.

Happé, F. G. (1994). An advanced test of theory of mind: Understanding of story characters' thoughts and feelings by able autistic, mentally handicapped, and normal children and adults. *Journal of Autism and Developmental Disorders, 24*(2), 129–154. https://doi.org/10.1007/BF02172093

Heider, F. (1958). *The psychology of interpersonal relations.* Wiley. https://doi.org/10.1037/10628-000

Heine, S. J. (2016). *Cultural psychology* (3rd ed.). W. W. Norton.

Hogg, M. A. (2016). Social identity theory. In S. McKeown, R. Haji, & N. Ferguson (Eds.), *Understanding peace and conflict through social identity theory* (pp. 3–17). Springer. https://doi.org/10.1007/978-3-319-29869-6_1

Hogg, M. A., & Reid, S. A. (2006). Social identity, self-categorization, and the communication of group norms. *Communication Theory, 16*(1), 7–30. https://doi.org/10.1111/j.1468-2885.2006.00003.x

Illes, J., & Racine, E. (2005). Imaging or imagining? A neuroethics challenge informed by genetics. *American Journal of Bioethics, 5*(2), 5–18. https://doi.org/10.1080/15265160590923358

Isenberg, D. J. (1986). Group polarization: A critical review and meta-analysis. *Journal of Personality and Social Psychology, 50*(6), 1141–1151. https://doi.org/10.1037/0022-3514.50.6.1141

Janis, I. L. (1972). *Victims of groupthink: A psychological study of foreign-policy decisions and fiascoes.* Houghton Mifflin.

Jones, E. E., & Davis, K. E. (1965). From acts to dispositions: The attribution process in person perception. In L. Berkowitz (Ed.), *Advances in experimental social psychology* (Vol. 2, pp. 219–266). Academic Press. https://doi.org/10.1016/S0065-2601(08)60107-0

Joyce, R. (2006). *The evolution of morality.* MIT Press.

Kelley, H. H. (1973). The processes of causal attribution. *American Psychologist, 28*(2), 107–128. https://doi.org/10.1037/h0034225

Kerr, N. L., & Tindale, R. S. (2004). Group performance and decision making. *Annual Review of Psychology, 55*, 623–655. https://doi.org/10.1146/annurev.psych.55.090902.142009

Kleinke, C. L. (1986). Gaze and eye contact: A research review. *Psychological Bulletin, 100*(1), 78–100. https://doi.org/10.1037/0033-2909.100.1.78

Knapp, M. L., Hall, J. A., & Horgan, T. G. (2013). *Nonverbal communication in human interaction* (8th ed.). Cengage Learning.

Kohlberg, L. (1969). Stage and sequence: The cognitive-developmental approach to socialization. In D. A. Goslin (Ed.), *Handbook of socialization theory and research* (pp. 347–480). Rand McNally.

Korsgaard, C. M. (1996). *Creating the kingdom of ends.* Cambridge University Press. https://doi.org/10.1017/CBO9781139174503

Kovács, Á. M., Téglás, E., & Endress, A. D. (2010). The social sense: Susceptibility to others' beliefs in human infants and adults. *Science, 330*(6012), 1830–1834. https://doi.org/10.1126/science.1190792

Kunda, Z. (1999). *Social cognition: Making sense of people.* MIT Press.

Lieberman, M. D. (2007). Social cognitive neuroscience: A review of core processes. *Annual Review of Psychology, 58*, 259–289. https://doi.org/10.1146/annurev.psych.58.110405.085654

Locke, J. (1980). In C. B. Macpherson (Ed.), *Second treatise of government*. Hackett.

Macrae, C. N., & Bodenhausen, G. V. (2000). Social cognition: Thinking categorically about others. *Annual Review of Psychology, 51*, 93–120. https://doi.org/10.1146/annurev.psych.51.1.93

Markus, H. R., & Kitayama, S. (1991). Culture and the self: Implications for cognition, emotion, and motivation. *Psychological Review, 98*(2), 224–253. https://doi.org/10.1037/0033-295X.98.2.224

Mikhail, J. (2011). *Elements of moral cognition: Rawls' linguistic analogy and the cognitive science of moral and legal judgment*. Cambridge University Press. https://doi.org/10.1017/CBO9780511780578

Milgram, S. (1974). *Obedience to authority*. Harper & Row.

Mill, J. S. (1863). *Utilitarianism*. Parker, Son, and Bourn.

Nisbett, R. E. (2003). *The geography of thought: How Asians and Westerners think differently … and why*. Free Press.

Nisbett, R. E., Peng, K., Choi, I., & Norenzayan, A. (2001). Culture and systems of thought: Holistic vs. analytic cognition. *Psychological Review, 108*(2), 291–310. https://doi.org/10.1037/0033-295X.108.2.291

Norenzayan, A., Smith, E. E., Kim, B. J., & Nisbett, R. E. (2002). Cultural preferences for formal versus intuitive reasoning. *Cognitive Science, 26*(5), 653–684. https://doi.org/10.1016/S0364-0213(02)00082-4

Pettigrew, T. F. (1998). Intergroup contact theory. *Annual Review of Psychology, 49*, 65–85. https://doi.org/10.1146/annurev.psych.49.1.65

Pettigrew, T. F., & Tropp, L. R. (2006). A meta-analytic test of intergroup contact theory. *Journal of Personality and Social Psychology, 90*(5), 751–783. https://doi.org/10.1037/0022-3514.90.5.751

Premack, D., & Woodruff, G. (1978). Does the chimpanzee have a theory of mind? *Behavioral and Brain Sciences, 1*(4), 515–526. https://doi.org/10.1017/S0140525X00076512

Prinz, J. (2007). *The emotional construction of morals*. Oxford University Press.

Roskies, A. (2002). Neuroethics for the new millennium. *Neuron, 35*(1), 21–23. https://doi.org/10.1016/S0896-6273(02)00763-8

Rousseau, J.-J. (1978). *On the social contract* (R. D. Masters, Ed. & Trans.). St. Martin's Press.

Saxe, R., & Kanwisher, N. (2003). People thinking about thinking people: The role of the temporo-parietal junction in "theory of mind". *NeuroImage, 19*(4), 1835–1842. https://doi.org/10.1016/s1053-8119(03)00230-1

Sayre-McCord, G. (Ed.). (1988). *Essays on moral realism*. Cornell University Press.

Sherif, M. (1966). *In common predicament: Social psychology of intergroup conflict and cooperation*. Houghton Mifflin.
Sherif, M., Harvey, O. J., White, B. J., Hood, W. R., & Sherif, C. W. (1961). *Intergroup conflict and cooperation: The Robbers Cave experiment*. University of Oklahoma Book Exchange.
Sidanius, J., & Pratto, F. (1999). *Social dominance: An intergroup theory of social hierarchy and oppression*. Cambridge University Press. https://doi.org/10.1017/CBO9781139175043
Singer, T., Seymour, B., O'Doherty, J., Kaube, H., Dolan, R. J., & Frith, C. D. (2004). Empathy for pain involves the affective but not sensory components of pain. *Science, 303*(5661), 1157–1162. https://doi.org/10.1126/science.1093535
Tajfel, H., & Turner, J. C. (1979). An integrative theory of intergroup conflict. In W. G. Austin & S. Worchel (Eds.), *The social psychology of intergroup relations* (pp. 33–47). Brooks/Cole.
Thomson, J. J. (1976). Killing, letting die, and the trolley problem. *The Monist, 59*(2), 204–217. https://doi.org/10.5840/monist197659224
Triandis, H. C. (1995). *Individualism & collectivism*. Westview Press.
Turner, J. C., & Reynolds, K. J. (2012). Self-categorization theory. In P. A. M. Van Lange, A. W. Kruglanski, & E. T. Higgins (Eds.), *Handbook of theories of social psychology* (Vol. 2, pp. 399–417). Sage. https://doi.org/10.4135/9781446249222.n46
Turner, J. C., Hogg, M. A., Oakes, P. J., Reicher, S. D., & Wetherell, M. S. (1987). *Rediscovering the social group: A self-categorization theory*. Basil Blackwell.

CHAPTER 12

Cognitive Development and Aging

Cognitive Development Across the Lifespan

Cognitive development refers to the changes in cognitive abilities and mental processes that occur as individuals grow and age. This includes changes in perception, memory, language, problem-solving, and other cognitive functions (Berk, 2022; Siegler et al., 2017). Researchers have studied cognitive development to better understand the mechanisms that drive these changes and how they are influenced by biological, environmental, and social factors (Bornstein & Lamb, 2021; Vygotsky, 1978).

Cognitive Milestones and Developmental Stages

Cognitive milestones are key achievements in cognitive abilities that typically emerge at certain ages. These milestones serve as markers of normal cognitive development and can vary among individuals (Siegler et al., 2017).

Infancy (0–2 Years)

Sensorimotor Stage (Piaget's Theory): Infants learn through direct interaction with their environment; they initially rely on reflexes and gradually develop intentional actions (Piaget, 1952);

H. Kankam, *A Brief Excursion into Human Cognition*,
https://doi.org/10.1007/978-3-031-89752-8_12

Object permanence: Recognition that objects exist even when out of sight; this typically develops by the end of the first year (Baillargeon, 1987);

Emergence of symbolic thought: The ability to mentally represent objects and people who are not present (Piaget, 1952);

Early Childhood (2–6 Years)

Preoperational Stage (Piaget's Theory): Children begin to use symbols to represent words, images, and ideas, which is why we see a surge in playing and acquiring language (Piaget & Inhelder, 1969);

Egocentrism: The child's inability to see situations from another's perspective (Piaget & Inhelder, 1969);

Limitations in understanding conservation include, for example, not recognizing that liquid remains the same volume regardless of the shape of the container (Piaget, 1952). Rapid vocabulary expansion and improved grammar (Berk, 2022). The beginning of logical reasoning, though this is often intuitive and not yet logical (Siegler et al., 2017);

Middle Childhood (6–12 Years)

Concrete Operational Stage (Piaget's Theory): Children begin to think more logically about concrete (not abstract) events. An improved ability to think logically about direct experiences and perceptions (Piaget & Inhelder, 1969);

Conservation Concept: Understanding that quantity does not change with alterations in shape or appearance (Piaget, 1952);

Classification and Seriation: The ability to sort objects and ideas and understand sequences (Siegler et al., 2017);

Adolescence (12–19 Years)

Formal Operational Stage (Piaget's Theory): Development of abstract and hypothetical reasoning (Piaget, 1970);

Abstract Thinking: The ability to think about possibilities, hypotheses, and abstract concepts (Flavell, 1979);

Metacognition: Thinking about one's own thought processes; improved problem-solving abilities; moral reasoning develops, often influenced by peer and societal expectations (Steinberg, 2014).

These stages, proposed by Jean Piaget, provide a general framework for understanding cognitive development, although researchers now recognize that cognitive development is more continuous and dynamic than initially proposed by Piaget (Case, 1992; Siegler, 1996).

Adulthood

Early Adulthood (20–40 years): Cognitive abilities peak in terms of processing speed, memory, and reasoning (Salthouse, 2004). Continued development of expertise in specific domains and increased ability to manage multiple tasks and synthesize information (Ericsson & Lehmann, 1996);

Middle Adulthood (40–65 years): Some cognitive decline in areas such as processing speed but continue to improve in areas on the basis of experience and knowledge (Schaie, 2013). Greater reliance on crystallized intelligence (knowledge accumulated over time) over fluid intelligence (problem-solving and reasoning) (Horn & Cattell, 1967);

Late Adulthood (65 years and above): Declines in certain cognitive abilities, such as processing speed, working memory, and episodic memory. Continued stability or even growth in other areas, especially knowledge-based areas or wisdom (Park & Reuter-Lorenz, 2009). Neuroplasticity remains, although it may decrease with age (Greenwood & Parasuraman, 2010). This means that older adults can still learn and adapt, though perhaps at a different rate or style.

Factors Affecting Cognitive Development

Biology and genetics: Genetic predispositions can influence cognitive strengths and weaknesses; *Environment:* Stimulation in early childhood, educational opportunities, and life experiences play major roles;

Socioeconomic status: Access to resources, educational opportunities, nutrition and healthcare can significantly impact cognitive development;

Culture: Cultural values and practices can shape cognitive skills and values.

Understanding cognitive development across the lifespan clearly provides insights into how individuals learn, think, and interact with their environment at different stages of life. It is also crucial for educators, psychologists, and healthcare professionals in tailoring interventions and providing support for individuals of different ages if a need arises.

Age-Related Cognitive Decline and Cognitive Reserve

As individuals age, some cognitive abilities may decline, particularly those related to processing speed, working memory, episodic memory, and attention (Salthouse, 2004). However, other cognitive functions, such as *semantic memory* (Chap. 4) and *crystallized intelligence* (Horn & Cattell, 1967), often remain stable or even improve with age.

Crystallized intelligence represents the wealth of knowledge and skills that one gathers over a lifetime. It is a testament to lifelong learning and the value of accumulated experiences. On the other hand, cognitive reserve refers to the ability of the brain to cope with age-related changes or damage (Stern, 2002), allowing individuals to maintain cognitive function despite potential decline. Factors contributing to *cognitive reserve* include education, occupational complexity, and engagement in cognitively stimulating activities (Stern, 2009). Individuals with greater *cognitive reserves* may experience slower *cognitive decline* and a reduced risk of *developing dementia* (Livingston et al., 2020).

Promoting *cognitive health* and preventing *cognitive decline* are important aspects of maintaining overall well-being and quality of life in older adults. Integrating a combination of these interventions into daily life can support cognitive health across the lifespan.

Interventions to Maintain Cognitive Health During Aging

As individuals age, they often experience changes in cognitive function and brain structure. Structural changes with aging are associated with a decline in gray matter volume and white matter integrity, particularly in regions involved in memory and executive function, such as the hippocampus and prefrontal cortex (Fjell & Walhovd, 2010). However, various interventions can help maintain cognitive health and prevent or delay cognitive decline in older adults.

Physical Exercise

Evidence: Regular physical activity reduces the risk of cognitive decline and diseases such as Alzheimer's disease (Erickson et al., 2011; Kramer & Colcombe, 2018);

Mechanism: Increases blood flow, promotes brain health hormones, and supports neurogenesis (Colcombe & Kramer, 2003);

Recommendations: Cardiovascular exercises, strength training, flexibility exercises, and balance exercises (WHO, 2020).

Cognitive Training

Evidence: Targeted cognitive training can hone functions such as memory, attention, and problem-solving (Rebok et al., 2014);

Mechanism: Reinforces the "use it or lose it" principle, strengthening brain pathways (Willis et al., 2006);

Recommendation: Puzzles, reading, games, learning new skills;

Diet

Evidence: Specific diets correlate with slower cognitive decline (Morris et al., 2015);

Mechanism: Antioxidants, vitamins, and certain fats can combat oxidative stress and inflammation (Scarmeas et al., 2006);

Recommendation: Embrace the Mediterranean, DASH, or MIND diets.

Social Engagement

Evidence: There is evidence that increased social interaction is linked to enhanced cognitive health (Berkman et al., 2000; Fratiglioni et al., 2004).

Mechanism: Stimulates multiple brain regions and maintains active neural pathways (Kelly et al., 2017);

Recommendation: Join clubs, volunteer, maintain friendships.

Sleep Hygiene

Evidence: Quality sleep is essential for cognitive health (Walker, 2017);

Mechanism: Facilitates memory consolidation and clears out metabolic waste in the brain (Rasch & Born, 2013);

Recommendation: 7–9 hours of quality sleep with a regular schedule (Hirshkowitz et al., 2015).

Mental Health Management

Evidence: Conditions such as depression can expedite cognitive decline (Ownby et al., 2006);

Mechanism: Chronic stress releases neuron damaging cortisol (Lupien et al., 2009);

Recommendation: Mindfulness, meditation, and seeking professional help when needed.

Chronic Disease Management

Evidence: Conditions such as hypertension can increase the risk of cognitive decline (Fiocco & Yaffe, 2010);

Mechanism: Reduced brain blood flow and micro- and macrovascular damage can affect cognition (Iadecola, 2013);

Recommendation: Regular health check-ups and lifestyle modifications.

Avoiding Neurotoxins

Evidence: Excessive drugs or alcohol can be neurotoxic;

Mechanism: These substances can cause direct neural damage or disrupt networks;

Recommendation: Limit alcohol use and avoid drug misuse.

Lifelong Learning

Evidence: Continuous education offers a cognitive shield (Stern, 2009);

Mechanism: Dense neural networks are formed to counteract age-related changes (Valenzuela & Sachdev, 2006);

Recommendation: Engage in courses, lectures, pursue intellectually stimulating hobbies.

Environment

Evidence: Stimulating environments bolster cognitive health (Hertzog et al., 2009);

Mechanism: New stimuli encourage neuroplasticity and resilience;

Recommendation: Travel, explore new environments, periodically rearrange living spaces.

Additional insights show that both genetic and environmental factors shape cognitive development and aging. As already expressed, genetics dictates cognitive ability, the risk of age-related decline, and intervention responsiveness. Moreover, factors such as education, nutrition, and toxin exposure play environmental roles. Understanding this interplay may lead to more personalized cognitive health strategies.

Notably, certain disorders, such as Alzheimer's disease, Parkinson's disease, or traumatic injuries, can disrupt cognitive trajectories, as mentioned in previous chapters. Research in these areas can reveal the mechanisms of cognitive decline and pave the way for specialized interventions.

While no single intervention can guarantee the preservation of cognitive health, a combination of the above strategies can optimize brain health and reduce the risk of cognitive decline (Livingston et al., 2020). Individual needs may vary, and it is essential to consult with healthcare professionals when tailoring an approach to cognitive health maintenance.

References

Baillargeon, R. (1987). Object permanence in 3 1/2- and 4 1/2-month-old infants. *Developmental Psychology, 23*(5), 655–664. https://doi.org/10.1037/0012-1649.23.5.655

Berk, L. E. (2022). *Development through the lifespan* (8th ed.). Pearson.

Berkman, L. F., Glass, T., Brissette, I., & Seeman, T. E. (2000). From social integration to health: Durkheim in the new millennium. *Social Science & Medicine, 51*(6), 843–857. https://doi.org/10.1016/S0277-9536(00)00065-4

Bornstein, M. H., & Lamb, M. E. (Eds.). (2021). *Developmental science: An advanced textbook* (8th ed.). Psychology Press.

Case, R. (1992). *The mind's staircase: Exploring the conceptual underpinnings of children's thought and knowledge*. Erlbaum.

Colcombe, S., & Kramer, A. F. (2003). Fitness effects on the cognitive function of older adults: A meta-analytic study. *Psychological Science, 14*(2), 125–130. https://doi.org/10.1111/1467-9280.t01-1-01430

Erickson, K. I., Voss, M. W., Prakash, R. S., Basak, C., Szabo, A., Chaddock, L., et al. (2011). Exercise training increases size of hippocampus and improves memory. *Proceedings of the National Academy of Sciences, 108*(7), 3017–3022. https://doi.org/10.1073/pnas.1015950108

Ericsson, K. A., & Lehmann, A. C. (1996). Expert and exceptional performance: Evidence of maximal adaptation to task constraints. *Annual Review of Psychology, 47*, 273–305. https://doi.org/10.1146/annurev.psych.47.1.273

Fiocco, A. J., & Yaffe, K. (2010). Defining successful aging: The importance of including cognitive function. *Aging Research Reviews, 9*(4), 212–222. https://doi.org/10.1001/archneurol.2010.130

Fjell, A. M., & Walhovd, K. B. (2010). Structural brain changes in aging: Courses, causes, and cognitive consequences. *Reviews in the Neurosciences, 21*(3), 187–221. https://doi.org/10.1515/REVNEURO.2010.21.3.187

Flavell, J. H. (1979). Metacognition and cognitive monitoring: A new area of cognitive–developmental inquiry. *American Psychologist, 34*(10), 906–911. https://doi.org/10.1037/0003-066X.34.10.906

Fratiglioni, L., Paillard-Borg, S., & Winblad, B. (2004). An active and socially integrated lifestyle in late life might protect against dementia. *Lancet Neurology, 3*(6), 343–353. https://doi.org/10.1016/S1474-4422(04)00767-7

Greenwood, P. M., & Parasuraman, R. (2010). Neuronal and cognitive plasticity: A neurocognitive framework for ameliorating cognitive aging. *Frontiers in Aging Neuroscience, 2*, 150. https://doi.org/10.3389/fnagi.2010.00150

Hertzog, C., Kramer, A. F., Wilson, R. S., & Lindenberger, U. (2009). Enrichment effects on adult cognitive development. *Psychological Science in the Public Interest, 9*(1), 1–65. https://doi.org/10.1111/j.1539-6053.2009.01034.x

Hirshkowitz, M., Whiton, K., Albert, S. M., Alessi, C., Bruni, O., DonCarlos, L., et al. (2015). National Sleep Foundation's sleep time duration recommendations: Methodology and results summary. *Sleep Health, 1*(1), 40–43. https://doi.org/10.1016/j.sleh.2014.12.010

Horn, J. L., & Cattell, R. B. (1967). Age differences in fluid and crystallized intelligence. *Acta Psychologica, 26*, 1–23.

Iadecola, C. (2013). The pathobiology of vascular dementia. *Neuron, 80*(4), 844–866. https://doi.org/10.1016/j.neuron.2013.10.008

Kelly, M. E., Duff, H., Kelly, S., McHugh Power, J. E., Brennan, S., Lawlor, B. A., & Loughrey, D. G. (2017). The impact of social activities, social networks, social support, and social relationships on the cognitive functioning of healthy older adults: A systematic review. *Systematic Reviews, 6*(1), 259. https://doi.org/10.1186/s13643-017-0632-2

Kramer, A. F., & Colcombe, S. J. (2018). Fitness effects on the cognitive function of older adults: A meta-analytic study—Revisited. *Perspectives on Psychological Science, 13*(2), 213–217. https://doi.org/10.1177/1745691617707316

Livingston, G., Huntley, J., Sommerlad, A., Ames, D., Ballard, C., Banerjee, S., et al. (2020). Dementia prevention, intervention, and care: 2020 report of the Lancet Commission. *Lancet, 396*(10248), 413–446. https://doi.org/10.1016/S0140-6736(20)30367-6

Lupien, S. J., McEwen, B. S., Gunnar, M. R., & Heim, C. (2009). Effects of stress throughout the lifespan on the brain, behaviour and cognition. *Nature Reviews Neuroscience, 10*(6), 434–445. https://doi.org/10.1038/nrn2639

Morris, M. C., Tangney, C. C., Wang, Y., Sacks, F. M., Bennett, D. A., & Aggarwal, N. T. (2015). MIND diet associated with reduced incidence of Alzheimer's disease. *Alzheimer's & Dementia, 11*(9), 1007–1014. https://doi.org/10.1016/j.jalz.2014.11.009

Ownby, R. L., Crocco, E., Acevedo, A., John, V., & Loewenstein, D. (2006). Depression and risk for Alzheimer disease: Systematic review, meta-analysis, and metaregression analysis. *Archives of General Psychiatry, 63*(5), 530–538. https://doi.org/10.1001/archpsyc.63.5.530

Park, D. C., & Reuter-Lorenz, P. (2009). The adaptive brain: Aging and neurocognitive scaffolding. *Annual Review of Psychology, 60*, 173–196. https://doi.org/10.1146/annurev.psych.59.103006.093656

Piaget, J. (1952). *The origins of intelligence in children.* International Universities Press.

Piaget, J. (1970). *Science of education and the psychology of the child.* Orion Press.

Piaget, J., & Inhelder, B. (1969). *The psychology of the child.* Basic Books.

Rasch, B., & Born, J. (2013). About sleep's role in memory. *Physiological Reviews, 93*(2), 681–766. https://doi.org/10.1152/physrev.00032.2012

Rebok, G. W., Ball, K., Guey, L. T., Jones, R. N., Kim, H.-Y., King, J. W., et al. (2014). Ten-year effects of the Advanced Cognitive Training for Independent and Vital Elderly (ACTIVE) cognitive training trial on cognition and everyday functioning in older adults. *Journal of the American Geriatrics Society, 62*(1), 16–24. https://doi.org/10.1111/jgs.12607

Salthouse, T. A. (2004). What and when of cognitive aging. *Current Directions in Psychological Science, 13*(4), 140–144. https://doi.org/10.1111/j.0963-7214.2004.00293.x

Scarmeas, N., Stern, Y., Mayeux, R., & Luchsinger, J. A. (2006). Mediterranean diet and mild cognitive impairment. *Archives of Neurology, 63*(12), 1709–1717. https://doi.org/10.1001/archneurol.2008.536

Schaie, K. W. (2013). *Developmental influences on adult intelligence: The Seattle Longitudinal Study* (2nd ed.). Oxford University Press.

Siegler, R. S. (1996). *Emerging minds: The process of change in children's thinking.* Oxford University Press.

Siegler, R. S., Eisenberg, N., DeLoache, J., Saffran, J., & Gershoff, E. (2017). *How children develop* (5th ed.). Worth.

Steinberg, L. (2014). *Age of opportunity: Lessons from the new science of adolescence.* Eamon Dolan/Houghton Mifflin Harcourt.

Stern, Y. (2002). What is cognitive reserve? Theory and research application of the reserve concept. *Journal of the International Neuropsychological Society, 8*(3), 448–460. https://doi.org/10.1017/S1355617702813248

Stern, Y. (2009). Cognitive reserve. *Neuropsychologia, 47*(10), 2015–2028. https://doi.org/10.1016/j.neuropsychologia.2009.03.004

Valenzuela, M. J., & Sachdev, P. (2006). Brain reserve and dementia: A systematic review. *Psychological Medicine, 36*(4), 441–454. https://doi.org/10.1017/S0033291705006264

Vygotsky, L. S. (1978). In M. Cole, V. John-Steiner, S. Scribner, & E. Souberman (Eds.), *Mind in society: The development of higher psychological processes.* Harvard University Press.

Walker, M. (2017). *Why we sleep: Unlocking the power of sleep and dreams.* Scribner.

WHO. (2020). *Guidelines on physical activity and sedentary behaviour.* World Health Organization.

Willis, S. L., Tennstedt, S. L., Marsiske, M., Ball, K., Elias, J., Koepke, K. M., et al. (2006). Long-term effects of cognitive training on everyday functional outcomes in older adults. *JAMA, 296*(23), 2805–2814. https://doi.org/10.1001/jama.296.23.2805

CHAPTER 13

Artificial Intelligence and Human Cognition

I begin this chapter with a brief reflection on B. F. Skinner's 1969 book, *Contingencies of Reinforcement: A Theoretical Analysis.* Skinner—a renowned American psychologist, behaviorist, author, inventor, and social philosopher—argued that the real issue is not whether machines are capable of thought, but whether human beings are truly engaging in genuine thinking. This poignant reflection by B. F. Skinner, often attributed to his incisive observations as an American psychologist and a pioneer in behaviorism, sets a contemplative tone for this chapter. Skinner's assertion challenges us in examining not the capabilities of our creations but the quality of our own thought processes. In an era where artificial intelligence and machine learning permeate every aspect of our lives, this quote feels more relevant than ever before. Are we, as a society, thinking critically about the tools we develop, or are we merely moving forward because we can?

Reflecting on Skinner's time, we see a world on the cusp of technological revolution, yet his words echo nostalgia for an era when human thought was paramount, undistracted by the digital noise that fills our current existence. His challenge to humanity was not to merely use thought to manipulate the environment—as he expertly demonstrated through his behavioral experiments—but to use it to understand and improve ourselves.

As we delve deeper into this chapter, we explore not only the capacity of machines to mimic human thought but also our own engagement with

H. Kankam, *A Brief Excursion into Human Cognition*,
https://doi.org/10.1007/978-3-031-89752-8_13

thought as a tool for greater understanding of ourselves, the environment we live in, and how we are an intrinsic part of this construct.

Skinner's work, which spans from inventive behavioral experiments to profound philosophical inquiries, invites us to rediscover our own capacity for deep reflection and critical thinking. His legacy, not confined to the annals of academic psychology, resonates through the corridors of modern technological enterprises and into the quiet moments of our personal introspection.

In this exploration, we are reminded of the delicate balance between leveraging technology to enhance our lives and relying upon it to the extent that we neglect our own cognitive faculties. Let us journey through the landscape of thought, guided by Skinner's timeless insights, to uncover how much of ourselves we have invested in the machines we have created and how much we might still reclaim.

In the 1950s, Isaac Asimov, a professor of biochemistry at Boston University and a prolific science-fiction writer, began to explore the topic of AI and robotics. His work has had a profound impact on both the field of AI and the general perception of AI to this day.

Let us look at how Asimov's science-fiction relates to today's AI development. Asimov is perhaps best known for his "Three Laws of Robotics" (Asimov, 1942, 1950), which are as follows:

- A robot may not injure a human being or, through inaction, allow a human being to come to harm.
- A robot must obey the orders given to it by human beings, except where such orders would conflict with the First Law.
- A robot must protect its own existence as long as such protection does not conflict with the First or Second Law.

These laws have been a topic of discussion and inspiration in AI ethics and in the development of safe and responsible AI systems. While they are not directly implemented in AI systems today, they represent an early and influential attempt to think through the ethical implications of intelligent machines—a challenge that remains pervasive and is unlikely to be resolved in the near future. Crafting a universal solution, regulation, or norm that accommodates the diverse motives of various stakeholders in our intricate geopolitical landscape is an ongoing and formidable task.

Asimov's works often depicted robots and AI as integrated parts of daily life, assisting humans in various tasks. This vision is becoming more of a reality today, as we see the integration of AI in homes, workplaces, and public spaces. Examples include virtual assistants, automated customer service, and robotics in manufacturing.

Reflection on Societal Impacts: Asimov's stories frequently explored the *societal impacts* of AI and robotics, including issues of job displacement, dependency, and the changing nature of work. These are extremely vital issues today as the rise of AI continues to transform industries and the labor market.

Ethical and Moral Dilemmas: Asimov's stories often presented complex ethical and moral dilemmas involving robots and AI, forcing readers to consider the potential challenges and responsibilities that come with creating intelligent machines. This has clear relevance to current debates around AI ethics, bias, accountability, and transparency.

The Limitations of Programming: Asimov's robots were programmed according to the "Three Laws," but his stories often explored how these laws could be interpreted differently or could come into conflict with one another. This relates to current challenges in AI with regard to programming for ethical behavior, dealing with ambiguity, and ensuring that AI systems can handle complex and unforeseen situations.

The Concept of Machine Learning: While Asimov's robots were not depicted as learning machines in the way that today's AI systems are, his work does touch upon themes of adaptation and learning. In the context of *machine learning*, "learning machines" refer to systems or models that have the ability to automatically learn and improve from experience without being explicitly programmed. This concept is central to artificial intelligence and is fundamentally about creating algorithms that can receive input data and use statistical analysis to predict an output while updating outputs as new data become available. Modern AI, especially machine learning, is all about learning from data to make predictions or decisions.

While Asimov's vision of AI and robotics was grounded in the scientific knowledge and imagination of his time, many of his themes and questions remain highly relevant today. His work encouraged us to think carefully about the potential impacts, both positive and negative, of AI on society and to consider the ethical responsibilities that accompany the development of intelligent machines.

AI Approaches Inspired by Human Cognition

Artificial intelligence (AI) has been heavily influenced by research into human cognition, as researchers have sought to develop AI systems that can emulate human-like thinking and problem-solving.

Some AI approaches that are motivated by human cognition include "connectionist models" (such as artificial neural networks). These are inspired by the structure and function of the human brain and consist of interconnected nodes or neurons that "learn" by adjusting the strength of connections between nodes on the basis of input data (Rumelhart et al., 1986).

Another approach termed "symbolic AI," also known as good old-fashioned AI (GOFAI), is based on the manipulation of symbols and formal logic, similar to the way in which humans use language and reasoning (Newell & Simon, 1976). This approach aims to represent and manipulate knowledge in a structured and explicit manner, allowing for complex problem-solving and inference.

What I would like to focus upon, in this context, is "Cognitive architecture and computational models." These are computational frameworks that aim to model the organization and function of human cognitive processes. Examples include ACT-R (Adaptive Control of Thought-Rational) and SOAR (State, Operator, And Result), both of which model human problem-solving, learning, and memory processes.

Cognitive Architectures and Computational Models

Cognitive architectures and *computational models* play crucial roles in understanding human cognition and developing AI systems that emulate human cognitive processes; these systems hold a special place in the study of human cognition because of their ability to provide detailed, testable predictions and explanations of cognitive processes. At this point, I present some of the prominent *cognitive architectures and computational models* and highlight the cognitive processes they represent and the contexts in which they are employed.

ACT-R, developed by John R. Anderson, is a cognitive architecture that models human cognition based on the interaction of declarative and procedural memory systems. It has been used to simulate various cognitive tasks, such as problem-solving, learning and language processing. The following is an example of how ACT-R can be used to model a specific cognitive task (Anderson, 2007):

Example: Mental Arithmetic

Imagine that we want to use ACT-R to model how a person performs mental arithmetic, specifically, by solving a simple addition problem such as 17 + 26

1. *Declarative Memory*:
   Storage of Number Facts: ACT-R stores basic number facts in declarative memory. For example, facts such as 7 + 6 = 13 or 1 + 2 = 3 are stored as chunks of information.
   - Retrieval of Number Facts: When presented with problem 17 + 26, ACT-R retrieves relevant number facts from declarative memory to solve the problem
2. *Procedural Memory*:
   - Application of Addition Strategies: ACT-R uses procedural memory to store production rules that guide how to perform addition. For example, a rule might specify that when adding two numbers, one should start by adding the unit digit first; for 17, the unit digit is 7; for 26, the unit digit is 6.
   - Sequential Processing: The model applies these rules sequentially, first adding 7 + 6 to obtain 13, remembering the '1' to carry over, and then adding 1 + 1 + 2 to obtain 4
3. *Working Memory:*
   - Storing Intermediate Results: ACT-R uses working memory to store intermediate results, such as the '1' that needs to be carried over in the addition example.
   - Maintaining Task Goals: Working memory also helps maintain the goal of the task, which in this case is to solve the addition problem.
4. *Learning and Adaptation:*
   - Strengthening of Memory Traces: As a person practices mental arithmetic, ACT-R adjusts the strength of memory traces in declarative memory, making frequently used number facts easier to retrieve.
   - Adjustment of Production Rules: ACT-R also learns to apply production rules more efficiently, adjusting the weights of different rules on the basis of their success in solving problems.

5. *Perception and Motor Modules:*
    - Input and Output: In a real-world setting, the model would interact with the environment through its perception and motor modules, reading the problem and writing down the answer
6. *Application and Validation:*
    - Predicting Performance: The ACT-R model can predict how long it takes to solve a problem, which errors might occur, and how performance improves with practice.
    - Comparing to Human Data: Researchers would validate the model by comparing its predictions to data from human participants performing the same task.

By simulating the mental arithmetic task via ACT-R, researchers can gain insights into the cognitive processes involved, understand how different aspects of memory and learning contribute to performance, and thus make precise predictions about behavior. This example highlights the power of ACT-R in integrating various cognitive processes to model complex human behavior.

SOAR, developed by Clayton Lewis, John Laird, and Allen Newell, is another *cognitive architecture* that focuses on the integration of multiple cognitive processes, such as perception, memory, and decision-making. It uses a production system to represent procedural knowledge and has been applied to tasks such as planning, problem-solving, and learning (Laird, 2012).

Example: Problem-Solving in Chess

Imagine a scenario where SOAR is applied to model a human player's cognitive processes during a game of chess. The system would go through several stages to make decisions and plan moves:

1. *Perception and Understanding of the State:*
    - Input Processing: SOAR takes in information about the current state of the chessboard, identifying the positions of all pieces, both its own and those of the opponent's.
    - Knowledge Integration: This method integrates this information with its stored knowledge of chess rules and strategies.

2. *Goal Setting:*
   - Objective Definition: SOAR sets a goal for the current situation, such as gaining material advantage, controlling the center, or putting the opponent's king in check.
   - Prioritization: It prioritizes this goal on the basis of the current game context and its knowledge base.
3. *Generating Possible Moves (Operators):*
   - Move Enumeration: SOAR generates a list of all possible legal moves on the basis of the current state of the game.
   - Strategy Application: It applies its internal strategies and heuristics to filter and rank these moves according to their perceived effectiveness.
4. *Predicting Outcomes and Evaluating Moves:*
   - Simulation: SOAR simulates the outcomes of different moves, projecting the resultant game states.
   - Evaluation: It evaluates these projected states on the basis of how well they fulfill the set goals and objectives.
5. *Decision-Making and Action:*
   - Best Move Selection: SOAR selects the move that it evaluates as most effective in achieving its goals.
   - Execution: It makes the move, updating the state of the game.
6. *Learning from Experience:*
   - Feedback Integration: After making a move and observing the opponent's response, SOAR integrates this feedback to update its knowledge base and strategies.
   - Adaptation: It adapts its approach for future moves and scenarios on the basis of this learned experience.

This example illustrates how SOAR can be applied to model complex cognitive tasks such as playing chess, integrating various cognitive processes, including perception, decision-making, planning, learning, and action. The strength of this cognitive architecture lies in its ability to model a wide variety of tasks via a common set of mechanisms, which in turn provides a unified theory of cognition.

Bayesian models use probability theory to represent uncertainty and update beliefs on the basis of new evidence (Tenenbaum et al., 2006). These models have been used to model various aspects of human cognition, such as perception, reasoning, and learning, and have provided insights into the rationality of human decision-making. These models are based on *Bayesian* probability, which provides a way of updating beliefs in light of new evidence.

Below is an example that illustrates how *Bayesian models* can be applied to a specific domain of human cognition:

Example: Visual Perception and Object Recognition

Scenario:

Imagine you are walking in a dimly lit room and you see a vague, blurry shape at a distance. Your brain needs to determine what that object might be.

Bayesian Model Explanation

Prior Beliefs (Prior Probability): Your brain has prior beliefs about the likelihood of encountering various objects in a dimly lit room on the basis of your past experiences. For example, it might have a higher *prior probability* of encountering a chair rather than a penguin.

Likelihood (Conditional Probability): Given the blurry visual input, your brain evaluates how likely it is to observe that input if each possible object is actually present. This is the *likelihood* of the data given the hypothesis. For example, if it were a chair, how likely is it that you would see the blurry shape you are observing?

Posterior Beliefs (Posterior Probability): Bayesian models combine these two sources of information (*prior beliefs and likelihood*) to compute the *posterior probability* of each possible object being the actual object you are observing.

Mathematically, this is expressed as:

$$P(Hypothesis \mid Data) \propto P(Data \mid Hypothesis) \times P(Hypothesis)$$

where:

$P(Hypothesis|Data)$ is the *posterior probability* (what you want to know),

$P(Data|Hypothesis)$ is the likelihood (the probability of observing the data given a specific hypothesis), and

$P(Hypothesis)$ is the *prior probability* (your initial belief before observing the data).

Decision-Making

The brain then makes a decision on the basis of these *posterior probabilities*, favoring the *hypothesis* (in this case, the identity of the object) with the highest *posterior probability*.

Real-Life Application

This *Bayesian* approach is thought to underlie many aspects of visual perception and object recognition. It helps explain how humans are able to make reliable and accurate perceptual judgments, even when faced with ambiguous or incomplete visual information. The model accounts for why our expectations and past experiences play crucial roles in perception, influencing what we see.

By using *Bayesian models*, cognitive scientists can gain a broader understanding of how the brain integrates prior knowledge with sensory information to make sense of the world, explaining phenomena such as visual perception, object recognition, and decision-making in a principled way. These models provide a quantitative framework for predicting human behavior and can be tested and refined through experimental data.

AI Applications in Cognitive Research

AI techniques play a pivotal role in *cognitive research*, assisting in the simulation of cognitive processes, the analysis of intricate data, and the crafting of innovative interventions. Key applications in this domain include the following:

Neural Networks and Cognitive Architectures: These tools, as mentioned before, enable the creation of computational models that replicate human cognitive processes. They shed light on underlying mechanisms and assist in formulating testable hypotheses for hands-on research.

Machine Learning in Brain Imaging: Techniques such as support vector machines and deep learning are increasingly employed to scrutinize brain imaging data, including fMRI and EEG scans. Their utilization has led to the identification of neural activity patterns linked to specific cognitive processes and disorders (Haynes, 2015; Orrù et al., 2012).

Personalized Cognitive Interventions: A significant breakthrough in the application of AI has been its role in formulating individualized interventions. Examples include adaptive cognitive training programs and brain–computer interfaces, which are designed to either enhance cognitive capabilities or mitigate deficits. Such deficits might stem from traumatic brain injuries or neurodegenerative disorders.

Human-AI Interaction and the Future of Cognition

As AI systems become more sophisticated and integrated into various aspects of daily life, understanding and optimizing *human–AI interactions* becomes increasingly important. In this process, it is essential to look at some relevant topics in *human-AI interactions* and the future of cognition. Importantly, *research on trust and collaboration* between humans and AI systems is essential for developing AI systems that can effectively support human decision-making and problem-solving. This includes understanding the factors that influence trust in AI systems and developing strategies to improve transparency and explainability. Another aspect worthy of consideration is the use of "augmented cognition," i.e., the use of AI systems to enhance human cognitive abilities, such as memory, attention, and decision-making. This can include applications such as personal cognitive assistants, AI-powered tutoring systems, and brain–computer interfaces that enhance cognitive function. This can help increase trust in AI systems by allowing users to understand the decision-making processes behind AI systems. In this way, it can allow users to better interact with AI systems, allowing them to use their cognitive abilities more effectively. Furthermore, AI-powered tutoring systems and brain-computer interfaces can be used to help people with cognitive disabilities, such as memory loss or attention-deficit hyperactivity disorder, reach their full potential.

Ethical Considerations in Human-AI Interaction

As AI systems become more integrated into various aspects of human life, ethical considerations related to their design, implementation, and impact upon cognition become increasingly significant. Some key ethical issues include the following:

Privacy and Data Security in AI Systems: AI systems often require substantial amounts of personal data to function optimally, which raises significant concerns about privacy and data security. It is imperative that these systems uphold individuals' privacy rights and safeguard sensitive information, as this plays a crucial role in maintaining trust and fostering ethical interactions between humans and AI (Jobin et al., 2019; European

Commission, 2019). To this end, governments must establish robust laws and regulations that mandate responsible and secure data usage. Furthermore, there must be ongoing vigilance in the form of regular monitoring and updates to AI systems to ensure that data usage remains responsible at all times. Finally, it is essential that companies bear the responsibility of protecting customer data. This includes providing clear, transparent privacy notices for users, ensuring that they are fully informed about how their data are both used and protected (Mittelstadt, 2019).

Bias and fairness: AI systems can perpetuate and even exacerbate existing biases if they are trained using biased data or rely on biased algorithms. Ensuring that AI systems are designed and implemented in a fair and unbiased manner is necessary for promoting equitable access to cognitive technologies and preventing unintended negative consequences. To achieve this, it is imperative to ensure that AI systems are trained using data that are representative of the population they are intended to serve and that algorithms are designed to minimize bias and unfairness (Wachter et al., 2017). AI systems can be designed to help identify and correct these biases, potentially leading to better decision-making outcomes. Examples of AI applications in this area include the following:

- *Decision support systems*: AI systems can be designed to provide decision-makers with objective information and analyses, helping to mitigate the impact of cognitive biases such as *confirmation bias*, *anchoring*, and *overconfidence*. Further techniques, such as resampling or reweighting techniques, are needed to identify and correct biases in the training data used to develop AI models.
- *Nudge interventions*: AI systems can be used to develop personalized "nudge" interventions that help individuals make better decisions by gently steering them toward better choices while still preserving their autonomy and freedom of choice.

It is paramount that companies should be legally held responsible to ensure that AI systems are tested and monitored for fairness and bias to be held accountable for transgressions.

Autonomy and agency: As AI systems become more capable of making decisions and taking action on behalf of humans, questions about the right balance between human autonomy and AI assistance become increasingly relevant. Ensuring that AI systems respect human autonomy and support human agency—rather than undermine it—is a key ethical consideration in *human–AI interactions* (Santoni de Sio & van den Hoven, 2018). We should strive to develop AI systems that are capable of supporting human autonomy and agency while also providing meaningful feedback and guidance to users. This will help us ensure that AI systems are ethical, responsible, and beneficial to society.

To encapsulate, it is imperative that AI systems are developed with transparency and receptivity to user feedback, fostering an environment where continuous learning and improvement are prioritized. Moreover, these systems must undergo consistent reviews and audits, verifying their adherence to ethical standards. Accountability is paramount; thus, both users and developers should bear responsibility for any misuse of AI technologies. With this in mind, it is necessary to reflect on the progress made thus far in implementing such regulatory measures.

At this point, let us discuss China, a global leader in AI, renowned for its advancement and the widespread application of this technology across various sectors. China not only stands out in domestic AI development but also plays a significant role in the global AI landscape through its export of technology and expertise. In its ambitious "smart city" initiatives, China has integrated AI into urban living, deploying AI-powered surveillance systems, facial recognition technologies in public areas, airports, and train stations, and advanced traffic management systems. These innovations aim to bolster public safety and enhance the quality of urban living (Puaschunder, 2020). However, the extensive use of AI in surveillance has ignited concerns around privacy and civil liberties, particularly regarding the monitoring of specific ethnic groups (Pramanik & Rai, 2023).

In a similar way as we turn our attention to the United States, we encounter pressing issues related to facial recognition AI, specifically its accuracy across different racial groups. Many systems have been identified as having higher error rates when identifying color individuals than when identifying white individuals, a discrepancy largely attributed to a lack of diversity in the training data. The systems are predominantly trained with a prevalence of images of lighter-skinned individuals, leading to inaccuracies and a heightened risk of misidentification for people of color (Johnson & Johnson, 2023; Turner Lee & Chin, 2022). This is particularly concerning in law enforcement settings, where the stakes are high. Notable sources, such as the Scientific American and the Brookings Institute, have reported on and analyzed these issues, underscoring the critical need for action. Addressing the biases present in facial recognition AI is imperative to ensuring fairness, protecting privacy and upholding civil liberties. It requires a concerted effort from all stakeholders—technologists, policymakers, and the broader community—to develop and implement these technologies responsibly and equitably.

Finally, I would like to highlight a crucial step forward taken in March 2023 by Max Tegman, a renowned professor of physics and AI researcher at the Massachusetts Institute of Technology, as well as a cofounder of the Future of Life Institute. Tegman spearheaded an initiative, drafting an open letter that called for a six-month moratorium on the development of large-scale AI systems. This pause was proposed to provide ample time for the careful consideration and implementation of necessary regulations and controls. Impressively, the campaign garnered support from over 30,000 individuals who signed the letter, including high-profile figures such as Elon Musk and Apple cofounder, Steve Wozniak (Tegmark, 2023). Despite these efforts and the notable backing, the appeal unfortunately fell on deaf ears and was ultimately ignored. Importantly, Tegman's endeavor to raise awareness about potential risks is not an isolated case; numerous esteemed researchers and influential thought leaders have expressed similar concerns in the past, albeit with little success!

This incident underscores a critical point: leading AI experts are acutely aware of the potential dangers posed by giant, unregulated, and uncontrolled AI systems. I personally liken the development of these colossal AI systems to opening a portal to an unknown dimension, given the sheer unpredictability and potential risks involved.

Regrettably, it appears that a majority of elected world and regional leaders remain largely uninformed about the profound impact that such AI systems could have on our civilization, particularly through unintended consequences. The prevailing mindset seems to be predominantly focused on potential political and economic gains in the quest for dominance. This is all the more surprising, given that the use of AI/Social media to influence our cognition—through manipulation and misrepresentation—has been demonstrated in the past. These critical concerns continue to be overlooked and ignored.

References

Anderson, J. R. (2007). *How can the human mind occur in the physical universe?* Oxford University Press. https://doi.org/10.1093/acprof:oso/9780195324259.001.0001

Asimov, I. (1942). Runaround. *Astounding Science Fiction, 29*(1).

Asimov, I. (1950). *I, Robot*. Gnome Press.

European Commission. (2019). *Ethics guidelines for trustworthy AI*. https://digital-strategy.ec.europa.eu/en/library/ethics-guidelines-trustworthy-ai

Haynes, J. D. (2015). A primer on pattern-based approaches to fMRI: Principles, pitfalls, and perspectives. *Neuron, 87*(2), 257–270. https://doi.org/10.1016/j.neuron.2015.05.025

Jobin, A., Ienca, M., & Vayena, E. (2019). The global landscape of AI ethics guidelines. *Nature Machine Intelligence, 1*(9), 389–399. https://doi.org/10.1038/s42256-019-0088-2

Johnson, T. L., & Johnson, N. N. (2023, May 18). Facial recognition software is biased against Black people. It's not hard to guess why. *Scientific American*.

Laird, J. E. (2012). *The Soar cognitive architecture*. MIT Press.

Mittelstadt, B. (2019). Principles alone cannot guarantee ethical AI. *Nature Machine Intelligence, 1*(11), 501–507. https://doi.org/10.1038/s42256-019-0114-4

Newell, A., & Simon, H. A. (1976). Computer science as empirical inquiry: Symbols and search. *Communications of the ACM, 19*(3), 113–126. https://doi.org/10.1145/360018.360022

Orrù, G., Pettersson-Yeo, W., Marquand, A. F., Sartori, G., & Mechelli, A. (2012). Using support vector machine to identify imaging biomarkers of neurological and psychiatric disease: A critical review. *Neuroscience & Biobehavioral Reviews, 36*(4), 1140–1152. https://doi.org/10.1016/j.neubiorev.2012.01.004

Pramanik, S., & Rai, S. K. (2023). AI take-over in literature and culture: Truth, post-truth, and simulation. *Rupkatha Journal on Interdisciplinary Studies in Humanities*. https://doi.org/10.21659/rupkatha.v15n4.12

Puaschunder, J. M. (2020). The future of artificial intelligence in international healthcare: An index. *SSRN Electronic Journal*. https://doi.org/10.2139/ssrn.3623530

Rumelhart, D. E., Hinton, G. E., & Williams, R. J. (1986). Learning internal representations by error propagation. In D. E. Rumelhart, J. L. McClelland, & The PDP Research Group (Eds.), *Parallel distributed processing: Explorations in the microstructure of cognition (Vol. 1, Foundations)* (pp. 318–362). MIT Press. https://doi.org/10.7551/mitpress/5236.003.0016

Santoni de Sio, F., & van den Hoven, J. (2018). Meaningful human control over autonomous systems: A philosophical account. *Frontiers in Robotics and AI, 5*, 15. https://doi.org/10.3389/frobt.2018.00015

Skinner, B. F. (1969). *Contingencies of reinforcement: A theoretical analysis*. Appleton-Century-Crofts.

Tegmark, M. (2023, March 29). *Pause giant AI experiments: An open letter*. Future of Life Institute. https://futureoflife.org/open-letter/pause-giant-ai-experiments/

Tenenbaum, J. B., Griffiths, T. L., & Kemp, C. (2006). Theory-based Bayesian models of inductive learning and reasoning. *Trends in Cognitive Sciences, 10*(7), 309–318. https://doi.org/10.1016/j.tics.2006.05.009

Turner Lee, N., & Chin, C. (2022, April 12). *Police surveillance and facial recognition: Why data privacy is imperative for communities of color*. Brookings Institution. https://www.brookings.edu/articles/police-surveillance-and-facial-recognition-why-data-privacy-is-an-imperative-for-communities-of-color/

Wachter, S., Mittelstadt, B., & Floridi, L. (2017). Why a right to explanation of automated decision-making does not exist in the General Data Protection Regulation. *International Data Privacy Law, 7*(2), 76–99. https://doi.org/10.1093/idpl/ipx005

CHAPTER 14

Conclusion: The Future of Cognitive Science

Current Trends and Emerging Areas in Cognitive Research

Cognitive science is a field that is experiencing rapid evolution, with new research areas and trends constantly emerging. Presently, *big data* and *machine learning* represent significant areas of growth and interest (Lake et al., 2017). The burgeoning availability of extensive datasets, coupled with the advancement of sophisticated machine learning methods, has provided cognitive researchers with unparalleled opportunities. They are now able to investigate human cognition on a scale and level of detail that was previously unattainable.

Another exciting field of study is *computational modeling of cognitive processes* (Sun, 2008). In this domain, researchers are working to create and refine complex computational models that simulate human thought processes. These advanced models are invaluable, as they not only shed light on the intricate workings of human cognition but also pave the way for developing AI systems. Such AI systems could either replicate human cognitive abilities or enhance them, fostering a new era of human-AI collaboration. Moreover, the field of *neuroimaging* is undergoing a transformative phase with the advent of groundbreaking techniques. Innovations such as optogenetics, multimodal imaging, and high-resolution brain mapping are at the forefront of this change, offering unparalleled insights

H. Kankam, *A Brief Excursion into Human Cognition*,
https://doi.org/10.1007/978-3-031-89752-8_14

into the neural underpinnings of cognition. These advancements not only deepen our understanding of brain function but also open new possibilities for practical applications in various domains, ranging from healthcare to technology.

Interdisciplinary Approaches and Collaborations

Given an ideal environment, the evolution of cognitive science is poised to be significantly shaped by interdisciplinary collaboration. Such collaboration allows for a vibrant exchange of knowledge, methodologies, and perspectives among researchers from diverse fields, all converging on the complex study of human cognition. The synergy between *cognitive neuroscience* and AI is particularly promising (Hassabis et al., 2017). Researchers from both fields are actively engaging in collaborative efforts to demystify the intricate mechanisms of human cognition. This interdisciplinary endeavor not only enhances our understanding of the brain but also drives innovation in AI, resulting in systems that can more accurately emulate human thinking or provide cognitive augmentation. Similarly, the bridge between *cognitive science* and *education* is yielding transformative results (Mayer, 2017). This interdisciplinary collaboration translates research insights into tangible educational practices, ensuring that teaching methodologies are aligned with our scientific understanding of how learning and cognitive development transpire. This alignment holds the potential to revolutionize educational systems and enhance learning outcomes for students worldwide. Furthermore, the integration of *cognitive science* with *humanities* is fostering a richer and more nuanced understanding of human cognition (Slingerland, 2008). Scholars from disciplines such as philosophy, linguistics, and anthropology provide invaluable insights, situating cognitive processes within broader cultural, historical, and social contexts. This multidimensional approach is crucial for grasping the full complexity of human cognition.

Ethical Considerations and Societal Implications

As emphasized in previous chapters, the rapid progression of cognitive science has brought with it a host of ethical considerations and societal implications that demand our attention and careful deliberation. Central to these concerns are issues related to privacy, data protection, and the manifold consequences stemming from AI systems that are designed to either replicate or enhance human cognitive functions.

In terms of privacy and data protection, it is imperative that we establish robust protocols and guidelines to safeguard individual information, particularly as we delve deeper into understanding and modeling human cognition. The data required for such endeavors are often sensitive, and the potential for misuse is significant (Yannopoulos, 2017). Researchers bear the responsibility of ensuring that privacy is uncompromised and that data are handled with the utmost integrity.

Furthermore, as we develop AI systems that mimic or augment human cognition, we must critically assess and address issues pertaining to fairness, accountability, and transparency (Jobin et al., 2019). These systems have the potential to influence a wide array of fields, from education and healthcare to employment and governance. It is crucial that they operate in a manner that is fair, accountable, and transparent to prevent any form of bias or discrimination and to ensure that their decision-making processes can be understood and scrutinized.

Another dimension of this ethical landscape revolves around *cognitive enhancement* and the quest for *equality* (Bostrom & Sandberg, 2009). This issue extends beyond the borders of individual societies and countries, manifesting on a global scale where disparities are even more starkly evident. As cognitive enhancement technologies evolve and become more accessible, there is a risk that they could exacerbate existing inequalities, both within societies and between different countries. Researchers, policymakers, and society at large must address these challenges, working collaboratively to ensure that access to these powerful technologies is equitable and just. This could involve the implementation of a global framework or policy that ensures fair access to these technologies across different societal and economic boundaries to ensure that advancements in cognitive enhancements are accessible and beneficial to all segments of the global population, particularly focusing on underserved and low-income regions. This could be organized and managed through various implementations, such as subsidized distribution, research and development grants, regulatory guidelines, public education and awareness campaigns, accessibility measures, and monitoring and evaluation of various outcomes. The overarching goal is to prevent a scenario where only the affluent can benefit from enhancements that could significantly improve cognitive functions, thereby potentially leading to a greater divide in global intellectual and socioeconomic disparities.

In essence, as we navigate the complex terrain of cognitive science and its applications, our commitment to ethical principles and societal well-being must remain steadfast. This commitment is central to ensuring that the fruits of our labor contribute positively to society, fostering a future that is inclusive, equitable, and respectful of the rights and dignity of all individuals.

Future Directions and Challenges in Understanding Human Cognition

The future of cognitive science will likely involve tackling a number of significant challenges and questions, such as understanding the neural basis of consciousness: one of the most enduring mysteries in cognitive science is the question of how subjective conscious experiences arise from neural processes in the brain (Koch et al., 2016). Another major challenge is integrating explanations of cognition at multiple levels, from the molecular and cellular levels to the cognitive and social levels. Researchers need to develop novel methods and frameworks for integrating these diverse perspectives.

To enhance our understanding of culture during a time when we are increasingly living in multicultural environments, incorporating a cross-cultural perspective into cognitive science research is beneficial (Nisbett, 2003). This approach can shed light on both the universal aspects and the variability of human cognitive processes across different cultural contexts. Potential research areas in this domain include exploring the extent to which cognitive processes such as perception, attention, memory, and decision-making vary across cultures. Additionally, it is crucial to examine ways in which cultural factors such as language, social norms, and values influence the development of cognitive abilities and skills throughout an individual's life. This investigation has significant implications for contemporary cultural settings, particularly in education and community life.

This line of inquiry is also relevant to understanding how people perceive, reason, and make decisions regarding environmental issues. Investigating the cognitive processes and biases that influence decision-making about climate change, resource consumption, and conservation is essential (Gifford, 2014). Furthermore, it is important to understand how individuals perceive and assess environmental risk and how these perceptions impact their behaviors and decision-making processes. This research can contribute to more effective communication and policy-making strategies aimed at addressing environmental challenges.

As our lives become increasingly mediated by digital technologies, we find ourselves facing a growing number of digital distractions and experiencing cognitive overload (Ophir et al., 2009). It is incredibly important to understand how the constant stream of digital information, notifications, and demands of multitasking profoundly affect cognitive processes such as attention, memory, and decision-making.

The cognitive consequences of social media use, particularly its effects on social cognition, attention, and emotional regulation, are rapidly becoming clearer. According to a Pew Research Center survey in 2023, 77% of teens reported using social YouTube daily, with 16% doing so almost constantly (Pew Research Center, 2023). Similarly, regarding gaming platforms, another 2024 Pew Research Centre report indicated that 85% of teens play video games, with 41% engaging daily (Pew Research Center, 2024).

On October 24, 2023, forty-one states (along with the District of Columbia) filed lawsuits against *meta-platforms* (Kelly, 2023). They claim that the company deliberately designed features on Facebook and Instagram known, through internal research, to be addictive and harmful to teenagers and young users but continued to employ these features.

Inherently, the rapid evolution of technology poses a challenge as more users adopt increasingly sophisticated products in potentially harmful ways. The overconsumption of digital media—further amplified by AI and the rapid development of *virtual* and *augmented reality* that creates hyperreal experiences tailored to individual preferences—will most probably lead to a higher incidence and prevalence of mental health disorders, manifesting as an intensified form of dependency that will challenge both individuals and society.

In clinical practice, cognitive science plays a crucial role in enhancing our understanding of mental health disorders and shaping effective treatment strategies. Current research focuses on developing cognitive biomarkers that can predict, diagnose, or monitor the progression of these disorders (Insel, 2017). Additionally, there are ongoing advancements in evidence-based cognitive interventions, including cognitive–behavioral therapy (CBT), mindfulness–based cognitive therapy (MBCT) (Beck, 2020), and computerized cognitive training programs. These interventions are being refined and adapted for delivery through telemedicine platforms, making them more accessible and potentially more effective for patients.

As the field continues to evolve, researchers will be challenged to integrate new technologies, interdisciplinary perspectives, and real-world contexts into their investigations of human cognition while also addressing the ethical and societal implications of their work. I believe it represents a challenge far beyond what we can currently envision.

References

Beck, J. S. (2020). *Cognitive behavior therapy: Basics and beyond* (3rd ed.). The Guilford Press.

Bostrom, N., & Sandberg, A. (2009). Cognitive enhancement: Methods, ethics, regulatory challenges. *Science and Engineering Ethics, 15*(3), 311–341. https://doi.org/10.1007/s11948-009-9142-5

Gifford, R. (2014). Environmental psychology matters. *Annual Review of Psychology, 65*, 541–579. https://doi.org/10.1146/annurev-psych-010213-115048

Hassabis, D., Kumaran, D., Summerfield, C., & Botvinick, M. (2017). Neuroscience-inspired artificial intelligence. *Neuron, 95*(2), 245–258. https://doi.org/10.1016/j.neuron.2017.06.011

Insel, T. R. (2017). Digital phenotyping: Technology for a new science of behavior. *JAMA, 318*(13), 1215–1216. https://doi.org/10.1001/jama.2017.11295

Jobin, A., Ienca, M., & Vayena, E. (2019). The global landscape of AI ethics guidelines. *Nature Machine Intelligence, 1*(9), 389–399. https://doi.org/10.1038/s42256-019-0088-2

Kelly, M. (2023, October 24). 41 states sue Meta over 'addictive' features aimed at kids. *The Verge*. https://www.theverge.com/2023/10/24/23930408/meta-instagram-facebook-child-safety-lawsuit-states-kosa

Koch, C., Massimini, M., Boly, M., & Tononi, G. (2016). Neural correlates of consciousness: Progress and problems. *Nature Reviews Neuroscience, 17*(5), 307–321. https://doi.org/10.1038/nrn.2016.22

Lake, B. M., Ullman, T. D., Tenenbaum, J. B., & Gershman, S. J. (2017). Building machines that learn and think like people. *Behavioral and Brain Sciences, 40*, e253. https://doi.org/10.1017/S0140525X16001837

Mayer, R. E. (2017). How can brain research inform academic learning and instruction? *Educational Psychology Review, 29*, 835–846. https://doi.org/10.1007/s10648-016-9391-1

Nisbett, R. E. (2003). *The geography of thought: How Asians and Westerners think differently...and why*. Free Press.

Ophir, E., Nass, C., & Wagner, A. D. (2009). Cognitive control in media multitaskers. *Proceedings of the National Academy of Sciences, 106*(37), 15583–15587. https://doi.org/10.1073/pnas.0903620106

Pew Research Center. (2023). *Teens and social media: Key findings from Pew Research Center.* https://www.pewresearch.org; https://pewrsr.ch/3LorQUG

Pew Research Center. (2024). *Teens and video games today.* https://www.pewresearch.org/?p=165467

Slingerland, E. (2008). *What science offers the humanities: Integrating body and culture.* Cambridge University Press. https://doi.org/10.1017/CBO9780511841163

Sun, R. (Ed.). (2008). *The Cambridge handbook of computational psychology.* Cambridge University Press. https://doi.org/10.1017/CBO9780511816772

Yannopoulos, G. N. (2017). The immunity of internet intermediaries reconsidered. In M. Taddeo & L. Floridi (Eds.), *The responsibilities of online service providers* (pp. 43–59). Springer. https://doi.org/10.1007/978-3-319-47852-4_3

The manufacturer's authorised representative in the EU is Springer Nature Customer Service Centre GmbH, Europaplatz 3, 69115 Heidelberg, Germany. If you have any concerns regarding our products, please contact ProductSafety@springernature.com

Printed and bound by CPI Group (UK) Ltd, Croydon, CR0 4YY
30/09/2026
02225565-0005